ALL THE
WORLD'S A STAGE

ALL THE
WORLD'S A STAGE

DENNIS WEAVER

WALSCH
BOOKS

an imprint of
HAMPTON ROADS
PUBLISHING COMPANY, INC.
www.hrpub.com

Cover design by Bookwrights Design
Cover author photos by Alice Billings
Cover background photo by Corbis Images

Hampton Roads Publishing Company, Inc.
1125 Stoney Ridge Road
Charlottesville, VA 22902

434-296-2772
fax: 434-296-5096
e-mail: hrpc@hrpub.com
www.hrpub.com

If you are unable to order this book from your local
bookseller, you may order directly from the publisher.
Call 1-800-766-8009, toll-free.
Library of Congress Catalog Card Number: 2001094963
ISBN 1-57174-287-5
10 9 8 7 6 5 4 3 2 1
Printed on acid-free paper in Canada

"This is not the darkness before the storm, this is the darkness before the dawn of the Golden Age of peace . . . ," of productivity, of creativity, and justice.

—Peace Pilgrim

Dedication

In January of 1946, Gerry and I had been married just three short months, when we packed our bags and headed for the University of Oklahoma at Norman. We were lucky to get a one-room apartment in the basement of the home of Dr. Lawton, a professor in the Radio Department. We shared a bath and a kitchen with another couple who also had one room.

We lived on ninety dollars a month courtesy of the G.I. Bill, plus the twenty-five-dollar stipend I received each month for sweeping out the track room at the university. What really saved us financially was Gerry's excellent typing skills. She was a whiz and soon became very popular with the geology students, typing and proofing their theses at fifty cents a page.

Our meager budget didn't allow much for entertainment, which was mostly seeing a movie with our dear friends Lonny and Erma Dean Chapman, or playing bridge with Cecil and Millie Pickett. Gerry passionately disliked card games of any kind and when we played bridge, she always prayed to be the dummy. But the two things she never seemed to tire of were the way I performed Shakespeare and the stories I would tell of my childhood. I often entertained her for hours in the seclusion of our one-room sanctuary. After each presentation, she would say, "You've got to write a book!"

She has continually encouraged me to do so for over fifty years, so I guess you could say this book started way back then in Lawton's basement when our lives had just begun to unfold.

But the past ten years, her loving nudges have become a little more intense. . . . "Get it down; get it on paper. If for no one else, do it for the kids and our grandchildren." And so, it is done.

I dedicate this book to our three talented sons, Richard, Robert, and Rustin, beautiful and good people of whom I'm extremely proud. And of course, to our grandchildren, Jennifer, Travis, and Jess, with the hope they might discover something in these pages that could give them purpose—make their lives a little easier and much more fulfilling. And I cannot forget our god-granddaughter, Bethany, who is like our own. Know that each of you is dearly loved.

And I especially dedicate and offer this book to you, Gerry, with my sweetest love, for without you it would never have been done. Ours has been an incredible journey together, and it excites my soul to know that it has just begun. Yes, we've known the highs and the lows, the victories and defeats, and there were times I stumbled along the way, searching for my own growth; but you were always there with your unshakable love and support, for which I am eternally grateful. There's a line in a song I wrote for you once that I'd like to remind you of, for it's just as true today, if not more so, than it was when it originally sprang from my heart:

> *"Like slippers and wine,*
> *and this feeling of mine,*
> *you get better with time."*

You're simply the best. You are precious to me, and I love you always.

—Rupe, 4/14/00

Table of Contents

Foreword xiii

Acknowledgements xvii

Introduction xix

Prologue: "Twenty Minutes Tops, and Counting" xxiii

1 Gotta Love a Farm 1

2 Lard and Mustard Wasn't an Option 19

3 "I Never Want to See You Again, You Hear?" 49

4 Buck Jones, Tarzan, and . . . Principal Deathridge 57

5 Miracles, Times Three 63

6 Mrs. Billy Dennis Weaver .70

7 "Look Out, Mr. Dillon, He's Gonna Shoot!" 95

8 . . . You're Turning Down Orson Welles? . . . Saying
    "Yes" to Spielberg . . . There Ya Go,
    Marshal Sam McCloud .105

9 "Never Mind the Earth,
    Let's Save Our Own Ass" 136

10 Lights, Revolutions, Action .146

11 Ecolonomics . . . Think Anew, Act Anew 163

12 The Ecolonomic Stool 181

13 The Earthship 189

14 One Person Can Make a Difference 193

15 The Tender Trap 198

16 Journey into Spirit 209

17 Soul and Consciousness 241

18 Death, Karma, and Reincarnation 263

19 Changing Consciousness 286

A Meditation 304

Epilogue 309

Afterword 311

Foreword

We read in the papers almost every day about some new atrocity: Third World nations melting into chaos, deeply in debt to the World Bank from boondoggle projects that made their former leaders rich; the widening hole in the ozone layer; species loss; the worldwide devastation of indigenous peoples; the massive over-consumption of the First World, while elsewhere in the world two billion people live on less than two dollars a day with no access to safe water or adequate food.

Sometimes, for those of us who are working to inform people about the state of the world, the situation can seem overwhelming. I remember a day in 2000 I'd spent compiling information on pollution, cancer, corporate crime, and greenwashing. I felt like I'd descended into the pits of hell, facing the monsters that threaten our world and my children's future. I needed to hear the voice of somebody positive, somebody who was doing something useful while still aware of the world's situation, somebody who could offer me a word of encouragement. I called Dennis Weaver.

"Dennis," I said, "how do you handle being over-whelmed when you look at the overall situation in the world?"

"Well," he said, a smile in his voice, "sometimes that happens. But I think we just each have to push our own wagons, you know? Without worrying about everybody else's. We do our part; there are others who are doing theirs. If we each keep our attention on our own wagons, and enough of us are doing that, then we'll get this wagon train through the tough times and over to the other side."

It was exactly what I needed to hear, and the common-sense wisdom of "we just each have to push our own wagons" spurred me to go back to the book I was writing.

The book you're holding in your hands is about Dennis' life pushing his own wagon—one that has led him from growing up in the dustbowl depression, to being a TV and movie star, to making a deep spiritual commitment, to living in an "earthship" house made largely out of recycled tires and cans, to starting the Institute of Ecolonomics.

Dennis Weaver's story is both informing and enlightening. Through it, you'll come to know the broad history of the best and worst of times during the twentieth century in America. You'll discover a wellspring of inspiration, thought-provoking discussions of theology, insights into how our economic and business structures can be reformed to heal the world, and even a vicarious glimpse into the fascinating world of Hollywood.

I first met Dennis almost thirty years ago at a Self-Realization Fellowship conference in Los Angeles. At the time, he was already a world-famous star, yet there was a quiet calmness to him that bespoke his years of daily meditative practice. A few years later, he and his wonderful wife

Gerry and his sons performed a fundraising concert for a community for abused children that Louise and I had started in New Hampshire, and through that I got to know him as an earnest man of integrity and compassion, one of those rare individuals who loves to help others for the pure joy of the deed itself.

Through this book, you'll come to know Dennis and his family, and I'm sure you'll be as touched as I was by the humility and love they carry in the world. They are examples of the power each of us has within to push our own wagons across the plains of life, helping to create a better world for our children and grandchildren. The challenges we face in this world are extraordinary, but so are the opportunities to create transformation. Read on and discover a few that may inspire you and perhaps even change your life.

—Thom Hartmann
Author, *The Last Hours of Ancient Sunlight*

Acknowledgements

When I sat down to try to acknowledge those who have been of great help to me and have contributed significantly to this book, their numbers were endless. Thinking of one person only reminded me of two more. It was very similar to trying to determine the starting point of a circle.

Every person that has crossed my path has had an effect on my life, has helped shape who I am, and in some manner has contributed to this book. And, so that no one is excluded, I sincerely and humbly thank God—for in doing so, I thank all, for we are all together in Her; no one is excluded.

I would be remiss, however, if I didn't acknowledge my friend, Neale Donald Walsch, without whose persistent and gentle prodding this book would still be slushing around in my imagination. And, of course, Dee Silverstein, whose special flare for the theatrical gave a unique flavor to the completed work. I am thankful that she was willing to do what I considered burdensome work, but work she seemed to love. She was invaluable.

And last but not least, I again recognize my wife, Gerry, for her assistance. She not only inspired me but made innumerable valuable suggestions, always kept me on course, and even accepted the tedious job of proofreading.

And finally, I'd like to thank my thesaurus.

Introduction

I'm Dennis Weaver and, chances are, you may have heard of me, although that's not really important. What is important is what I'd like to share with you in this book. If you're like me and find the business of entertainment fascinating, we're going to have some fun together, because in this book I'm going to share with you some personal, humorous, and memorable moments. Moments I have experienced over the five decades that I've been a stage, television, and film entertainer. You'll get an insider's glimpse of Hollywood, a peek at the many stages on which I've had the privilege of performing. Then, I will share with you my most important role to date and the most important stage I've ever trod—the grandest stage of all, the stage on which we are all playing out the stories of our lives—planet Earth.

It was Shakespeare who said, "All the world's a stage and all the men and women merely players: They have their exits and their entrances; and one man in his time plays many parts." He was right. But what he didn't tell us was how to keep the show going. I suppose he thought we'd figure that out for ourselves, that we'd have more sense than to pull the curtain before the final act was finished. We all agree that "the show must go on"; we just haven't figured out a way to stop ourselves from slapping the closed sign on the marquee.

My passion for these past twenty years has had to do with this larger "show" that we call life on Earth and how we keep it going. How to do that? Well, I have to be honest with you. That's why I've written this book. I'm hoping to use it as one more stage from which I can speak the most important lines I've ever been asked to deliver. The script calls for me to say, "Join with me to save our planet." But the planet's not in jeopardy. It's been around for billions of years and it will continue. The question is, will we still be along for the ride? We're talking about saving our own hide, not the planet. We're talking about preserving our life as we know it. But along the way I want to tell you some stories, share some anecdotes, and weave a few tales of the many times you and I have shared together.

Oh, yes, this is not the first time we've shared a common experience . . . at least, I hope not. It all began for the two of us—this delightful dance we've had—many years ago when you invited me into your home as Chester in the pioneering television western series *Gunsmoke*. It continued when the entertaining "fish out of water" *McCloud* caught your fancy. And it gathered momentum with the many other film, stage, and television appearances, through which we have shared a common moment in time—a moment in which our paths crossed in a real and tangible way.

We've been friends for a long time, you and I. At least, I feel that way. Because I've known that without you, without your friendly and warm reception, I could never have had the wonderful career that you have given me. We've shared a great deal together, and I'm going to ask you to join me once again as an important player in the greatest show on Earth. Together, we can produce a final extraordinary extravaganza. And in this production you will be just as big a star as I intend to be . . . we get equal billing.

I have a wonderful friend, Dee Silverstein, whom I've asked to help me with this book, because well, frankly, my strong suit is acting, not writing. I know what it is I want to say, but Dee has the talent to draw it out of me. So, I asked her if she would just "interview" me and, through that process, help me pull this book together. And that she's done. So, you'll hear her voice in this book as well as mine—along with some of her observations. Since she, too, is fascinated about life at all levels, and, like most of us, with life in the entertainment business, she has asked many of the same questions that I'm sure you might ask.

I have a strong feeling you're going to enjoy the journey we're about to take together. But before you turn the first page, let me thank you one more time for the wonderful years you have given me, and that you have allowed me to give you, for life is a game of give-and-take. As one great sage said, "The purpose of life is to Love and be Loved." We've done a pretty good job of it. It's been a good run. Let's keep it going. Lights—camera—action. . . .

—Dennis Weaver

Prologue

"Twenty Minutes Tops, and Counting"

The first time I met Dennis Weaver I was living in Dallas, Texas. I remember it being a particularly hot summer day and I had taken a rare moment away from my writing to take a swim in our pool, thinking a dip now and then into cool water would help ease the onslaught of the baking heat. A sunbath would not be bad either; I could use a little color on my skin. Yes, I had read the reports of the depleting ozone layer, and yes, I knew it wasn't good to lie in the sun for very long. But it was August and I was sick of air-conditioned air—I needed a break. Unfortunately, the pool water was nearly as hot as the air. There was no relief.

I must have dozed off, because the ringing of the phone startled me. I was even more shocked to hear the voice on the other end. It was Jim, a friend of mine, with whom I had recently finished working on the editing of his novel. He was calling from his cell phone, gingerly reporting that he had just picked Dennis Weaver up from DFW (Dallas–Fort Worth Airport) and was heading my way. *Dennis Weaver, the actor?* The thought pulsed through my brain, bolting me upright. I quickly assessed the situation: swimsuit, wet hair—and *baby oil* ! Twenty minutes tops, and counting. I began to panic.

"We'll be there in about twenty minutes." I heard sound coming to me from some long tunnel. "I can't wait for you two to meet." Jim's cheery voice rang off, and the phone went dead in my hand.

After a beat, I sprang into action and dashed through my bedroom door and across the room—shedding the suit as I went. At the end of my run was an ice-cold shower. I found cooling relief from the heat, after all. I should have just taken a shower in the first place!

Jim McCormick was a well-known businessman in Dallas. He was successful, erudite, and kind, and had been a friend of our family for many years. I had known for several weeks that he was planning to bring Dennis Weaver to Dallas to speak on behalf of the environment but had not expected to actually meet him—much less have a talk with him at my house! Jim informed me later that he had wanted me to meet Dennis, thinking that, since I was a screenwriter, there might be some future project we could work on together.

Twenty minutes later, I was waiting on the front porch, just in time to see Jim's shiny, white Lincoln-Continental pull slowly into the driveway.

Dennis emerged from the car—a tall, lanky, handsome cowboy with salt-and-pepper hair. His long-legged, rocking-horse gait gave him an air of casual arrogance and superlative command. He seemed to drift to the porch while mumbling something about not being able to unpack his shirts.

When he smiled and shook my hand, his worry over the shirts seemed to pass, and I was immediately transported from the Dallas heat through time and space to a world filled with possibilities. I studied him curiously—wondering who he was, exactly, and why did he have such an immediate effect on me?

His eyes danced over me with an enthusiasm for life, and I caught Jim's smile in the background as Dennis slipped past me and into one of the three rocking chairs on the porch. It seemed as if the conversation started in that same moment, and I was instantly engaged. We talked with an ease that usually only complements old friendships.

ॐ

Years later, as I walked up a gravel driveway in Colorado toward the home of Dennis and Gerry Weaver, called an "Earthship," I smiled because I knew this man now and, finally, we were working together. We were going to put his thoughts, dreams, visions, and experiences down on paper.

I stopped on the lawn to study the Earthship—ten thousand square feet of adobe and glass, nestled in the Uncompahgre River Valley and ringed by the magnificent San Juan Mountains. The Weavers built it as an environmental house into the hillside of their twenty-five-acre property. It was made out of aluminum cans, old tires, dead-standing timber, and adobe. It was beautiful—all three hundred feet of windows glowing from within with benevolent light.

Moments later, the front door opened, and the warmth

of a pair of Van Erp copper sconces and an effervescent smile greeted me. Gerry, Dennis's spunky, beautiful wife of fifty-three years, threw her arms around my neck. I hugged Gerry back with equal enthusiasm. We were friends—four years now—but this was the first time I'd visited their home. As Gerry ushered me inside, I heard the distant rumble of thunder. I could smell the rain. It was coming.

"Dennis is waiting in his study for you," she said in a chipper voice. "He's very excited about the book."

She led me down a lengthy, flagstone-floored hallway past rich terra-cotta walls of adobe, which opened to a modern kitchen, the countertops adorned with turquoise, orange, and black tiles patterned in an Indian mosaic. The polished wood cabinets sported silver Indian-head pulls. I marveled at it all as I passed a vaulted-ceiling living room with a curved flagstone staircase. As I ambled along, banks of enormous, colorful geraniums caught my eye, along with unruly vines of Australian spinach, zucchini, and tomato plants that filled planters running the length of the house under huge slanted windows. I passed the billiards room, which housed, among its many treasures, an old player piano and Navajo loom, and pushed open a handmade oak door with a blue stained-glass star on it. I was entering Dennis's private office. The room was comfortable and fashionably decorated in the Southwest style, showcasing different hues of blue—primarily denim—and anchored by a large kilim rug. Dennis stood up and walked around his desk and, with a warm handshake, said, "Hey—you're here! Come in—sit down. Let's go to work."

I eagerly removed my backpack and sat on the sofa.

"Did you bring the tape recorder?" he asked in a raspy, enthusiastic voice.

"Yes—it's right here." I reached into my pack and pulled out a handheld tape recorder and placed it on the Indian drum coffee table between us.

Dennis settled back in a chair and relaxed. "Okay, I'm ready—ask away."

"What is this book going to be about?" I asked.

He paused as if to get his motor revved up, leaning forward, elbows on knees, his expression pensive. Then, his face softened and his eyes focused, he pressed his lips together with that firmness that precedes speech.

"Planting seeds." He smiled and leaned back, letting the statement settle on me like a tiny beacon of light.

"Okay. Where do we start planting?"

He smiled. "I think we should begin with the Great Depression. . . ."

—Dee Silverstein, 1999

1

Gotta Love a Farm

The Great Depression was a frightening force. It affected people in ways they could never have imagined. It made them probe their consciences and delve into the depths of their souls.

Fortunes were lost overnight, and the unemployment rate soared to 24 percent. Breadlines offered the only food for millions of people. There were no societal safety nets, such as unemployment benefits, social security, or welfare programs, to catch the desperate people who had fallen on hard times. Proud men sold shoelaces and pencils in an effort to put bread on the table.

My family was not immune to the pain that rippled through the nation and the world. I remember seeing, when I was five years old, looks of intense concern on my Mom and Dad's faces, talking in hushed and worried tones. I wasn't old enough to appreciate their dilemma, but kids have great intuitive power, and I sensed that something was terribly wrong.

My dad worked for the Empire District Electric Company in Joplin, Missouri, and I later learned that the small amount of money he had saved had been invested in company stocks. With the crash of '29, it all evaporated.

Dad worked for the electric company for thirty-five years. We were luckier than most, for all through the depression years, he never joined the ranks of the unemployed, although, at the height of the depression, his monthly pay was sixty dollars. It was hardly enough to sustain a family of five, which in 1929 included my sister Jerry, who was six years my senior, and my brother Howard, who was three years older than I.

Jerry was a gentle soul, very kind and considerate, with a heart as sweet as a vine-ripened tomato. She fell in love with a boy named Denzil Bell at an early age and was married before graduating high school, despite Dad's pointed objection. Many relatives and friends warned my sister that choosing a lifetime partner before her seventeenth birthday was not wise, and that she was just too young. "It'll never last," they sanctimoniously assured each other. But her love for Denzil, and his for her, never dimmed, and they celebrated their sixty-first wedding anniversary before she passed in 1996.

Since Howard was the closest to me in age, we shared more together than I did with Jerry. Everybody should have a sibling like Howard, and you'll understand why I say that when you get deeper into my story. He was strong-willed and set goals for himself that he began to accomplish early on. He was very gregarious and very much into service.

In Vista, California, where he was a builder/contractor, he joined Rotary International. It wasn't long before his leadership qualities were recognized and he eventually became governor of the San Diego District. He still actively attends weekly rotary meetings.

On December 28, 1932, our mother sent Howard and me down to our neighbor's house, the Stevenses, to stay all night. We had never done that before, and for a fleeting moment I thought it was very strange. I quickly dismissed the thought though, because the idea of staying overnight in somebody else's house had the ring of adventure about it.

The "why" we stayed the night at the Stevenses became clear the next morning when we came back to our house. Mom was still in bed—unusual for her—and snuggled next to her, pink and wrinkled, was my brand-new baby sister. It was a total shock to me, as my folks had not prepared me for a such a wonderful happening. As a matter of fact, sex was not something that was openly discussed between my parents and us kids—at least not with me. Consequently, early on in my mind, I thought sex was something that God didn't look upon too kindly. It even bordered on sinful.

Isn't it sad that the most intimate of physical relationships, the most wonderfully loving physical exchange between two individuals, has been pronounced "dirty" in the eyes of much of society? Perhaps we should take a page from the lives of "primitive" societies that still exist on the planet where the sexual experience is honored and glorified, where it is not spoken of in whispered tones but openly accepted as a normal function of the human experience. In those societies, rape is unheard of, as well as battered women. And a television ad promoting a cure for "erectile dysfunction" would be laughed at. Sex? It's the shame and guilt we place upon it that is so destructive.

I remember very vividly, when I was about six or seven, an evening on the farm when my mom and dad were discussing an article in the newspaper concerning a rape victim. It got our attention, because I'd never heard the word and I guess Howard wasn't really sure either, so we innocently asked, "What's rape? What's that?"

The room fell deathly silent for a good ten seconds as the color drained from Dad's face. It was quite obvious that he was in a state of mental turmoil trying to figure out the best way to satisfy our question without getting too graphic. He cleared his throat a couple of times, but the words just wouldn't come out. Finally, Mom said, "Well, go on, Walter, take them into the kitchen and explain it to them." You see, she didn't even think it was appropriate for that subject to be discussed in front of her.

So Dad summoned up his courage and said, "Okay, boys, come with me." I followed him and Howard into the kitchen, thinking, "Boy, this is going to be something. Mom can't even hear this!"

When we were safely out of earshot from her, Dad lowered his voice, apparently hoping even God wouldn't hear what was about to be said, and made a very painful attempt at clarifying things.

"Rape is . . . uh . . . what it is, is . . . uh . . . it's like . . . well, let's . . . let's say a man sees a woman and . . . and what he does is . . . uh . . . and he doesn't even ask her . . . he just . . . uh . . . he just . . . ." And at this point, Dad demonstrated to us visually by grabbing at the sleeves of his shirt. "He just tears all her clothes off!" The light bulb flipped on in Howard's head, and he quickly relieved Dad of any further agony.

"Oh, I understand, I know, I understand," he said.

Dad breathed a sigh of relief. He had passed the test. The ordeal was over. I just stood there dumbfounded, wondering if I should admit my bewilderment. I understood zero! What in thunder was rape? I was still totally in the dark.

Thankfully, afterwards, in the secret sanctuary of our bed, where we were sure no one else could hear, Howard cleared it up for me.

"That is truly amazing. I was raised the same way—no one talked about sex. So, you were talking about your new-born sister . . . ?"

Oh yeah. She was eight years my junior and we all thought she was the cutest thing ever to drop down from Heaven. The way we doted over her, it's a wonder she didn't become a spoiled brat. To her credit, she overcame all our coddling. It's hard to believe she is now a great-grandmother.

I think to make the bond between us stronger, Mom asked Howard and me to name her. He was to select her first name and I would pick her middle name. Howard chose Mary. I could have followed that with Beth, Louise, or Jane, but I thought Ann fit much better, so she had no choice in the matter. She went through life as Mary Ann Weaver, until she met and married her life's love, Lee, and became Mary Ann Greenly.

My mother was a fixer by nature, a true provider, so when things got rough, she was looking for a way to help, to make things easier for Dad. I'm not sure her efforts were always appreciated. Looking back, I think he may have felt her well-intentioned suggestions and frequent prods were a bit irritating.

However, something had to be done, and undoubtedly her voice was a big reason they decided to go back to their roots. They were both raised on farms, and in 1930 they bought a ten-acre piece of land about ten miles south of Joplin, to ensure that the family would be fed.

The property didn't have a house on it when we bought it; it had no electricity or plumbing—only an old cowshed. We converted that cowshed into a house and that is where we lived, in a made-over cowshed.

They say every cloud has a silver lining. Well, for me, the silver lining for the "depression cloud" was our move to that farm. It seems like my whole childhood was spent on it, but it was only four years—yet what a glorious four years it was.

"Hey, do you want to see a picture of the farm house?" Dennis asked modestly.

"Sure," I replied.

He jumped up from his chair and walked across the room. I got up and followed him. He stopped at a bookshelf filled with awards and picked up a relatively small oil painting of a shed-like house.

"This is it," he whispered.

I studied the picture, then his face. It was as though his smile held just a hint of apology and yet there seemed to be amusement behind it, like a joyful declaration that said he would not hide his childhood struggle. In that tiny frozen moment, I felt an unsolicited compassion for this man.

"It's cozy," I managed.

We sat back down and continued. . . .

The time that shapes our consciousness, that molds our character, is those formative years of early childhood. There is no doubt in my mind that the time I lived on the farm was greatly responsible for what I am today. Children need role models to give them life direction and purpose—and healthy surroundings to help them become the best they can be, to help them secure that state of happiness for which we are all reaching. I was blessed, beyond measure, to have been born and raised in an environment that served me well in my early years. I was surrounded by an abundance of positive role models.

First of all, my family gave me the feeling of belonging to something special. That is not to say that we didn't have our differences. Oh yes, we had our quota of spats and disagreements, but the stabilizing and overriding glue that held us together was love.

"What was your father like?" I asked, curious about both the people who had raised him.

Through my dad, I was exposed to a delicious sense of humor. He was an incurable tease. (Gerry says that I, for sure, picked that up!) He always carried his tools in a satchel that looked very much like a doctor's bag and, as a result, the gang down at the electric company called him "Doc," a nickname that stuck with him the rest of his life. I think my mother was the only one who called him Walter, usually when she was peeved.

One of the special treats for us kids was the Sunday edition of the *Denver Post*.

"The *Denver Post*? How'd you guys get the *Post* and why didn't you read the Joplin paper?" I interrupted him.

His eyes twinkled. "The *Denver Post* came by rail all the way to Joplin. We liked it best because it had the best funny papers in it."

"Comics?" I ventured.

"Yeah—some people called them comics. We called them funny papers."

So, we would get dibs on the funny-paper section to get up to speed on the exploits of Dick Tracy, Flash Gordon, Buck Rogers, Mutt and Jeff, The Katzenjammer Kids—my favorite—and then there was Maggie and Jiggs. Dad would always bring the paper home on Saturday night, and we kids waited for it with great anticipation. However, this one time it wasn't in plain view under his arm, which is where he normally kept it. I was stunned.

"Dad, where's the funny papers?" I squealed. The look on his face was a cross between pain and disbelief.

"How in the world could I have forgotten?" he said with an intense look on his face. "When I left the shop, I said to myself, now don't forget this is Saturday and I've got to pick up the *Denver Post*." He hesitated, then said, "I guess I was worried about the weather and just forgot."

He looked at the painful expressions on our faces for about ten seconds, but he could hold it no longer. A twinkle crept into his eyes, and the slightest trace of a smile warmed his face.

"Or maybe I absentmindedly stuck it in my tool bag."

The game was up! We pounced on the bag like a dog on a bone. And there, well hidden underneath his tools, was our weekly treat—the Sunday *Denver Post*.

Dad could not contain his giggle, and I heard Mom say from the kitchen, "Walter, shame on you!"

I think my dad was a frustrated entrepreneur, or perhaps just a dreamer with a good dose of Walter Mitty in him. He tried a grocery store in the early '20s, but it failed because of poor management by his brother-in-law. He talked of starting a mattress company and his own electrical service, but they remained only dreams, never coupled with action. He clung to his security at the electric company and, on retirement, he received his pin, which read, "Thanks for 35 years of loyal service."

He decided the community needed a place to dance, so he gathered a group of men together and, between them, they built an open-air dance platform on the southeast corner of our ten acres. He got the local talent to contribute their musical skills and on Saturday night, we had square dancing. There were no drums, but the banjos, guitars, and the stand-up bass really got our feet tapping. I really perked up when my granddad's fiddle woke up the crowd. Once in awhile, Dad would hit a hot lick on his harmonica. I can still hear the caller splitting the warm summer air with: "Bounce all, everybody whirl . . . up the center and back . . . up the center and cross the track . . . do-si-do right . . . do-si-do left . . . get her by the bobtail and shake her to death."

I had the best, reserved seat in the house, perched high up in my favorite post oak tree. From there, I could see everything going on—the dancers, the lovers, and the inevitable fight that always broke out when the booze took charge and two guys had their caps set for the same girl.

Between sets, Dad would show off by performing his famous turkey trot shuffle. It was a real crowd-pleaser, and he bathed in the attention. He was the life of the party.

"I think Gerry was right—you did get a bit of the showman from your father—I can see you doing that," I said, giggling, having seen both Dennis and Gerry perform at the

"Big Barn" here, in our little town, turning the packed house inside out with laughter.

A coyote was howling somewhere out in the impending darkness. It seemed close and, for a moment, distracted us from what we were talking about. Then, as quickly as the sound had pierced the night, it was gone, vanishing into the mysteries that held other secrets for only those creatures that are wild.

Dennis turned to me and said, "I like the sound of the snow goose the best. Did you know they fly in every spring and land on our pond?"

"I didn't know that," I said softly. Then I felt the need to move on. "Did your dad ever do any other kinds of performing?"

Many times I heard my mom say, "Your dad should have been an actor." But, with his situation and age, it was impossible for him to be another Will Rogers—and, I think the fact that his chance had slipped by him, made me determined that that wouldn't happen to me.

Dad did appear in a couple of plays at the local school. One of them got enough attention that it was booked in the Electric movie house in Joplin. I remember at one point in the play, a robber drew a pistol on Dad and, to show how frightened he was, his hands began to shake and his knees began to knock—it wasn't inspired by the Stanislavsky method of acting, but it got a huge laugh.

The room fell silent for a moment; only the rat-tat-tat of the rain at the windows could be heard.

"You told us that your mother was a fixer by nature—what was she like on a personal level?"

He squirmed around in his chair, and for a moment I thought he might be uncomfortable with the personal subject of his mother—but the submerged intensity that brought his voice down to a gentle softness told me that was not the case. Then, a smile turned the corners of his lips, and he started to speak.

My mother's heart was pure gold. But her Scorpio stinger was always lurking in the shadows. She was the disciplinarian, the one who made the rules and the one who enforced them. If I got out of line, she would tell me, "Go cut your own switch." This had a twofold benefit. It allowed me to find a weak switch and to take enough time for her fury to cool. She was quick to anger, but just as quick to forgive.

She had great sympathy and compassion for others—and, if someone needed a helping hand, she would quickly and willingly extend hers. During the depression, there were many strong-bodied men looking for "handouts," and not a few of them came knocking at our back door. They asked for food, not because they were unwilling to work, but because there was no work to be had. My mother never turned a single person away. Our cupboard was sparse, but it wasn't empty, and in her heart she could do nothing but share. However, she insisted they work for it. She always found a little job they could do to earn their food. Often I heard her say, "It's important they keep their pride."

Housework was not her thing—she would much rather be outside with her hands in the warm, rich earth, tending her flower beds or planting her vegetable garden. She was also very handy around the house. It seemed to me that she could fix anything.

Mom loved her children and fiercely supported us in anything we chose to do—as long as it was honest and didn't damage others. I can still hear her say, "Walk straight, shoulders back, and hold your head up high!" Sometimes, I think she believed in us a little too much.

For example, when we lived on the farm, I spent the first and second grades at a school in Spring City, but then we found out that we really lived in the Greenwood School District. The following year, when she enrolled me, Mom told the teacher (who taught grades one through four) that I was in the fourth grade. It was never questioned, so I skipped the third grade altogether! I handled it all right; however, I wouldn't advise anyone to do the same—for I was always a year younger than my friends and it affected me socially, and because I was always trying to match speed and strength with others (in sports) one or two years my senior! It made competing rather difficult.

She always made sure that her kids never went without anything they needed, even if she had to sacrifice her own needs.

Her tears came easily and sometimes often, but it was her joy for life and ready laugh that I remember above all else. I thought my mom was the best possible of all mothers and felt sympathy for kids not so lucky. As a youngster, she was my rock. No matter what the problem was, she gave me a wonderful sense of security—I always felt everything would be all right as long as she was near.

Since Dad had his day job, it was Mom's responsibility to run the farm. She taught us how to plant, to clear the brush, plow the fields, milk the cows, and cultivate and tend the garden.

In the summer, we "made hay while the sun shone." We prepared for the winter by stacking up a huge supply of wood and canning almost everything we grew. Since my hand was small, I was given the job of cleaning the jars used for canning and preserving. I always wondered why it was called "canning" since all we ever used were glass jars.

About a mile from our farm was a massive wild-blackberry patch. I don't know whose land it was on, but as far as the blackberries were concerned, they were common property. Everybody was welcome to take what they could pick. I took many trips to the blackberry patch with my Mom to fill my bucket with sweet juicy berries, ripened perfectly by the warm sunshine. They were delicious and by the time my bucket was filled, so was my stomach.

Those four years on the farm have provided me with a wealth of memories. I remember . . .

. . . an open fire in the back yard, heating water in a large washtub used to wash our clothes. It was my job to stoke the fire to keep the water hot. In those days, a washboard was a necessity that we used to scrub our clothes clean—not just a musical instrument in the country bands of today. We used the same tub to bathe in—of course, we changed the water!

. . . drawing water from our well to fill the bucket that I carried into the house. We had no indoor plumbing and no electricity.

. . . sitting on the wet, cold gunnysack of the ice cream maker to keep it stable while Granddad turned the handle.

. . . plunging the dasher of our butter churn up and down, up and down, up and down, until I could see little golden flecks of butter forming around the hole in the lid of the butter crock—which told me that I had beaten the butter out of the sour cream inside and my job was finished.

. . . crunching through the snow to the "two holer" outhouse.

. . . neighbors coming from miles around to fill their wooden barrels with our well water—which was considered the best in the county. The idea of charging for it was unthinkable. What nature gave freely to us was given to others without cost.

. . . jumping out of bed on a crisp, cold winter morning and huddling around the "king heater"—a thin, metal drumlike stove which a short time earlier was shoe-polish black and was now glowing red from the roaring fire inside which Dad had built moments earlier.

. . . the piping hot biscuits baked in a woodstove oven, slightly overdone just enough to make them deliciously crunchy on the outside, flaky and soft in the center. Breaking one open and watching the steam explode was a delightful sight. Then, slapping on a large dollop of freshly churned butter and watching it immediately disappear . . . and then covering it with Mom's special milk gravy. Oh me, they sure don't make them like that anymore.

. . . tramping through the woods with Howard in search of an old abandoned house which old-timers claimed was a hideout for Jesse James. After a couple of hours of meandering through the oaks and hickory trees freshly painted with bright autumn reds, oranges, and yellows, we suddenly came upon an impressive two-story dwelling in the middle of nowhere. If there was a road leading to it, Mother Nature had long since taken it back. It was eerie-looking, and we cautiously entered, not knowing if someone still occupied the premises. As we slowly examined room after room, it became obvious that it had long ago been abandoned. The only evidence of its past life were photo albums strewn on the floor. We quickly flipped through them, hoping to find a likeness of the famous outlaw that would confirm the old-timers' contentions. There were a lot of photos from the 1800s, but none matched the image of Jesse James this eight-year-old had come to know. And then, we noticed the walls . . . bullet holes! The walls were full of them. Eureka! It was as if we had found gold. Our imaginations took off like a runaway train. The old-timers were right—they knew what they were talking about, after all! We had found the secret hideout of Jesse James!

. . . keeping the cookstove supplied with wood, which had to be small enough to fit into the firebox. I loved the challenge of splitting the log pieces. It was very satisfying to strike the big chunks with all my strength and hear the sharp sound of a perfect hit as the mighty ax split it clean. Of course, if I had to work with a log full of knots, the wood could be very stubborn and my job frustrating.

. . . taking a salt shaker into the garden and gorging on the first vine-ripened tomatoes of the summer.

. . . Dad cutting the back half of our '27 Dodge off and converting it into a pickup. Howard and I loved to ride in the back of it all the way to Joplin to get our weekly treat—a Saturday matinee double feature, mostly westerns, at the Rex Theatre. Buck Jones with his horse "Silver" was my favorite, although Ken Maynard and Bob Steele were close seconds. Admission was a dime, and popcorn was a nickel.

. . . Shoal Creek, where my family and neighbors went swimming on hot summer days. A cable was attached to a large sycamore tree, which had branches reaching out over the river. We could hold on to a wooden bar, tied to the end of the cable, and swing out to the middle of the river and drop.

. . . Howard and I picking watermelons, breaking one open, eating the sweet, succulent center, then having a watermelon fight with the rest.

. . . our two cows. Morning and night, Howard milked one, and I milked the other.

. . . riding on the harrow to give it weight so that it could efficiently break up the clods of dirt and level the plowed ground. Eleven-year-old Howard handled the reins of our only horse, guiding him and the contraption expertly. He assumed, very early in life, the responsibility of a man.

. . . the droughts. Days of scorching hot sun. We watched the crops wither and die for lack of life-giving rain. Our garden only survived because we drew water from the well and hand-carried buckets of water to the thirsty plants.

. . . watching the dust storms gather, blowing precious topsoil away. Mom hanging water-soaked sheets over the windows to catch the fine dust that found its way through the tiny cracks around the window frames.

Early in the depression, it became clear that people had to come together and support each other, or many would just not survive. Not being cooperative and neighborly was not an option. If our neighbors were in trouble, we would not think twice about helping them—we just did it.

I remember a family, named Hardy, bought the ten acres next to our farm. There was nothing on the land except woods. . . .

Dennis leaned forward in his chair then and smiled, but not at me—he was looking through me—at a virgin piece of land filled with gnarled hickory trees and mighty oaks. He closed his eyes, lost in the fondness of the memory for a beat. Then, he opened them again and spoke.

The men in the surrounding area got together on weekends and cut down the trees and made logs to build a house—a real "log raising." And within six or seven weekends, they built a log home for the Hardy family to live in and a shed for their cow.

The children had lots of fun. We played games and jumped from stump to stump like leaping frogs while the men sawed logs and hammered nails. The ladies brought covered dishes of food, like potato salad, baked beans, and Jell-O, and we had a picnic at lunchtime. It was a community thing—a gathering of friends—and to this day, I still carry the feeling of it with me.

In those times and those moments—despite the depression—we thought we had the best of life; and, in a way, we really did. Life was simpler. We knew how good it felt to be neighborly—to share our lives with each other.

The stillness of the room was accentuated by a silence. Then he began again. . . .

The national economy was shredded due to the crash of '29, but in our area, including parts of Missouri, Oklahoma, Kansas, and Texas, the problem was exacerbated by what was known as the "Great Dust Bowl."

Continuing droughts had dried up the earth and the fierce winds picked up the defenseless topsoil and made huge clouds of thick, swirling dust. Visibility often shrunk to a few yards. The most skilled and determined farmers were humbled before its wrath. The nutritious topsoil was all blown away, and agriculture came to a screeching halt.

At the time, I didn't understand it, but it is crystal clear to me now that our economy and our environment are interdependent. When the environment (at that time) was destroyed and the farmers could no longer farm, they weren't the only ones who suffered. The economic disaster for the farmers spread like a raging virus . . . to carpenters, plumbers, shop owners, and even bankers. "Okies" by the thousands piled whatever possessions they could salvage into trucks, cars—any jalopy that would run—and headed for California, which Dust Bowl victims considered to be the land of milk and honey. Perhaps the only one who profited from the Dust Bowl was John Steinbeck when he wrote *The Grapes of Wrath*.

2

Lard and Mustard Wasn't an Option

Because of the Dust Bowl, our farm wasn't financially successful. It certainly helped to feed the family, but the extra income my folks had hoped it would generate didn't materialize.

Mom, always trying to find a way out, heard from neighbors, who had fled the Dust Bowl and our devastated economy earlier, that the strawberries were good in Oregon—there was money to be made just for the picking. So, we gave up on the farm and moved back to my birthplace in Joplin—619 Brownell—to get ready for the trek west. For a kid just turning ten years old, this was pretty exciting stuff. The farthest west I'd ever been was Blackwell, Oklahoma. Would I see a real-live cowboy? I wondered. What would Oregon be like? I might even see the Pacific Ocean!

Our budget for the trip was minimal at best. Like the pioneers who crossed the Great Plains a hundred years earlier, we were obliged to carry our own supplies, because motels and restaurants were out of the question. Unlike those earlier settlers, the horses that carried us were not hitched to a wagon, but were under the hood of a '28 DeSoto.

Our plan was simple—Mom, Howard, Mary Ann (two years old by this time), Jerry, Denzil Bell, and I would go to Oregon and pick strawberries, or do what other jobs we could get. We would save our earnings and come back to Joplin in time for Howard and me to go back to school. Dad would stay behind, keep his job at the Empire District, and serve as a safety net for us; in case we broke down or got stranded, he could bail us out.

Denzil was a carpenter by trade and he put his skills to good use. He built a cupboard on the back of "Ol' Betsy" (our DeSoto) where we could store an ample supply of canned goods and food staples. By releasing a fastener, the back side of the cupboard opened up and a leg swung down to support it, and, lo and behold, we had a table on which to prepare the food and off of which we could eat.

We jammed the "storeroom" with supplies, gave Ol' Betsy a final mechanical check, said our farewells, and headed west for the "wild blue yonder." Although she never hinted at it, I'm sure Mom must have had a few qualms and trepidations. For me, it was just the beginning of what I imagined to be a great adventure.

We started out for Oregon in the late spring of 1934.

In those days, there were no four-lane interstates, just two-lane roads that were often in need of repair and full of detours. Our top speed was forty miles an hour, so driving to Oregon was no walk in the park.

Not long after crossing into Colorado from Kansas, we could see, on the horizon, what looked like a triangular cloud. It was strange, because, while the other clouds moved, this one didn't budge. We used it as a guiding star for more than two hours before we realized that it wasn't a cloud at all—it was the snowcapped top of Pike's Peak!

As we drove deeper and deeper into the Rocky Mountains, I was moved more and more by their sheer beauty and breathtaking grandeur. It was awesome.

I loved the majestic granite mountains, the tall pines, the quaking aspens, the crisp, dry air—it was all very magical to me. I guess I am back in Colorado today because I was so impressed with it as a child. I was not only impressed by the beauty, but by what it had to offer. This was the first time I had ever seen a real-live working cowboy. And it was the first time I had ever seen a real deer.

We were driving over Wolf Creek Pass at dusk, coming around a bend, and there, right in front of us, was this wild deer, running down the road in and out of the shadows. He was a young buck, his antlers just out of velvet, and everybody in the car screamed! It was one of the most exciting things this ten-year-old kid had ever seen. It is funny how life works. Now there are deer all over our front yard—I see them every day.

Going through Utah, Ol' Betsy sputtered and stopped. Kids have a wonderful ability to not worry a whole lot. At least I didn't. I just knew that somehow things would turn out okay. After all, Mom would take care of it. So, while Denzil had his head stuck under the hood trying to find the problem, I was throwing dirt clods at prairie dogs to see how fast they could duck into their holes.

I don't remember what was wrong with the car, but Denzil evidently found the problem, for the next thing I heard was Mom calling, "C'mon, you kids, Ol' Betsy's ready to roll."

To pass the time, Howard and I would try to see who could guess the make of an oncoming car first—by the time we got to Oregon, we knew all the front grills of all the cars made in Detroit!

We also sang a lot. We just about wore out "Home on the Range." I kept looking for a buffalo, but by that time they had practically been slaughtered into extinction. Fortunately, a few were protected in Yellowstone National Park, so today they're making a comeback.

The day finally came when we crossed the Oregon border and we "whooped and hollered," for we could feel that our destination was in reach. Unfortunately, the rugged mountains, hot desert sun, rough roads, detours, and the heavy load that she carried proved to be too much for Ol' Betsy. She had given us her best, but in the mountains of Oregon, she had no more to give. She just pooped out. This time, Denzil's magical mechanical hands could not revive her. We looked at the map and realized help was not just around the corner. We were in a real pickle—up the creek without a paddle, so to speak.

Denzil decided that he would flag down a car, get a lift to the next town, and bring back help. The first car that came along was a late-model Buick. Lo and behold, when Denzil signaled that we were in trouble, it pulled over.

A middle-aged man got out and asked, "You folks got a problem?"

Mom immediately took over and explained where we had come from, where we were going, that a job was waiting for us, and our car had given out. The man's eyes scanned our motley-looking group, stuck his head under the hood—for a quick examination—looked once again into our eyes, and gave us a generous offer.

"Let me give you a push to the next garage, where you can get this fixed."

A grateful sigh escaped Mom's lips, and it was one of those rare times when she was speechless.

Recovering from disbelief, Denzil softly said, "Thank you, sir, we truly appreciate it."

I doubt if the man would have been so quick to offer had he known that the next garage was forty miles down the road. But he was as good as his word and pushed us through the mountains all the way to town.

The depression was a great equalizer. Everybody suffered to some degree, and it was natural to identify with a struggling neighbor. Shared troubles and pain have a way of bringing people together, of lifting them to a higher level of compassion and understanding. There was a feeling of togetherness. A shared crisis is fertile soil in which kindness can grow.

It seems a shame to me that in the years which followed, the more affluent our society became, the more a consciousness of separation prevailed. But that is changing. The pendulum is swinging back the other way. There is a great shift in mass consciousness towards "oneness." We can feel it. It's in the air. We can see it in spiritual organizations, books, movies, personal-growth seminars, tapes, and symposiums. We have realized that all the material pleasures the world has to offer will not satisfy the craving in our soul. The tide is shifting. The only question is, will it shift soon enough—before, as the Union of Concerned Scientists has warned us, we have "*irretrievably mutilated*" this incredibly beautiful Earth we call home?

We had no contingency plan that covered the fixing of Ol' Betsy. So, after paying the garage bill and topping off the gas tank (which amount we calculated would now get us to our journey's end), we had forty cents left.

The last rays of sunlight were filtering through the beautiful pines of Oregon. It was an exhausting day, and Denzil was dog-tired. Since Mom didn't feel comfortable driving at night and since our estimated time of arrival would be well after midnight, we pulled into a roadside park and gave thanks for the blessings we had received that day. Mom said a special prayer for the man who had pushed us the forty miles—a stranger who had saved our hides, and who we would never see again.

Mom unfastened the drawbridge door and opened up our cupboard, but the larder was beyond sparse. This was a mealtime we planned to spend with our friends, and we would have, had we not been sidetracked by car trouble.

All the cupboard could offer was part of a loaf of bread, an almost-empty jar of mustard, a quarter-pound of lard, and a couple of tablespoons of sugar. Mom didn't skip a beat. You would have thought she was a waitress at the Ritz-Carlton. "Alright, children, what'll it be, a mustard-and-sugar sandwich or a lard-and-sugar sandwich?"

Howard and I just looked at each other—but not for long. I heard Howard's stomach gurgle as he said, "I'll take mustard and sugar." Well, I never did care much for mustard, so I ordered lard and sugar. I guess Mom didn't figure lard and mustard was an option.

We slept on the ground in bedrolls. I remember how great it felt sleeping outdoors and looking up into the night sky, filled with millions of stars. I loved being that close to nature, listening to the night noises of the animals in the distance.

We were up and on the road before daybreak. By the pale glow of blue on the eastern horizon, we knew that the sun would soon start its daily trek across the sky, awakening the Earth from its nightly slumber . . . warming and energizing all living things.

Early morning was our preferred driving time, before the sun beat down on Ol' Betsy and made her a rolling oven. Air conditioning was still on the distant horizon, so by ten o'clock all the windows were down and Ol' Betsy was a veritable wind tunnel.

We gave "Home on the Range" one last shot as we pulled into the Collier's place. . . .

"That song, over and over again, must have driven your mother nuts!" I just blurted out—couldn't help myself.

"What—are you kidding? She was leading us!"

"Leading you—?" I shook my head in amazement. "What an incredible woman!" We were both laughing now.

"Yes—yes, she was," he chuckled. "Now, where was I? Oh, yes . . ."

We were a ragtag bunch—dirty and hungry as we emerged from the DeSoto shortly after twelve noon. Mrs. Collier took pity on us and started throwing food together. Mom immediately rolled up her sleeves and did what she could to help—all the while relating the dramatic stories of our trip. I could hear peals of laughter coming from the kitchen as she recited the scary details, which at the time were anything but laughable. After the fact, the worst problems are often amusing and it gives us a great deal of pleasure to recall them. Wouldn't it be wonderful if we could react to scary or hurtful situations while we're going through them just as we do after we've distanced ourselves from them? It would help if we realized it's all just God's great motion picture in the sky, and that pain is just God's loving prod to help us consider another option.

We were relieved when Mrs. Collier assured us that the strawberry farm needed pickers, and she felt it would be no problem for us to start in the morning. Looking back, I'm amazed at the tremendous faith my mother had. As I felt secure and had faith in my Earthly mother, she had the same faith in her heavenly Father/Mother. She often said, "God doesn't give us a test that He doesn't also give us the strength to overcome."

That night, pallets were strewn all over the living room floor of the tiny Collier house as the Weaver clan hunkered down to get a good night's sleep before challenging the strawberry patch.

After being assigned to small worker's cabins, we stowed our belongings and reported to the "Straw Boss." He explained to us that her strawberries went straight to a nearby plant, where they were made into jam; therefore, the berries had to be stemmed as they were picked.

I didn't mind the challenge. In fact, I remember being quite good at picking those Oregon strawberries—even at ten years old. I took great pride in the fact that I could keep up with the adults.

Now in order to understand what came next, you need to know that my mother was a Scorpio. She would always tell us kids, "You beware of my stinger." Yes, she was kind— but she also had a terrific temper, *and* she was very protective of her brood.

One day the Straw Boss—the foreman of the strawberry patch—had a problem with the way Howard was picking his strawberries. He claimed that he was mashing them. My mother was quick to point out that they were going to be jam anyway, so what was the difference? Well, somehow that comment did not sit well with the Straw Boss. He insisted that he had a problem with Howard, and my mother insisted that she had a problem with *him*. Finally, they got into a real row. Mom said something like, "Well, if that's the way you feel about it, we're out of here! I'm taking my gang and we're all leaving! And you know what you can do with your strawberries!"

We picked up my sister Jerry at the shack they provided for the workers and loaded everything up in the DeSoto. Within minutes, the strawberry patch was eating our dust. We got about three or four miles away, and someone asked, "Where's Mary Ann (my little two-year-old sister)?" With a sickening feeling we realized that we had left her behind— in the strawberry patch!

My mother said, very matter-of-factly, "Well, we've got to go back and get Mary Ann."

So, Denzil turned the car around and headed back. The more Mom thought about it, and the closer we got to the strawberry patch, the funnier the whole situation got, and her stiff veneer started to crack. We could see that she was beginning to smile, and we all starting laughing. By the time we got back to the field, we were hooting and hollering . . . tears were running down Mom's face. It was so ridiculous that she made up with the Straw Boss, and we all went back to work.

We were both laughing at the story. It took a moment for Dennis to compose himself, somewhat astonished at the depth of humor he had found in it.

The work in Oregon ended with the strawberry season and, on everyone's advice, we loaded Ol' Betsy and headed for the land of opportunity—California. There, in the warm sunshine, crops were abundant and jobs were plentiful.

In Manteca, Denzil got lucky. He found a job as a carpenter. His income increased considerably, and we were able to rent the old Duval house at the edge of town. Manteca was in the center of the fertile San Joaquin Valley, a huge agricultural district. The land was very flat, and irrigation waterways crisscrossed the valley to form a patchwork of ditches that fed the thirsty soil.

Mom was always one to pull her own weight, so it wasn't long before Howard, Mom, and I were working in the peach and apricot drying sheds in nearby Escalon. Our job was to cut and pit the peaches, and lay them out on a tray so they could be carried to the sulfur houses, where they were treated to keep them soft to the palate and appealing to the eye. (I have no idea what the sulfur did to the nutritional value of the fruit!) The trays of peaches would then be placed in the sun to dry.

We didn't get paid by the hour. It was piecework, and we were paid according to how many peaches or apricots were pitted. There were two kinds of peaches—Freestones and Clings. Freestones were easy to pit; we just cut the peach, popped it open, and flipped the pit out with our thumbs, placing the fruit on the tray with our right hand, while our left was reaching for another. Developing a rhythm was very important.

"That reminds me of the 'Lucy Show,' when Lucy and Ethel were working in the chocolate candy factory. . . ," I interrupted.

"Yeah—only we never ate any. Could have . . . should have. Didn't," he said with a laugh.

Anyway, the Cling peaches were a different matter altogether. First we had to cut them, then take a special spoon-like knife and drive it into the peach and twist the pit out. This was time-consuming.

On a good day, I could cut a box, about half a bushel (or "lug" as they called it), of Freestones in twenty minutes and collect five cents for my effort. Yes, that was the going rate—five cents for Freestones and ten cents for Clings. If I averaged a lug every twenty minutes, a pace I could not maintain, it doesn't take a rocket scientist to figure that's fifteen cents an hour. After eight hours, my take-home pay was closer to seventy-five cents a day! Now, that's not going to get you rich, but—hey—it was better than a breadline, and it did do wonders for my self-esteem.

The move to the Duval house proved to have an unpredictably strong effect on my life, for just across the irrigation ditch that bordered the Duval place lived an old German family, the Hogrefes. The mother and father had migrated to America when they were young and raised a family of seven kids here. The next to the youngest was George, who at the time of our meeting was in his early twenties. I think, because of a birth defect (a cleft palate) which most would describe as homely, he felt awkward around adults, particularly women. So, he lived the life of a bachelor. But with kids, he felt comfortable, and we all loved him.

I actually went to school in Manteca one year—in the eighth grade. When everyone went back to Joplin, I got to spend the entire winter with George and his family. I used to work for him, doing lots of odd jobs around the house. He made sure that I did the job thoroughly, that I was honest . . . he encouraged me to be the best I could be. He also taught me to play chess. And, something that was really important, he taught me how to drive his 1928 Essex!

A lot of the kids I ran around with would congregate at his place, because he was good at woodworking and had a workshop at the back of the house. He made beautiful inlaid pieces—like chessboards. It was a fascinating place to be. He was also a writer and a poet.

One day, he stuck a dollar bill on the wall of his room and said, "Whichever one of you guys beats me first (at chess) gets the dollar bill." I learned the importance of incentive and perseverance. I won the dollar.

George was the janitor at the El Rey Movie Theatre. He hired me as his assistant, cleaning up the theatre—and nothing gets dirtier than a theatre! The good part was that I got to see all the movies that came to town for free, and that stimulated my love of acting.

George had a big influence on my life. He was a wonderful human being, and I will never forget him. I am sure that I have incorporated his work ethics into my life. He was a positive role model who has contributed greatly to what I am today.

"Sounds like George was a great guy." The expected nod was there, followed by a moment of introspection. I hesitated, then started again. "So, did you stick to your plan? Did you go back home?"

Yes. We were back in Joplin in time for school the next year. But California was in our blood, and for the next four summers we made our annual pilgrimage out west. Mom had a special incentive: since carpentry work was plentiful, Denzil and Jerry stayed in California and soon had their first son, Jimmy. Donny and Larry quickly followed, and Mom wanted to see her grandsons.

One year, I think it was '36, we got Dad to take an extended vacation and come with us, hoping he would find a better-paying job in California. I don't think he made much of an effort to get one, which, no doubt, didn't please Mom very much. But it was a fun and challenging trip, because we left Ol' Betsy behind and took up residence with sixteen others in a large 1934 Chevy truck—it looked like one of those army vehicles with a tarpaulin strapped over it to protect us from inclement weather. There were twenty-one of us, including our family. On one side of the tarp we painted "California or Bust" and, with great expectations, we confidently pulled out onto old Highway 66 and headed west, leaving Joplin in our rearview mirror.

In 1938, Mom decided she wouldn't make our annual summer trip to California. But for Howard and me, it was now in our blood and we were itching to get on the road. Howard had worked at the Parkway Pharmacy in Joplin as a soda jerk and felt he had saved enough money to make the trip. All that was needed was an automobile. He found a '29 Model A Ford convertible on sale for fifty dollars, and Dad was willing to sign for him—guaranteeing payment to the bank. Howard would pay it off at five dollars a month.

With that done, we went to Mom for permission, which she promptly denied us.

"You kids are a little young to be making that trip by yourselves," she said, thinking she had just put an end to the conversation.

But Howard had anticipated her reaction and countered with, "Well, Mom, we won't be going by ourselves. Preston Stahlsmit (son of a local osteopath), who is twenty-two, will be going with us. He needs to go to Phoenix, and he'll also pay half of the expenses!"

Mom hesitated, and Howard seized the moment. "It's not as though we haven't done this before, and Monte (the nineteen-year-old son of our next-door neighbor) also wants to go—he has to get to Los Angeles, and can chip in some."

Mom was still hesitating, so I threw in my two cents. "Aw, come on, Mom, it'll be a good experience for us. And I can work for George while I'm there. We may never get this chance again."

It was very difficult for our mother to deny us anything, and I could see her melt.

"You just be sure and take care of yourselves and don't get into any trouble. And let us know where you are, you hear?"

Howard and I were overlapping each other. "Oh, sure, Mom—of course, we will! And thanks a lot, Mom. Thanks—you won't be sorry!"

So, in late May—of my fourteenth year—the Model A Ford was loaded and ready for another go at the western coastline. Howard was behind the wheel, Preston was riding shotgun, and Monte and I were tucked away in the rumble seat. Baggage? Oh yes, we had a luggage rack attached to the running board which held all our gear, except for Preston's tennis racket, which he clutched guardedly in his lap. The fact that he couldn't open his door, because it was blocked by the luggage rack, was a source of some irritation for him.

The final hugs and kisses were delivered, and we pulled away from the curb singing, "California, here we come. . . ." I gave a final look over my shoulder, and I could see Mom and little Mary Ann, by her side, still waving. Then, we rounded a corner and they disappeared from view. I was at once excited about the adventure that lay ahead and a little misty-eyed, knowing I wouldn't see them again until the fall.

As we turned onto old Highway 66, I could not contain the thrill of anticipation that tingled through my body. We were really doing it! We were on our way to California. The sun shone generously on us, the sky was an endless blue, and the Model A cut through the fresh morning air, creating gentle puffs of wind that ran like soft silky fingers through my hair and over my face. Oh yes, for a fourteen-year-old, it was pure bliss. Of course, I had no idea of what really lay ahead.

We arrived in Phoenix without incident, but fell into deep shock when Preston refused to pay his half of the expenses. Howard, his anger level rising rapidly, confronted him.

"You promised to pay. We've got to get to California. I was counting on that money!"

But no amount of pleading dented Preston's conscience. "Well, I'm sorry, but I just don't have it," he said flatly. Then, he simply picked up his bag and tennis racket and walked away, practicing his serve with an imaginary tennis ball.

I think that nothing infuriates a person more than injustice, and I saw steam coming out of Howard's ears. He was as mad as an old wet hen, but what could he do—call the district attorney? After a few choice expletives, his mindset shifted from anger to concern. I'm sure he was wondering if we could reach our destination on our limited funds or whether we would have to pick up some work first.

I felt about Howard much the same as I felt about Mom . . . if he was around, he'd handle whatever problem came up. And so, as he leaned against the left front fender and pondered the situation, I tried to figure out how he was going to get us out of this mess.

Heaving a sigh of frustration, he pulled himself up to his full height, kicked the Model A tire to vent the last residue of his anger, walked around the car, and retrieved a map of Arizona and California from the glove box. He spread it out on the sun-heated hood and began to calculate the miles to go against miles per gallon, and the cost of gas.

His math complete, he pulled his wallet from his left hip pocket, split it open, and started thumbing through his well-worn bills. Monte and I—all eyes and ears—were respectfully silent and hoping for the best.

After what seemed like an endless pause, he looked us in the eye and reported.

"It's going to be a little tight, but I think we can make it."

Monte and I both yelled, "whoopee!" and danced a little jig. We were on the road again, and I had the rumble seat all to myself.

After dropping Monte off in Los Angeles, Howard told me he wasn't sure we had enough money to get to Manteca, so we opted to go to Oceanside, north of San Diego, where Uncle Rex, our Mom's brother, had a small beach house.

When we arrived, the front door was locked and no one was home. Luckily, we found easy access through an unlocked back door. Since we were eating very lightly on the road, we quickly headed for the kitchen. It looked like Uncle Rex ate out most of the time, because the pantry only produced a box of saltines, and the icebox didn't yield much more—a half bottle of French dressing and a couple of "on the edge" avocados. Growing up in Missouri, I had hardly ever seen an avocado, and I sure hadn't acquired a taste for them. But I did that day. If you're hungry enough, a lot of things you don't like can suddenly taste really good, especially if you mix them with enough French dressing and spread them on saltine crackers.

A neighbor told us that Uncle Rex, who was a lineman for Bell Telephone Company, was injured on the job and needed to recuperate in the hospital for a few days. He was somewhat startled when we walked into his hospital room.

"What are you kids doing here?" he asked, genuine surprise in his voice.

"We're heading up to Manteca—for work," Howard replied.

"Manteca? That's way north, near Sacramento." And, with a little chuckle, he added, "You've come a far piece out of your way."

Then, Howard explained in detail our present plight.

Uncle Rex listened with some amusement, and when Howard was finished with his tale of woe, he made us an offer we couldn't refuse.

"I've got an account at the Safeway store. You get the food you need to get you to Manteca—you hear?"

"Yes, sir." We both answered in unison.

"I'll call the manager and tell him it's okay—to charge it to me."

We stayed long enough to thank him profusely and as we started out the door, he stopped us.

"Oh, another thing—if you need a couple of extra bucks to make sure you've got enough gas money, I'll tell him to give it to you and he can put that on my bill also."

Howard and I could not believe our good fortune, and we rushed to give him a hug and another thank-you.

We headed for Safeway and loaded up on tins of sardines, cheese, crackers, mustard, and Oreo cookies—just what growing boys need. We stopped by a roadside stand, bought a half a bushel of oranges for a dollar, and were on the road again.

That summer was a memorable one for me. I worked with George cleaning the El Rey Movie Theatre and in return I got my room and board and a little pocket change. And of course, I got to gorge on free movies—and in those days they changed the bill every two or three days! Soon I became very familiar with Melvyn Douglas—he later played my father in *Intimate Strangers*, a movie-of-the-week—Barbara Stanwyck, Tyrone Power (who I worked with in *Mississippi Gambler*), Spencer Tracy, Irene Dunne, Gary Cooper, Jimmy Stewart, James Cagney—who tried to teach me to dance like he did in *Yankee Doodle Dandy* between shots on the set of *Gallant Hours* . . . nobody could dance like Cagney. He was special.

Howard worked in Stockton as a fry cook all summer and saved enough money so that going back to Joplin wouldn't be a white-knuckle trip. We left plenty early so that our journey home could be a tour of the West. And indeed it was. We roamed from Arizona to Wyoming and visited places of interest we had only heard older folks talk about. We saw the painted desert and the petrified forest; I was a little disappointed in that—it didn't look like much of a forest to me. Not one of the trees was standing; every single one of them had fallen over.

In Nevada we stopped to see the Hoover Dam (Boulder Dam). I had remembered seeing a movie about the building of it, starring Ross Alexander. What stuck with me as a young kid was the fact that this extremely talented actor took his own life. I couldn't understand that—why would someone at the peak of his movie career, able to have everything he could possibly want, commit suicide? It puzzled me greatly.

Anyway, Howard and I decided to drive up to the dam and take a look. Wow! What an awesome piece of work! Standing on the road at the top of the dam and looking over the rail at the river 726 feet below made the backs of my knees turn to water. We just stared down in silence for a long time. Finally, we left what was at that time the largest man-made structure in the world behind and headed for Salt Lake City—all the while wondering if we could really float in the lake.

We were seventy-five miles out of Ely, Nevada, with the next town—according to the map—a good seventy-five miles down the road, when it happened. The Model A choked, sputtered, and died, right there in the middle of the desert. Howard jumped out and threw open the hood, scrutinizing its innards. After a few minutes, he declared that the points of the distributor were no longer making good contact and needed to be replaced. He tried for half an hour to prove himself wrong, to no avail.

He first tried to get it to fire up by using the starter but, after several minutes of grinding the battery, it had only enough power to barely turn the motor. It was growing dangerously low on juice, so Howard took out the hand crank. While I was in the driver's seat operating the spark lever according to Howard's instructions, I could see his head bobbing up and down as he desperately tried to crank the dead Ford alive.

The cool morning air began to quickly dissipate as the sun climbed higher in the sky, beating down hot on the desert floor. With beads of perspiration dripping from his nose, my brother gave it one last futile crank, wiped his brow on his sleeve, and sat in the shade of the Model A to catch his breath and ponder our next move.

It was ten o'clock when Howard hitched a ride to Ely. The plan was for me to stay with the car while he picked up a new set of points from the Ford dealership. He figured the roundtrip would take no more than three hours. Fortunately, we carried food and water with us, so I wasn't very concerned.

I really don't know how I spent the next three hours—I was just thankful that we had the top up on the convertible; otherwise, without shade, the hot desert sun could have baked me to a fare-thee-well. By 12:30, I was thinking that the next approaching car might be the one carrying Howard, but by one o'clock—the time he had calculated his return—the cars were still whizzing by. I began to get a little uneasy. Then, two o'clock came and went. Still no Howard. By 2:30, I was getting seriously worried and started wondering what I would do if Howard never returned. Finally, at 3:15, I held my breath as a big black Chrysler began to slow. When it pulled in behind the Model A and Howard stepped out, I heaved a huge sigh of relief.

Howard immediately began to replace the points, and the driver of the Chrysler offered to hang around to make sure we could get it started. It's a good thing he did, because the new set of points didn't remedy the problem. The car still refused to start.

While we tried to figure out what to do next, the driver of the Chrysler suggested that he push us to a filling station he said was just over the next hill. We quickly accepted his offer.

The Chrysler gave us one last push and as we coasted to a stop by the gas station, I saw a weathered sign that announced "Bard's Café—home-cooked meals." It turned out to be a combination filling station and restaurant. It reminded me of the one in the movie *Petrified Forest*, starring Leslie Howard and Humphrey Bogart—and I expected Bette Davis to walk through the swinging doors that had an "employees only" sign hanging above them; but instead, a pleasant-looking woman, rather plump, with a kind face, the same age as my mother, came out wiping her hands on her flour-sack apron. This was Mrs. Bard. The aroma of cooking food followed her—wafting under my nose and reminding my stomach that I hadn't eaten since early morning—as she stood there and listened sympathetically to our story.

"We can give you an oil change and a fill-up, but that's about it. There is no mechanic on the premises," she said apologetically.

Howard had already determined that he had to go back to Ely, before the Ford dealership closed, and get the whole distributor—which, of course, he should have done in the first place, and he kept berating himself for trying to save a couple of bucks.

"There's a truck driver ready to pull out now. I'll get you a ride with him and with some luck—it'll be close, but I think you'll make it before the dealership closes," Mrs. Bard informed him. Then she turned her attention to me and said, "And you, you'll help me with the dishes for your supper."

I said, "You bet I will." I was good at that. Howard and I often helped Mom do the dishes at home.

By 7:30 p.m., the summer sun was beginning to drop and Howard had not yet returned. I began to think that he probably got to Ely after the dealership had closed and I wondered where he would be staying the night.

Mrs. Bard detected the concern in my face and said in a confident, almost jovial tone, "Oh, it's early yet. He'll be back. In the meantime, you've had a long day, and I'll show you where you can bunk." She led me out back to their pump house in which she had placed a bed—that had seen better days—and explained, "Sometimes I can rent it to a trucker that gets all wore out and feels he can't make it clear into Ely. It's not the Ritz, but it'll beat the floor." It looked like heaven to me, and I thanked her kindly. I was dog-tired and almost before I pulled the covers over my shoulder, I was sawing logs.

It was midnight when Howard woke me with a start. "Move over. You're hoggin' the bed," he said as he crawled in, exhausted, beside me.

In a flash, I was quickly awake. "Did you get it?"

"Yeah. I got it."

"What took you so long?"

"Nobody wants to pick up a stranger at night. Not many people even drive at night."

I was quiet for a long moment, then I asked, "Do you think we'll get it started?"

"We'll know in the morning. Now knock it off—I'm tired."

Mrs. Bard's dog was yapping loudly outside the pump house as the sun peeked over the horizon. I slowly woke from a deep, satisfying sleep, and for a brief moment couldn't figure out where I was . . . then, as my brain focused, I quickly sat up. Howard was already gone, so I threw off the covers and reached for my pants. I stuck my head out the door, as I jammed my clothes on, and could see Howard was already working on the car. Somehow he knew that I was there, watching, and yelled at me without turning his head.

"When you finish breakfast, come out and give me a hand—and we'll see if she's got any life in her."

I was just finishing up my bowl of oats when Howard yelled through the screen door of Mrs. Bard's kitchen, "I need you to help me start it; let's go."

My self-esteem always went up a notch whenever I felt Howard needed my help, so I gulped the last two spoons full and hurried out the door to see how I could assist.

Howard was at the front of the car with the crank in hand, and he carefully explained to me what to do.

"As I give it a couple of cranks, you give it some spark, and if it kicks over, choke it a little, okay?" Now, realizing that the success of this operation depended on me, I braced myself for the task and confidently replied, "Okay!" Cooperating and working with Howard gave me a real high.

As he gave it a couple of cranks, he yelled, "Now!" I responded by pulling the spark lever down and up a couple of times. Nothing happened. Cranking a Model A is not easy, and Howard soon took a breather to rest his arm.

A moment later, he was ready to give it another try.

"Now, try choking it when I crank and just pull the spark lever down and leave it."

"You got it," I yelled back. And Howard began to crank it again. After three or four vigorous turns, the old Ford coughed and coughed again—the distributor was firing and Howard screamed at me.

"Push the choke in! You're going to flood it!"

I quickly did, and the coughs came closer together. Howard ran around the car, disengaged the spark, and reached in and started pumping the foot feed with his hand, all the while coaxing the Ford to keep firing.

At first it was hitting only on two cylinders and Howard had his ear to the engine, whispering encouragement, . . . "C'mon, baby, c'mon." And baby did. She started hitting on three cylinders! Howard turned to me with a big smile on his face and said, "Get your stuff, that's good enough—three cylinders will get us home."

I dashed back to the pump house, grabbed my little satchel, and the both of us bid Mrs. Bard farewell—thanking her for all her help. By eight o'clock we were on the road again. About a mile down the highway, Howard turned to me and smiled.

"Do you hear that? She's hittin' on all four now."

I just smiled and thanked God.

We did stop at the Great Salt Lake and took a dip in the briny water. Sure enough, we couldn't sink, but it took us the better part of an hour standing under a freshwater shower to wash the salt off of us.

We drove to the center of Salt Lake City and took in the museum, which gave us a real sense of early pioneer life and the settling of the valley by Brigham Young and the Mormons.

We also visited the Tabernacle. The thing that impressed me the most was its acoustics. Our guide had us stand next to the back wall while he stood near the pulpit, which seemed to separate us by at least two hundred feet. He then lightly rubbed his hand on his sleeve and the sound was clearly audible. Amazing! The building was designed so well that no sound amplification was needed. Even at fourteen, it became obvious to me how important design was in the things we make.

We heard that "Cheyenne Days" was in full swing and calculated we could get to Wyoming before they ended, if we didn't dally around. I had never been to a rodeo, and the possibility of seeing real cowboys on bucking broncos was an irresistible pull. I guess Howard felt much the same way, because we headed the Model A northeast and set sail for Wyoming.

I wasn't disappointed. Cowboys and horses inundated the entire town. The scent of the Old West was everywhere, permeating every nook and cranny of Cheyenne. My excitement was nonstop. I loved the sound of creaking saddles and the smell of sweaty mustangs. The urge to get on one of those cow ponies was intense. I've always felt that desire is to fulfillment what cause is to effect.

"Wait just a minute—that came out of nowhere. What are you talking about?" I interrupted. My facial expression must have been askew, because his left eyebrow shot up, then settled back into its normal position.

"Desire. It is the beginning of fulfillment. How quickly the fulfillment comes depends on the degree of desire, and the intensity of the action that you give to it. It took me a few years to prove that axiom true, but I eventually had that desire satisfied."

"You're talking about riding cow ponies—right?"

"Yeah—but I learned to apply the principle to other things as well."

Before we left Cheyenne, a man approached us with a bucket, paintbrush, and a stencil of a bucking bronco—it's still the logo that can be seen on Wyoming's license plates—and asked if he could stencil our car. He assured us that the paint would wash off with a little soap and water, so we said, "Hey, why not?"

As we left Wyoming and headed south to Colorado, a passing motorist, at quick glance, might have thought the Model A had chicken pox. There were no less than one hundred bucking broncos covering it bumper to bumper. It was a rolling billboard for "Cheyenne Days."

I breathed a sigh of relief as we picked up Highway 66, which would deliver us back to Joplin. We were both eager to get home and took turns driving, day and night, nonstop.

We were halfway through Oklahoma, ten o'clock at night, and Howard was pretty well spent. He pulled over and said, "Your turn. I'm beat. I need some sleep."

I was delighted. As you can well imagine, at the age of fourteen, I felt pretty special to be the captain of the ship.

Feeling confident and very grown up, I commanded the Model A down the road at a good clip. Twenty minutes later—Howard was fast asleep—I noticed that the road was wet with frequent large puddles of water. I could hear the ominous rumbling of thunder off in the distance and knew that we had just missed some heavy rainstorm. I rounded a curve and was confronted by bright red, flashing lights. Trouble was ahead. I glanced at Howard, hoping he was awake, but he was still long gone. I pulled up to the lights and discovered that it was a sign—bridge washed out; detour ahead. The arrow pointed to an old country road full of Oklahoma red-gumbo-mud. I hesitated, should I wake up Howard? Should I try it myself? Then, with unlimited self-confidence, the kind reserved for an adolescent with one year's driving experience under his belt, I decided to go for it. After all, Howard needed his sleep, and I could see the tracks of others that had gone ahead of us. It seemed to be no problem, so I steered the Ford off the highway and challenged the Oklahoma gumbo. Not too smart.

I've never gotten into such a mess since. The mud was slicker than Granny's okra stew! Luckily, I didn't try to fight it. I just went with the flow, and I'm here to tell you I knew if I ever stopped, it was all over and I'd never get started again. Several times I chewed myself out for not waking Howard, but it was too late for that now. There was nothing to do but plunge ahead and pray for the best. I'm sure that the Ford's high center of gravity saved my butt. I chugged along, slipping and sliding past late-model Buicks and Chryslers with their low-slung chassises off in the ditch stuck up to their hubcaps—I thanked God I was still moving.

I finally came to a small town where the detour ended. I felt total relief. I was exhausted, but at the same time, exhilarated . . . I did it! I really did it! I can't tell you how secure I felt when I was once again back on good old Highway 66.

Howard woke up to ask if everything was okay. I assured him, "Oh—yeah, sure. Everything's fine. It's all under control." In two minutes he was gone again. It wasn't until midmorning, the next day, that I bragged about how I got us through the perilous red-gumbo-mud of Oklahoma.

That day we pushed hard to get home in the early evening, but by ten o'clock, passing through Miami, Oklahoma—thirty miles outside of Joplin—exhaustion overtook us both. We pulled over to the side of the road, figured we'd catch a couple of winks, and still make it home by midnight.

The next thing we were conscious of was the morning sun beating down on our faces. We fought our way out of dreamland, only to discover that the folds of the soft-top convertible were filled with water. Our clothes were drenched. We were like two drowned rats. We were so road-weary, so completely drained, that we were totally unconscious of what must have been a real cloudburst that night. We gave thanks for the warm morning sunshine and laughed as we pulled out onto the highway. Our clothes dried in the wind and sun over the next thirty miles, and by the time we arrived home we felt exhilarated.

Mom, Dad, and Mary Ann welcomed us with hugs and kisses. That night, after dinner, you can imagine the stories that were spun and the tales that were told. A most memorable and thrilling summer had ended for me.

"Have you been back to Joplin since you left?" I asked.

In 1985, Gerry and I took a trip back there. I was very eager to see the old farm again. However, it wasn't easy to locate, for the washboard gravel road that I had traveled so many times going to and from Joplin had long since given way to an interstate—a four-laner—that came perilously close to our ten acres. We finally found the old farm by circling and approaching it from the opposite direction. The old converted cowshed that was once our home was gone. But the one landmark that allowed me to identify the farm for certain was my favorite post oak tree in which I had spent so much time pretending to be Tarzan. Glory be, it was still standing! Such a flood of memories raced through my mind as I ran to the tree and grabbed the lowest branch and began to climb. I was a kid again, and it felt so good.

I looked down to catch Gerry's reaction. She just stood there frozen—open-mouthed. Was she afraid I was going to break my neck? I think she was dumbfounded that I could still shinny up a tree so fast at the age of sixty-three!

I didn't have such luck finding the blackberry patch. It had, years ago, been obliterated by the interstate highway. I was sad, for I realized that many kids growing up today would not have the same close contact with nature that I once had. I became acutely aware of the fact that humans were gobbling up more and more of the Earth's soil and I understood in a very personal way that we are on a collision course with that which gives us life—our environment. The experience prompted me to write this song:

Where have the wild blackberries gone that I picked
when I was a boy?
Where's the creek where I cooled my feet?
Where's the country store?

CHORUS
They're gone, they're gone.
The wild berries are gone.
They fought 'til their defeat.
They were no match for the brain of man
And his highways of concrete.

We chopped and burned our trees away
Where nature did reside.
We stilled her laugh
By the barefoot path.
Now to each other we cry.

CHORUS

This land once grew the things we need.
The water was pure and sweet.

Now the town is dirty brown
And the air is not fit to breathe.

CHORUS

For what we think and say and do
There always is a tax
And in a trice we pay the price
For our foolish acts.

CHORUS

The connection with the Great Depression and the destruction of the environment—the Dust Bowl—made me realize as a little boy that the environment was very, very important to life on the planet, and to our economic welfare as well.

When the environment is destroyed, it affects the economy and vice versa—it is an ugly cycle of both economic and ecological destruction. What we have to do is break that cycle—and we can do that through the philosophy and the power of Ecolonomics. It is interesting how one thing impacts us and propels us into something else.

"What is Ecolonomics?" I asked.

"It's a word I coined, several years ago—the marriage of the ecology with economics. But that's for later—we'll work into that subject a few hours from now," he said with a voice that left no doubt that this subject was far too important to merely touch on—it would require time.

"Okay—," I said, my own voice sounding tentative in comparison. "So what happened next?"

3

"I Never Want to See You Again, You Hear?"

After we moved back to Joplin in 1934 and started our annual summer trips to California, we never lived on the farm again. The depression was winding down and Dad's salary had increased. But to make sure there was enough money for the necessities of life, Mom and Dad divided our small (city) house at 619 Brownell and rented out the front portion to the Hastings family, who operated the corner grocery store. We closed in the back porch so Howard and I could have a place to sleep. Most of the kids I ran around with lived in a whole house, and it was awkward and embarrassing to invite them over to a house that was divided.

At the time, I didn't really appreciate my parent's struggle to provide for us kids. I more or less knew that we would be taken care of.

I also was aware that, although my parents were compatible for the most part, they were not an overly loving couple. Underneath the façade, particularly on Dad's part, all was not well. However, it was easy for me to push this aside and live in denial. I assumed what troubles they had would be smoothed over and life would go on—after all, that had always been the pattern.

As a kid growing up, I felt secure because I had a mother and a father, and in my perception their good moments together certainly outweighed their bad ones, and I definitely felt that they would always be together for me; and they were until I was nineteen.

I was training in the Naval Air Corps when I got the news from my sister Jerry, who by this time had moved back to Missouri with Denzil and their three kids, that Dad had left Mom. I was stunned—why, after twenty-seven years of marriage? I felt Mom's embarrassment, and I knew the fear of being alone would leave her distraught and deeply depressed, and my heart went out to her. Even with their ups and downs, Mom was very attached to Dad. Attachment and expectation always sets us up for pain and disappointment.

Shortly afterward, I was on my way home for Christmas from Saint Mary's College in California, where I was in pre-flight training. The train ride back to Missouri was very somber. In my mind, I created all kinds of scenarios of how I would deal with the circumstances and what I would say to Mom. Of course, when I was faced with the real situation, none of the scenes I had planned worked—it didn't matter how many times I had rehearsed them.

Mom had moved in with Jerry and Denzil and their three young boys. As I had suspected, living alone was not something she could readily face—especially since Dad had left her for another woman, which I learned upon my arrival. It was a crushing blow to her ego.

It was Christmas Eve, 1943, and we were in the spirit of the season, pretending all was well, and doing a remarkable job of it, when the doorbell rang. Jerry answered it, and there stood Dad, hat in hand, looking sheepish and forlorn, with three crisply wrapped Christmas presents tucked under his arm for his grandsons. There was a very pregnant pause. The air was heavy with silence.

Finally, he broke the awkwardness with, "I've got some gifts for the boys." Jerry quickly glanced at Mom, who responded with an "it's okay" nod. Then she invited him in. After placing the packages under the tree and attempting some awkward greetings, Mom and Dad disappeared into the upstairs bedroom to talk.

We all looked at each other questioningly, hoping maybe they'd work things out. Ten minutes passed and I turned to Jerry and said, "Do you suppose they are getting back together?" But before she could answer, the upstairs bedroom exploded with angry voices, and the door flew open, and Dad came bursting out with Mom right on his tail, pummeling him with a stream of heated accusations. All I could hear him say was, "All right, Lenna. All right," as he hastily retreated down the stairs, with Mom venting her rage on his backside.

With distance and time I can look back on the situation and see both the drama and the humor in it—the remembrance of it actually provokes a smile. But isn't that the way it is with most situations that seem so sad and near tragic? So often, that which at the time seems so difficult proves to be a stepping stone to bring value and benefit to our lives.

The problem is that, at the time, we can only see a very small portion of a very large picture. We cannot see the perfection of the individual pieces of the puzzle.

And I certainly couldn't see the "perfection" that Christmas Eve in 1943. All I could see was what appeared to me to be the injustice that my mother was suffering, and I responded with all the righteous indignation befitting a nineteen-year-old who perceived himself to be his mother's protector.

As Dad hurried through the living room, heading for the front door, Mom stopped at the coffee table and grabbed the Christmas oranges, apples, and bananas, neatly arranged in a fruit bowl, and flung them at him—one right after the other. Dad ducked and dodged, as he bolted through the door. He still tried to calm her rage, muttering, "All right, Lenna. I know, I know. All right." The sound of his pathetic voice did not diminish her fury! Fruit was still flying after him as he disappeared around the corner of the house.

I was totally swept up in the emotion of the moment and ran through the house and out the back door to head him off. I confronted him in the driveway and blurted out, "How could you do this? How could you do what you've done?"

He just looked at me and said quietly, "I understand, yeah—I know what you're saying—I understand."

In an emotional outburst, I shouted, "I never want to see you again, you hear? I never want to see you again!"

He just turned and walked away, all the while saying, "I understand, I understand . . . I understand."

"Wow—that was a powerful scene," I said, my voice cracking with emotion. It wasn't so much the story that had gotten to me—it was more the way he told it. His voice got softer and softer as he repeated his father's lonesome words, "I understand." It touched me—it touched him, too.

I had a lot of time to think about that incident—that Christmas Eve in 1943—and after the war was over. I had a very strong urge to see my dad again . . . to talk to him, and let him know that I also understood. I wanted him to know that I knew everything wasn't black and white, that there might have been situations and feelings on his part that I wasn't privy to.

My sister Jerry and brother Howard shared my feelings, so together we made the trip to Aurora, Missouri, where he was then living, to connect with him again. He had married Grace, the woman he left Mom for, and they had had a son, Gary. I now realized that one of the reasons he left Mom (I'm sure there were others) was that it was the "honorable" thing to do—with Grace being pregnant.

It was an emotional gathering, to say the least. We were all eager to forgive—letting bygones be bygones and starting anew. The hugs and kisses were real and the healing process was well on its way. As we said "good-bye" and headed back to Joplin, a warm feeling of gratefulness filled my heart. I had my dad back.

Mom, on the other hand, was still feeling the pain of Dad's rejection. We knew it would take time and some special turn of events before they could once again relate as friends. I really thought it would never happen. What actually brought them back together again was an event in Hollywood.

It was 1957 and I was filming my third season of *Gunsmoke*. I had become very popular as "Chester" and was getting a number of requests for personal appearances. Bill Hayes, my business manager, felt it would enhance my career to make a guest appearance on the *Dinah Shore Show*. Being a variety show, it required rehearsals. So at my first rehearsal, I showed up, guitar in hand, prepared to record. Dinah also had an interview segment and it was during this section that I heard the familiar phrase, "Dennis Weaver, this is your life!" My head spun around and, sure enough, there was Ralph Edwards, mike in hand, and my "life" book under his arm. All I could think of was, no, no— I haven't lived it yet. There is more to come. And then, another familiar sound caught my attention; it was the sound of a '28 DeSoto. I looked to my left and, to my utter disbelief, there was the spitting image of Ol' Betsy motoring directly toward me on the stage of the *Dinah Shore Show*! Inside the car with their arms waving frantically out the windows were Howard, Jerry, Mary Ann, Mom *and* Dad! I was stunned, because that was the first time I'd seen them together since she had pelted him with fruit that Christmas night so long ago.

From that moment on, they became better friends than they ever were when they were married—it was remarkable. Shortly after that reunion, Grace—Dad's new wife— was killed in a tragic train accident. After Grace was gone, Dad often visited Gerry and me in California. And because Mom worked in a health-food store in nearby Bellflower, it was convenient for her to pick up Dad in her little Hillman and find interesting places to visit and new ways for them to share time with each other. It always gave me a kick to see them drive off together with Mom at the wheel. There was a healing between them, which I greatly appreciated.

They both lived to an old age.

Dad passed in 1974. He was eighty-four years old. Howard and I were with him just before he died. When we went into his hospital room in Aurora, I hardly recognized him. His body had depreciated greatly and he was terribly weak—feeble. He had always been very prim. His appearance was particularly important to him—he even combed his hair a special way. It saddened me to see the nurse had combed it with a washcloth.

When we approached his bed, he hardly moved. He just looked at us with sad eyes that had seen so much and knew they were not long for the light of this world. We spoke to him of our love and tried to lift his spirits. But he just stared at us for a moment, and then said in a weak voice, "It all goes by so fast."

I got the strong sense that he was trying to apologize and that he wished he had done something to make the world a little better, that he wished he had another chance. I thought to myself, he will—he absolutely will, for through God's grace we are given endless chances . . . until we get it right.

"It all goes by so fast . . . ," was the last thing he said to me. It had enormous impact.

Mom passed in 1992, when she was ninety-five. I took care of her the last ten years of her life. The last few years she needed constant help, and I spent many hours at the nursing home doing what I could to make her comfortable. By this time, she was legally blind and she could only hear me if I got close enough to speak into her ear. I would whisper my love for her and tell her she didn't have to hang around, that she wasn't her body, that it only housed her real self, the eternal part of her—her soul—and that it was all right to leave her worn-out house and move on.

55

I told her, "Mom, just as the caterpillar sheds its cocoon and becomes a butterfly, you can shed your worn-out body and become a spiritual butterfly—an angel of light."

I let her know that she had done her job and done it beautifully, and what was waiting for her was nothing but pure light and love.

While Gerry and I were in Taos, New Mexico, consulting with Michael Reynolds, the architect of our Earthship, we received word that Mom had passed. She waited until I was gone, to go.

Friends and family gathered at our Malibu home to celebrate her life. Each told a story that was special to them. Something they had done with her, something she had said—some special moment they had shared together. It was a most uplifting occasion, with a tear now and then sprinkled in between the laughs.

Suddenly, Gerry cried, "Look! Look out the window!"

I turned towards the picture window and there, fluttering by, was a Monarch butterfly. It was strange, for I couldn't remember ever seeing a butterfly at the beach before. I turned to Gerry and said, "Do you think Mom is sending us a message?"

Gerry replied, "I wouldn't put it past her."

The tale of the butterfly didn't end there. Exactly one year later, on the anniversary of the celebration of her passing, another Monarch butterfly flittered by the same window. We hadn't seen one since her party celebrating her life, and we've never seen one again.

At her request, her tombstone reads, "Not gone, just movin' on."

4
Buck Jones, Tarzan, and . . . Principal Deathridge

Rain was lashing at the windows now, and the sky was completely dark. The thunder had stopped, but lightning was still dancing off in the distance beyond the Cimarron mountain range.

The office door opened, and Gerry came in carrying a tray of food. The raw vegetable salad she'd made was piled high in two bowls, mixed with a special homemade dressing. A plate of flat brown bread accompanied the salads with two glasses of fresh water.

"I thought you might be hungry," Gerry said in her sprightly voice. "They say it's snowing in the mountains."

Dennis glanced up at her from under his broad forehead and said, "Thank you, honey." He stood up and took the tray from her. "Do you want to join us?"

"No, I've eaten. You two keep working." With a deep admiration, they touched each other with their eyes. Then she left the room.

"How nice," I said as I looked at the food, then to the window. "How about that—the first snow of the season."

"Yeah—." He took a bite and so did I. It was delicious.

"When did you first know you wanted to be an actor?" I asked, while still chewing.

He took a few more bites, then set his bowl down—temporarily.

My first real acting experience was when I was four years old.

I was in a Christmas program at our church, and I was supposed to recite the poem "Little Jack Horner." Mom had spent a week helping me memorize it. So, I was pretty confident when I got up on the stage. I stood there and began, just like this: "Little Jack Horner sat in a corner eating his Christmas pie . . . he stuck in his thumb and pulled out a plum and said, what a good boy I am."

The audience just cracked up! At the time, I had no idea why they were laughing, but as I looked out into the sea of faces and saw how excited they were—all smiling, laughing, clapping—I thought: Man this feels good! This feels great! I think I like this!

That experience, coupled with watching Saturday matinees, did it.

Buck Jones, my favorite Hollywood cowboy star, and Tarzan mesmerized me. Back at the farm, Howard and I would act out certain scenes from the movie we had just seen.

Howard would tie a rope tightly around the belly of our half-grown calf and hold her, while I climbed on the calf's back. I would get a good hold on the rope and then he would turn the calf loose and see how long I could stay on— pretending to be Buck Jones. It took about two jumps and I was in the dirt! Somehow, the fact that I always ended up on the ground didn't discourage me. But thinking back now, I feel sorry for that poor calf!

As I've mentioned, on the corner of our property, we had this large post oak where we acted out scenes from Tarzan. We climbed that tree so much that the limbs, because of the oils and friction of our hands, were absolutely slick. People would stop their cars to watch us jump from limb to limb yelling, "Ah-ahhhh—ahhhh." My love for acting was in full bloom.

Some people have asked me when I first knew that I wanted to be an actor, and I would have to say that I cannot remember a time when I didn't have that desire! I have wanted it all my life. But I kept that dream to myself— because I was born in Joplin, Missouri. Wanting to be an actor was just something you didn't go around announcing, because in those days people thought acting as a career was simply not an option.

My mother, however, supported the dreams of all her children. Somehow she always got together enough money, from someplace, to give us lessons. Howard got clarinet lessons, Jerry got piano lessons, Mary Ann got dance lessons, and I got, what they called back then, "Expression Lessons."

I remember my teacher giving me little "pieces" to learn, and I would recite them for family and friends.

My favorite was "The Italian Immigrant." I was supposed to be this immigrant who was trying to figure out what American football was all about. I still remember a couple of lines: "Dese a games dey call foooot-a-ball, she's a crazy as can be. I like-a da game dey call-a base-a-ball, but she's uh no foooot-a-ball for me."

Dennis was giggling—tickled by the memory. He picked up his salad bowl and ate some more, giggling all the while. Then, he sobered.

That is all I can remember of my expression lessons.

By the time I got to high school, I had already acted in several one-act plays. Once, I played the part of a wounded soldier in a play that we thought was pretty good, so we decided to perform it before the entire assembly of Joplin High School.

I was lying on a cot in an army hospital and I had three nurses taking care of me—I was in bad shape.

Right in the middle of the most dramatic part, while I was moaning and groaning on my deathbed, the Principal, Mr. Deathridge (we called him "Bulldog" Deathridge), yelled out, "All right! All right! That's enough! Stop—!"

We thought he was talking to us, so we stopped. But he was talking to the kids in the assembly, who were all laughing uncontrollably at us—especially the football team, of which I was a member. They were getting a real "honk" out of my "performance." And this was supposed to be a serious play! I didn't even know they were laughing, I was so absorbed in what I was doing.

Deathridge said to the entire student body, while pointing a stubby little finger at us, "These people are doing the best that they can up here. It is not polite for you to be out there laughing at them!"

Well, being laughed at didn't seem to bother me, because that incident in no way stifled my urge to act.

However, there was another incident in high school that could have squelched it.

We were required to fill out a form that asked us what we wanted to be when we finished school. Everybody wrote in normal professions like banker, storekeeper, lawyer, farmer, doctor, teacher, and scientist. I knew very strongly at that time that I wanted to be an actor, but could I really let people know that? Could I really write it down, and declare it to the world? It was a moment of decision for me. It wasn't easy, but I mustered up my courage and filled in the blank with the word: actor.

The next day, I got a notice that Principal Deathridge wanted to see me. I had avoided him like the plague all through school and I had never been asked to come to his office. Needless to say, I was a little bit shaky walking down the long hall toward his office. I had no idea what I had done.

When I walked in, his expression was anything but warm and inviting. He quickly ushered me to a chair. I sat down and waited. He broke the tension-filled silence with a flap of a piece of paper and a troubled accusation.

"This form," he said, while still flapping the paper, "this form that we've asked you to fill out, (flap, flap) this is a serious thing. We don't like it when people make jokes about it!"

I was silent for a minute, then in a small and trembling voice, I said, "Oh . . . oh, well, sir . . . that's the truth. That's what I want to be."

There was another moment of silence, after which he gave me some well-intentioned advice. "I think, for your own future, you should choose something else. People in Joplin don't make a career out of acting." To which I responded, "Sir, what about Bob Cummings? He's from Joplin."

He said nothing. I wish you could have seen the look on his face . . . it was priceless.

Dennis looked at me then. His lips held the hint of a smile, but his eyes were earnest and, for just an instant, disturbingly perceptive. "I learned that when you give a public pronouncement of your intention, it gives strength to your resolve."

He looked out the window then. The storm had passed, and I followed his gaze. We could see the dusting of snow on the peaks.

"That was a day I will never forget," he said simply, no emotion in his voice. "Then the war came along and I had to put the dream away for a few years."

I relaxed back into the soft cushions, very much into his history. "Tell me about your role in the war."

"It wasn't much, I'm afraid," and he smiled, "but it *was* interesting."

5

Miracles, Times Three

I joined the Naval Air Corps at eighteen and entered the V-5 flight training program, comprised of academic studies, physical training, and flying, and which took over two years to complete.

While I was stationed at the University of Colorado at Boulder, I learned to fly a Piper Cub near the foothills of the Rocky Mountains. It was there that my instructor okayed me for my first solo flight.

It was a special day and I was alive with excitement—everything seemed perfect. The sun shone brightly and the sky was clear and calm; it was an ideal day for flying. My instructor explained the maneuvers I was to complete, slapped me on the back, and encouraged me with, "you're on your own, kid, and don't forget to spin" . . . the most dreaded maneuver.

As I climbed to 6,000 feet over the brown fields east of Boulder, I kept going over in my mind the sequence of actions I was to take to initiate the spin and then the sequence to recover from it. I was clear. I had it nailed. I was ready.

I pulled back on the stick and nosed the plane up. Then I cut back on the throttle and immediately lost airspeed. As it began to stall, I kicked left rudder and jerked the stick as far back as it would go, cutting the throttle to idle. The plane immediately tipped to the left and went into a beautiful spin. I did it! I was spinning, and it was magnificent! After three or four revolutions, it was time to come out of it. All I had to do was reverse the process—which I did. I kicked right rudder, pushed the stick forward, and gave it full throttle. Lo and behold, it *kept spinning!* What had I done wrong? Nothing. I did it right. Just as I was told! I'll do it again, I told myself, with a bit of panic rising in my throat. And I did it again . . . and again . . . and *it kept spinning* . . . down, down, down toward Earth.

Overlapping thoughts of terror raced through my mind . . . am I going to eat it on my first solo flight? Should I bail out? Will I get washed out? Will the damn parachute work? I decided to give it one more try—and when that didn't work, and I could see the ground coming up to meet me fast, I opted to jump. I let go of all the controls and, as I reached for the release on my safety harness and was ready to open the door of the Piper Cub, a miraculous thing happened—it came out of the spin all by itself and flew straight and level. By this time, I was totally wrung out. I took a deep breath and feebly muttered, "Thank you, Lord! Thank you, Lord!" And I didn't try any more fancy maneuvers that day.

Now, that was not normal—planes do not just come out of spins like that. I had no idea what had just happened— but it sure got my attention.

When I landed back at the airport, I went into the hangar and looked up at the board—which scheduled the different cadets and their flights, their plane, etc. I saw my plane, number twenty-three, and next to it in very bold letters, it warned, "Do not spin plane 23!"

I hadn't read the board before going up, and nobody had told me!

"Well, it's clear that you were not supposed to die that day!" I said with a laugh. He joined me. "No—I guess not."

"So, that was it—after that you went to war?" I asked.

"No." His expression sobered, and he continued.

I still had pre-flight at St. Mary's College near Oakland and primary at Livermore, California. It was in Corpus Christi, Texas, where I finally got my wings.

After that, I was stationed at Opalaka Naval Air Station outside of Miami, Florida, where we had target practice in F-4F Wildcats—the kind of plane Joe Foss, our first ace of World War II, flew. They had this big, long tube target made of cloth, and we were supposed to dive down and fire on it with our machine guns. Each pilot's bullets were different colors so when we got on the ground and examined the target—we would know who had hit it and who hadn't.

Sometimes on the way back from target practice, we would do a little fun stuff—we would stage mock dogfights and try to get on each other's tail. We never shot at each other, of course. We were just playing around.

I remember this one time, I made a dive on my buddy, Lamont Davis, or maybe it was Don Rickard. Anyway, I went screaming past him. I was looking back to see where he was so he wouldn't get on my tail, when, suddenly, something made me turn around and look straight ahead. Holy cow, there was this pink stucco house—I am telling you—it was about two seconds away and I was headed right for it!

You never saw anybody jerk a stick back so fast—I damned near broke it! The nose of the F-4F arched skyward as it screamed past the pink house, missing it by a whisker. With trembling hands and a thankful heart, I flew straight and level all the way back to the base.

"Wow—two miracles!."

Dennis gave me one of those "there's more" looks, and my mouth dropped open.

I was still at Miami making touch-and-go landings at an auxiliary field some distance from Opalaka N.A.S., pretending that we were landing on an aircraft carrier.

One day, I flew back to the main base, moved into the landing pattern, and prepared to set my Wildcat down, finishing my day's work. Down on the runway was a landing signal officer who gave us certain signals, guiding us in to the landing. He always gave us the "roger" sign if everything was okay to land—getting us used to what we would experience on a real flattop.

The F-4F's didn't have automatic-powered landing gear. You had to crank it down manually, which I did before making my final approach to the runway. I looked down, got a "roger" from the L.S.O., and prepared to land. But, there was one little problem . . . I didn't have the wheels locked in the last notch, so as soon as I hit the tarmac, the landing gear folded like a tent, causing me to make a belly landing!

It felt much like a horse when it steps in a gopher hole and crumples to its knees. I thought I was dead for sure, because the F-4F has a belly fuel tank, which can very easily explode—especially landing on asphalt. A stream of sparks came from under the Wildcat's belly and I braced myself for the inevitable explosion.

All I could think of while my plane was skidding down the runway was—I've got to leave this baby as quickly as I can before I'm engulfed in flames. In the distance I could see the flashing lights of the fire truck as it came screaming towards me—full throttle.

As soon as I felt the plane stop, I quickly flipped the latch which loosened my safety belt and stood up to jump out. There was a slight hitch, however. The Wildcat hadn't come to a dead stop. It had one last lurch left, which sent me headfirst into the instrument panel, laying my head open just above the eyebrow. Blood trickled into my eyes. Boy, did I feel stupid! I had just survived an almost fatal crash and nearly had a clean getaway; then I had to go and hit my head on the instrument panel! Fortunately, that was the only injury.

I explained the accident to the officer in charge and filled out an accident report. If I hadn't been commissioned, the accident would probably have "washed me out" of the program—they go a little easier on you when you're an officer. But that didn't take the sting out of the embarrassment.

And there was still one more incident!

When I was in Livermore, California, in primary, we were flying Steermans—which we called "Yellow Perils." They were biplanes. They had two wings and open cockpits—similar to the planes the Great Waldo Pepper flew at carnivals. They are so much fun to fly, the closest I came to feeling like a bird. You can really maneuver them. It was great fun flying out there with your scarf flapping in the wind, your goggles on, wearing the Red Baron-type helmet, and all of that.

One particularly nice day, I walked across the field and stepped up onto the wing to get into the cockpit. A little indentation in the body of the plane is where you put your foot to stabilize you while you swing the other leg over into the plane. I put my foot into that little indentation and, as I swung my leg over, my foot slipped out of it and my knee went right through the skin of the Steerman.

I was horrified. I stood there for a moment, trying to figure out what to do—take the plane up and just go ahead and fly it with the possibility of the wind catching the skin and ripping it off . . . or report it? Well, I quickly dismissed the idea of flying it, so the only other option was report it as an accident. Another really embarrassing moment; reporting to my superior officer that I slipped and my knee went through the airplane!

As I look back, I realize how fortunate I was to get through that program and get my wings—then, survive! It was amazing, because many of the cadets that I started out with dropped like flies at different bases—some not even getting a chance to fly.

Many of my friends washed out of the academic courses, failing navigation, engines, or "blinker" (a signaling procedure, Morse code with lights).

You have to reach a certain speed with "blinker" (like typing) before you can pass—and I almost didn't make it. It was tough. Fortunately, I had a nice relationship with the blinker instructor, a sympathetic Wave named Patricia O'Connell. She helped me through it, giving me some extra attention—or they would never have pinned the wings on me.

Finally, I had carrier checkout at the Great Lakes and was assigned to a squadron. They gave me orders to go to Pearl Harbor. But before going overseas, they always give you a final leave to go home, to say "good-bye" to family and friends. While I was there, the U.S. dropped the A-bomb, and that pretty much took care of that—it was all over for me, thank God. I had deep compassion for the citizens of Hiroshima, but at the same time I was thankful I didn't have to engage anyone in deadly combat.

I reported to San Diego, but everything was shut down. I was a buck ensign, and on "the list" that they felt they could do without—so, when they said I could get out and go home, I snapped up the offer.

6

Mrs. Billy Dennis Weaver

I went through Joplin (Missouri) on my way to being mustered out of the Naval Air Corps at Grosse Ile, Michigan. As always when I came home, I was looking forward to seeing my steady girlfriend, Gerry Stowell.

Gerry and I met at a Joplin Junior College sock-hop. She was dancing with her good buddy Bobby Dunn, and I was hanging out by the stage with my best friend, Bob Prince, checking out the girls—looking for some good dancers.

Apparently, Gerry noticed me and asked Bobby, "Who's the handsome guy, standing by the stage—the tall one?"

"Oh, that's Bill Weaver, the halfback of the football team," he happily replied, without hesitation.

"Dance me over there in front of him, please, Bobby— and give me a big whirl."

Well, Bobby did, and that act changed my life forever.

Now, what you've got to know is that Gerry was a figure roller skater and a darn good one. Her mother made her this real cute roller-skating outfit—with real short, red tights that went under the skirt—which she was wearing that night. It was the kind of skirt that, when you whirled around, didn't leave much to the imagination.

When she was right smack dab in front of me, Bobby gave Gerry a powerful whirl and her skirt twirled up, exposing the neatest pair of legs I'd ever seen. I got a glimpse of those red tights, and it was all over!

Gerry was a great dancer—she spoiled me for anyone else; she was the only one I danced with the rest of the night. That was the beginning of a grand partnership that has lasted over fifty years. She has truly blessed and enriched my life.

The junior college yearbook, like all yearbooks, had pictures of different students with comments by the staff written underneath them. Below a picture of Gerry and me dancing, they wrote, "The couple that always Weaved across the floor and Stowell the show."

Three years later, after I'd left the Naval Air Corps, I was back in Joplin and decided to take in a Joplin High School football game one Friday night with Gerry. In the middle of the second quarter, I turned to her, and in a very businesslike tone said, "Gerry, I'd like to know something."

"What?" she answered.

I continued in my serious mood. "I'd like to know if you'd marry me."

Her response was instantaneous; she didn't miss a beat. "Yes! Yes, I will."

I was taken aback by the quickness of her response. "No, no—no. This is not the way they do it in the movies! First of all, I should be more romantic, and this is a big decision for you. You've got to show some doubt. Hesitate a little bit—pondering the seriousness of the moment. All right?"

She gave an understanding nod.

"Shall we try it again?"

She agreed.

I summoned up my most romantic posture and softly whispered, "Honey, will you marry me?"

Before I hardly finished the question, she blurted out, "Yes, yes! I said I will!"

She was so cute. She just cracked me up. "Well, if that's the way you feel about it, what are we waiting for? Let's do it tonight."

She smiled. "Let's do it!"

In those days, Missouri had a waiting period after you applied for a license before you could get married, but not so in Kansas. Just over the border, we could get hitched on the spur of the moment. So we crossed over into Kansas with our friends Morris and Louise Cole, woke a justice of the peace in Columbus, and got married. We didn't even have rings, so when it came to the part where I said, "With this ring, I thee wed," I took off my navy ring and slipped it on her finger.

The next day, the first thing I did was to get her a real ring. Of course, I hadn't received my mustering-out pay yet, so I was close to flat broke, and Gerry had to pay for both our rings. She always says I married her for her money.

By the time we got back to Joplin on our wedding night, a hint of daylight was discernible in the east. We felt the first people we should tell were Gerry's parents. I'm sure she had some trepidation, because she had always promised her mother that she would never do anything so rash, so foolhardy, as to elope—that was out of the question. She vowed she would have a beautiful church wedding as her mother had wished.

We cautiously opened the front door and headed for her parent's bedroom—the door was open. Gerry took a deep breath, I squeezed her hand for support, and she walked to the foot of their bed. Coward that I was, I hung back in the doorway.

Her mother woke up—by this time it was morning—took one look at Gerry and then at me (still in the doorway), and realized exactly what had happened. No words were necessary. She began to softly cry. This woke Mr. Stowell, who quickly surveyed the situation. Gerry simply stated that we had gotten married. I stayed where I was, because I wasn't sure how her dad would react. I think he felt as though he should support her Mom and also cry—but he just couldn't bring himself to do it. Instead, he pulled the sheet up over his mouth, trying to hide the huge smile on his face. But his twinkling eyes gave him away, and I knew we were okay.

I'm sure a couple of things pleased him . . . first of all, he was a rabid sports fan and now he had an athletic son-in-law (Gerry had no brothers, only her sister Elaine), and secondly, he now wouldn't have to drop a chunk of money on a fancy wedding.

I don't think anyone thought it would last—eloping like that—and I wouldn't recommend it for everybody. But it's been over a half century and we're still hanging out together, and over the years, our love, like fine wine, has grown sweeter with time. These are really the most love-filled days of our lives, and we are truly blessed, for that love continues to deepen.

"Dennis, what do you think is the secret to the success of your marriage?" I asked after a moment's pause.

He looked away. The slight straightening of his shoulders was like a stiff salute to a form of completion. The gesture marked an opening in his face, anticipated, and yet at the same time, totally unexpected. I sat back, intrigued, wondering what was coming. He fixed his eyes on me.

Well, there isn't just one secret—there are many. First of all, it's not a contest of longevity. The length of a marriage has little to do with the success of a marriage. But we normally shower a couple with applause and congratulations if they make it to their fiftieth wedding anniversary—although the love in the relationship may have expired years earlier.

Relationships are an extremely important part of the human experience. They give us the greatest chance to grow. We have a relationship with everything—our dog, our neighbor, the homeless person, the Earth, our boss, our student, etc. It is only through relationships that we have the opportunity to define who we are and what we're doing here—and to announce that to the world.

By the nature of marriage, because the husband and wife live in such close proximity, it is by far life's most critical relationship, and the one that allows us the grandest opportunity to express the purpose of life, which is to love and to be loved. Any marriage that does not have mutual usefulness as its foundation will be difficult.

The word "allow" is very significant in any successful relationship, whether it be between family members, friends, or husbands and wives. When we truly love someone, we allow them their own thoughts, interests, and space. We give each other room to breathe.

No one person can satisfy all the needs of another—that only happens in overly romantic love novels. So, don't expect that kind of perfection, or disappointment will surely follow. Gerry and I developed an understanding of each other, a feeling of compassion and patience that has run quiet and deep. We each enjoy our own sense of freedom. We try not to walk in fear, for from fear comes all the destructive stuff, like jealousy, possessiveness, and suspicion. We somehow knew that if we couldn't hold on to each other with love, we certainly couldn't hold on to each other with jealousy. If the feeling of ownership creeps into a marriage, it will blow out the strongest flame of love.

What I can offer from these years of experience is, be happy with yourself. Be content with who you are. That doesn't necessarily mean we should be finished with ourselves, for we should continually seek to improve. It simply means that we should love ourselves at our present level of development while reaching for the next highest wrung on the ladder of consciousness. For it is only when we own that love, only when it is ours, that we can truly give it to others. And, as we give, so shall we receive. Therefore, that which you would have for yourself, give to others.

And, for goodness sake, express your love in thought, word, and action. Let your partner and the world know that you are the lover of all lovers. Unless, of course, you are not—in which case the world will discover it very quickly.

Sometimes people just can't make a marriage work, no matter how hard they try. If all attempts fail and you feel all efforts to salvage the relationship have been exhausted, then understand that everyone has a right to happiness, including you and your partner. If part you must, do it with the dignity befitting children of God. Bless your spouse for the good intentions you both had in the beginning and the

good moments you've shared, and wish each other well—
that you both may find the relationship that serves you
better.

‿

When the war was over, there was no question in my
mind—I was going to pursue an acting career, although it
wasn't clear to me exactly how to do that.

Providence stepped in and gave me a little help. I was
offered a football scholarship at the University of Oklahoma, which fit into my long-range plans perfectly, because
I was told by a friend, Lonny Chapman—who had majored
in drama there before the war—that its drama department
was one of the best in the country. Lonny was also from
Joplin, and I had always admired his athletic ability. He was
a very strong reason I chose O.U. So, in January of 1946,
Gerry and I packed our bags and headed for Norman,
Oklahoma.

I arrived ready to make a name for myself both on the
stage and on the gridiron . . . but, as they say, a funny thing
happened on the way to the forum.

The coach that had offered me my scholarship was
replaced by Jim Tatum, who during the war had coached
football at the Great Lakes Naval Station and brought with
him a whole slew of players he had promised scholarships
to . . . he didn't know me from Adam. Bottom line—he
wouldn't honor the promise made by the departing coach.
I asked him what I had to do to earn the scholarship, and
he told me if I made one of the first nine teams, he would
give it to me. That's right, first nine. There were a lot of guys
returning from the service that wanted to play football, but
I accepted the challenge. I suited up for spring practice and

immediately was relegated to the thirteenth or fourteenth team. By the time spring practice was over, I was alternating with (the later famous coach) Darryl Royal at quarterback on the third team. When I asked the coach about my scholarship, he said there weren't any left.

I just stood there, stunned, unbelieving, and pissed. He had broken a promise, and he made me feel like dirt. Trying to suppress the anger steaming within me, I told him he could shove his football and abruptly turned and walked away. I knew I could get some help from John "Jake" Jacobs, the track coach, and besides, my buddy Lonny was on the track team. Of course, track is a spring sport, and by the time I made my move, the season was over, and the only event scheduled for fall was the two-mile team race, which was run during halftime at football games.

The race consisted of five runners from each school. As each athlete crossed the finish line, he was given a number . . . first got number one, second got number two, and third number three, etc. At the finish of the race, the numbers were added up and the team with the lowest score won.

I had never run as far as two miles before, but I wanted to earn my oats, so I trained diligently and became the number-one two-miler for Oklahoma. The rest of the team did well, too. We won the Big Six (which is now the Big Twelve) two-mile team championship in 1946. Besides Lonny, there was Canaris, Burns, and R. C. Slocum.

I would always run until there was no gas left in the tank, and after each race I had to practically be carried into the field house. I was not a fast rebounder. I never saw the second half of a football game the entire first year I was at Oklahoma. I spent my time throwing up or collapsing on the training table, wondering why I chose to punish myself.

Winning the Big Six championship made us eligible to run in the national cross-country championship, which was held in Lansing, Michigan.

It was an honor I would have just as soon skipped. It wasn't a two-mile race, it was four miles, and it wasn't run on a flat track. It was a very challenging course, laid out over fields, roads, ditches, and hills. It seemed as though every conference in the country was represented. The starting line was a good tenth of a mile long. I noticed many of the runners were oiling their bodies, and I thought to myself, "Do they think they are going to swim the English Channel?" But then, just before the gun went off, I realized they had a very good reason for the oil—it began to snow.

There were over three hundred entries in the race. Lonny finished in the top fifties, and I wound up in the sixties. The last quarter mile was like a bad dream. I was hardly conscious. My legs were like so much rubber. I staggered across the finish line and wobbled towards a nearby tree. With one final lurch, I made it to the shelter of its limbs and fell flat on my back. I couldn't move. As the soft snowflakes pelted my face, I didn't care whether I lived or died. It was the last time I ever ran cross-country.

"Jake" Jacobs was one of the most colorful characters I've ever known. When asked to be an honorary pallbearer at a friend's funeral, he said, "I guess that means I'm too old to carry the casket!"

Ol' Jake had trouble remembering names, so he gave everyone on the track team nicknames, like: Crowhop, Punkin-Butt, Tooslow, and Kickass. Because Lonny was in the drama department, he called him "Barrymore." When I came along, and was also in drama, Ol' Jake was stumped. Barrymore was the only actor he knew. Now, the head of the drama department was a fellow named Rupel J. Jones, and for Jake that was good enough. He started calling me Rupel, which got shortened to "Rupe." And, to this day, Gerry still calls me Rupe, as do Lonny, Joe Sargent, Lou Antonio, John Randolph, and other longtime friends.

I was a talented track man, but not good enough in any one event to make the Olympic team, so Jake suggested that I try the decathlon—ten events rolled into one, performed over two days.

Some of the events I had never tried before, such as the weights and the pole vault. Time was short—six months until the trials—so I started training immediately.

My first test was at the Colorado relays, where I competed in the septahlon—seven events. The septahlon is the indoor equivalent to the decathlon. The discus, javelin, and 1500 meters are not part of it because of the confined space.

Athletes from all over the Midwest were attracted to the event, and, to my amazement and most everybody else's, I won it rather easily.

The next day, the sports page of the *Denver Post* boldly announced: "Weaver Candidate for Olympics."

That really pumped me up and I started training big time while I was working on my degree in Fine Arts in Drama, and when the Olympic trials rolled around—which were held in Bloomfield, New Jersey, in early June—I was ready.

Now, Bloomfield was only a subway ride from New York City, and Lonny had gone to New York the year before to pursue his acting career and had experienced some success with an Off-Broadway acting group. He met me at the train in New Jersey (that shows how long ago it was—I didn't fly, I took a train).

We threw my bags in my hotel room in Bloomfield and immediately headed for the bright lights of New York City.

Even though the Olympic tryouts were the next day, Lonny and I spent the whole afternoon walking around Broadway, gawking at the marquees and studying the pictures of the actors on the outside of theaters. We picked a scene from a play called *Thunderock* and rehearsed it all afternoon. I was so excited, I simply dismissed the Olympics.

That evening, I auditioned for Lonny's Off-Broadway group. When we finished, it was so late that I did not even get back to my hotel. I slept on somebody's floor in Manhattan.

I got up the next morning and took the subway to New Jersey and got to the stadium just in time to suit up and go to the starting blocks for the hundred-meter dash.

The whole scene reminded me of Robert Taylor in *A Yank at Oxford*, in which he ran to the starting line at the last minute, didn't have time to suit up, and won the race in his street clothes. Folks, let me tell you, that only happens in the movies—not in real life!

It was the worst first day of decathlon competition I had ever had! My legs were totally dead from walking around on the concrete the day before.

Normally, if I had made my usual marks, I would have been in second or third place, but after that first day, I was in ninth. The next day I improved a bit, and I ended up finishing sixth in the nation out of thirty-six entries. Not bad, but not good enough—only the top three made the Olympic team.

The last two events of the second day were normally my two best events—the pole vault and the 1500 meters. I was vaulting with an aluminum pole—not the fiberglass type they use today, which makes it a totally different event. With that aluminum pole back at the University, I was making 13 feet 9 inches, steadily.

I had only been vaulting about six months, and I was improving all the time. Now, back then if a pole-vaulter went 14.6 he would be on the Olympic pole-vaulting team. So, I really had the possibility of making some major points in that event.

But just before the pole vault started, the skies opened up and the worst deluge of water I had ever seen swamped the stadium. I cannot even begin to describe the kind of rain that came down that day . . . it was just . . . it was a flood! When it stopped, the runway to the crossbar (of the vaulting pit) was absolutely mush. The officials tried everything to dry it. They soaked wood chips in kerosene, spread them on the runway, and burned them, put on fresh sand, packed it down, everything; but it was useless. The runway remained treacherously soggy.

I got over ten feet and they raised the bar to 10.6. I made that mark along with Al Lawrence from Southern California—and his specialty was the pole vault. We were the only two in a field of thirty-six who cleared 10.6. They raised it to eleven feet, and I hit the bar on the way up twice. The coach from Arkansas said to me, "You've got plenty of height—what we should do is move the standards back just a little bit so you won't hit the crossbar on the way up, and you can clear it easy."

I prepared for my last jump. I eyeballed the crossbar. It looked easy. As I sped down the runway, I was confident. I hit my jump mark perfectly and pulled my body up with all my strength. It was a perfect jump. I sailed up, up, and over, clearing the bar by a good eight inches. What a great feeling. But because they had moved the standards back, I hit the damn crossbar on the way down! That bar flipped off the standards and sailed ten feet in the air! My hopes sunk. I lost a lot of points that I was counting on.

And then, of course, in the 1500-meter race, we were running through mud puddles. By that time, the spirit had gone out of me—I was totally discouraged by the pole vault. I won the 1500 meters, but in very slow time. It was all over. Needless to say, I did not make the Olympic team—but I was accepted by the Off-Broadway group.

I got so excited about what was going to happen in my life, with acting, that not making the Olympic team didn't crush me like it otherwise would have. Throughout my life, this has happened a lot—when one door closes, another opens. Those two days in Bloomfield taught me an important lesson . . . to achieve a certain goal, three things are necessary, focus, focus, and *focus*. Don't let yourself get distracted!

৵

I had a round-trip ticket back to Oklahoma, but instead of using it, I cashed it in and stayed in New York.

It wasn't an easy time for us. While I was there, I did everything from selling real silk hosiery *and* magazines, to taking janitorial work—anything I could do to support myself.

The worst part was knowing Gerry was in Oklahoma, living with her parents. I was up in New York trying to make it and she was back home pregnant with our first son, Rick. It was a touchy situation. I don't think her mother and father thought very highly of me for staying in New York and pursuing the "dream." But I did ride the bus all the way home for Rick's birth. After he was seventeen days old, I went back to New York.

I was doing well Off-Broadway and making somewhat of a name for myself. In those days, it was really "off" Broadway. There were no Actors Equity contracts and no union to stand up for the interest of actors.

"New Drama," the group that I was with, produced *They Shall Not Die*, a play based on an actual event in which nine black youths were accused of raping a white girl. It happened in the South and, since a southern accent came easy for me, I was cast as General Dade, the prosecutor of the nine youths. He was a true-blue bigot, and my character didn't gain much sympathy from the audience . . . lots of hisses and boos. However, it was gratifying to know I was effective.

While putting makeup on one night, word came backstage that Lee Strasberg was in the audience. The announcement created an electrical buzz through the whole company. Strasberg was one of the originators of the prestigious Group Theatre of the '30s, along with Cheryl Crawford and Harold Clurman. At that time, he was the artistic director of the "Actors Studio," with actors such as Marlon Brando, Anthony (Tony) Quinn, Shelley Winters, and Paul Newman on its roster.

One of the biggest thrills of my life as an actor came after the curtain came down. Strasberg came backstage and sought me out. I was so excited that I was speechless. But I do remember with great clarity that he applauded my work and told me, "You're in the right profession." You can't imagine how that brief encounter and those few words boosted my morale and pushed me on to better things. I was floating on "cloud nine" for days.

It was during the run of *They Shall Not Die* that Gerry joined me in New York. In order to do that, she had to leave Rick with her mother and father. This was really painful stuff—being separated, first from me, then her son. But I doubt I could have made it alone—she was a big support to me emotionally and financially.

Gerry started working in the accounts-receivable department at the American Tobacco Company (Lucky Strike), and then at Hoover Uniforms as a secretary. It was hard for both of us. I worked in television sporadically, but it didn't pay much. I remember doing a commercial for Pall Mall cigarettes. (Can you believe that?) It paid twenty-five dollars, with no residuals. That was it, a flat fee.

My first break on Broadway was understudying Lonny in *Come Back, Little Sheba*, which became a major movie. Bill Inge was the writer, and Shirley Booth won an Oscar starring in it.

Lonny was playing the young athlete, Turk—the juvenile lead—and he suggested to the producers that I understudy him. They agreed. So for six months I had a steady job.

Gerry and I had acquired an "apartment" in the Bronx at 124 East 146th Street. It was actually one room on the second floor of an old mansion that was built in the 1800s when 146th Street was nothing but cow pastures. It appeared to be in a time warp as it stubbornly resisted the industrialization that had grown up around it. A fence guarded the unkempt lawn that reminded passersby of another era long gone, which refused to give in to the march of time.

The mansion was a wonderful study in social behavior and tolerance. The three-story building had been broken up into apartments by its owner, Eric, a Jehovah's Witness from England. When the World Revival was held in 1950, Eric offered the lawn to those Witnesses who either couldn't find rooms or couldn't afford them, and the mansion's lawn became tent city.

The first floor was occupied by Pedro and Rosita, a young couple fresh from Puerto Rico, and Rosita's younger sister, Teresa. We shared the kitchen with them and several dozen friendly cockroaches—which scurried away into the cracks and crannies whenever the light was switched on. We also shared the bathroom, with a Jewish couple, Herb and Ruth Armstrong, who were trying to make it in show business. The top room in the building was occupied by a Frenchman who spoke with a very romantic accent. We never saw him sans his perky little beret. Gerry and I, being from Missouri via Oklahoma University, were the odd couple! They referred to us as the "foreigners."

In the wintertime, we took turns stoking the furnace with coal. It was a dirty job, but someone had to do it. A large closet joined our room, big enough for Rick's crib, and that was where he slept. The rent was twenty-five dollars per month. Here's the good part . . . lightbulbs and toilet paper were furnished.

When Gerry's mother and father brought Rick up to us, Lonny pretended to be sick so that I could do the part and they could say their son-in-law was a Broadway actor.

When it came time to do the road show, Lonny didn't want to do it, so the producers gave me the part. I toured all over the United States, playing Turk for another six months. When I returned to New York, I was accepted by the Actor's Studio and finally got to work with Lee Strasberg, Danny Mann, and the best of New York's actors.

Shelley Winters was in town and happened to be at the studio while I was doing a scene from Tennessee Williams' *27 Wagons Full of Cotton*. She was with Universal International at the time and, after seeing the scene, suggested the studio put me under contract. Well, it didn't happen that easily, but I appreciated the recommendation.

Later, I auditioned for a play that Elia Kazan was directing. I was all wrong for the part, but the reading impressed him, and his assistant again suggested to Universal International that they sign me. Later, Universal sent a talent scout to see me in summer stock in *A Street Car Named Desire* and *All My Sons*. I must have impressed him, because when Bob Goldstein, the head talent scout at U.I., came to New York, he called me in and asked if I'd read something for him. The next day, I came back and did Tom from *The Glass Menagerie*. As soon as I was finished, I quickly looked at him to try to detect a reaction. He silently returned my look for a moment. My heart was in my throat and my gut was churning. He simply said, "Would you like to go to Hollywood?"

"Would I?" I asked incredulously. "You bet your bippy I would!"

As I look back, I was really naïve. I didn't have an agent and I innocently said, like a true artist would, "Mr. Goldstein, it's not the money I'm interested in. I just need enough to take care of my family. What's really important to me are the roles—not the money."

He obliged me by signing me to the Screen Actors Guild's minimum contract for studio players, at $125 a week.

At the time, that amount seemed huge . . . and then, of course, there was security. Oh yes, security that had to be considered, security was important. I signed for seven years.

Coincidentally, the next day was Christmas—what a gift. I could hardly wait to tell Gerry.

Before we moved to California we spent Christmas in the Bronx, in our little apartment at 124 East 14th Street. Christmas was a very important time when I was a kid. If we had nothing but oranges, bananas, and nuts to fill the stocking, that was still exciting for me. It was a very warm, family oriented time where we exchanged a lot of love, a few presents, but mostly, it was just a feeling of togetherness.

Gerry and I were always living from day-to-day and had spent everything we had on a train set for three-year-old Rick. I was excited about that, but I didn't have anything to give Gerry, and she had nothing to give me.

A couple of days before Christmas, I was down at the little market where we shopped and saw these beautiful, very colorful Seagram boxes that had a velveteen finish on the outside. They were nice to the touch, and I asked the storeowner if he would give me one that was already used, and he did.

My family always enjoyed jokes, and at Christmastime we played fun pranks on one another just for the laughs. So, I thought that I would play a joke on Gerry—to give her a laugh. I bought some potatoes and put them in the whiskey box and wrapped it up in holiday paper. I knew she would think when she unwrapped it, "What is he giving me whiskey for, when we don't have any money and I don't drink?"

As she began to open it, part of me was inwardly tickled and another part was thinking maybe I'd gone too far. As she opened the velveteen box and the potatoes rolled to the floor, she had a stunned expression on her face, which, much to my relief, soon turned into a smile and then to an understanding laugh . . . I readily joined in. Through our laughter came the tears. I held her close and kissed her warmly and whispered, "We're going to Hollywood, honey, and you can have all the potatoes you can eat."

We've held the memory of that moment in our hearts for lo these many years.

We arrived in Hollywood in 1952, and I can't go on without mentioning my friend John Randolph, who at that time was playing in *Paint Your Wagon* and loaned me $200—so I wouldn't arrive in Hollywood broke.

After working for one year and appearing in fourteen films, the studio opted not to renew my contract and I no longer had a steady acting job—as a matter of fact, I had no steady job at all! For two years I freelanced, picking up what acting jobs I could . . . and the pickings were slim. To help put bread on the table and pay the rent, I tried a lot of jobs I could do on my own time, so that I would be available for interviews.

I tried selling Electrolux vacuum cleaners and discovered I was not born to be a salesman. Before I knocked on a door, I was already defeated. I assumed the lady of the house couldn't afford the vacuum any more than I could. The only person that bought one was Lew Brown—an actor and a longtime friend from my college days.

I put dual controls on our '47 Studebaker and tried teaching driving lessons. In those days, people had to learn to use the clutch and shift manually. The only student I had was a 63-year-old lady from the Bronx who had never driven before and whose husband had had two heart attacks. She wanted to be sure she could get him to the emergency room if he had a third. Either I wasn't a good teacher or maybe it's true that "you can't teach old dogs new tricks." It took us three trips to the Department of Motor Vehicles before they finally gave up and issued her a driver's license. For months I lived in fear that the *Los Angeles Times* would announce a horrible car crash involving a 63-year-old woman from the Bronx driving her husband to the emergency room!

We were both laughing at that horrible and hysterical image. Then, he sobered and gave me a look that abruptly silenced my giggles.

"I don't think I would have made it through that time if it weren't for my overriding desire to act and a feeling deep inside me, perhaps naively, that somehow, someway, it would happen; and, of course, Gerry's encouragement and willingness to stay the course."

"When did you start doing *Gunsmoke*?" I asked, thinking this was going to be fun.

"It was in 1955—three years after we arrived in Hollywood. But I have to tell you, those two years before *Gunsmoke*, our faith was severely tested and our will was challenged." Then his eyes left me, seeing some distant memory.

"What happened?" I asked.

It was a hot day in June and we had gone to Bob's Big Boy Drive-In for a fast burger. Robby (our second son) was only ten weeks old as he lay in Gerry's lap listlessly on a pillow. He had been quiet all day and when it was his feeding time, Gerry couldn't wake him. As we drove home from dinner, she became more and more concerned. I tried to assure her that it was probably just the heat and with a good night's sleep he would be fine in the morning. However, her mother's intuition was strong, and she asked me to please go down to the drugstore and get a thermometer so she could check his temperature.

It was Sunday, and when I arrived, the doors were locked. I must have been just minutes too late, for I could still see bodies moving around through the glass. I pounded on the door to get their attention. A lady turned and gave me a "we're closed" sign. I yelled, "It's an emergency!" The plea in my eyes was evidently convincing. I got the thermometer.

Robby's temperature was 104 degrees and Gerry put in an emergency call for Dr. Lucius "Lucky" Lindley, our pediatrician . . . hoping and praying he was reachable on Sunday. Her prayers were answered . . . he was on call.

When Gerry explained Robby's condition, his temperature, and that he had only wet four diapers all day, Dr. Lindley, with great urgency in his voice, said, "I'll meet you at the hospital. Get him there as soon as you can."

We pushed our '47 Studebaker to its limits, racing through North Hollywood over Cahuenga Pass and to Children's Hospital in Hollywood. I stayed in the car with five-year-old Rick while Gerry, with Robby in her arms, hurried to meet the doctor.

I waited anxiously for what seemed like an eternity, and when she finally came out of the hospital doors, her arms were empty. As she ran across the busy street, oblivious to oncoming traffic, she was crying, "The doctor says it's either polio or spinal meningitis . . . and he hopes it's polio. His temperature is now 109!" A shudder went through my body. I couldn't conceive of anything worse than polio. We held each other for a long moment, absorbing the dreadful turn of events and trying to comfort each other.

We drove quietly home, hoping for the best. A telephone call later that night confirmed the worst—Robby's chances of surviving the night were not good. It was the longest night of our life, but he made it.

For eight days, he was in the isolation ward, his temperature remained extremely high, and his fragile life hung by a thread. It was painful for us to visit him, because we really couldn't. We could only look through the cold plate-glass window at his small form lying there spread-eagled with his tiny arms and legs attached to IVs. The feeling of helplessness that overwhelmed us was very hard to deal with.

Two doors down from us lived our good friends, Marge and Jim Swift—both strong followers of Christian Science. By the eighth day, Robby's temperature still hadn't broken and the doctor warned us that he probably couldn't hold on much longer. It was then that we got a phone call from Marge suggesting that we try talking to her friend who was a Christian Science practitioner, and Marge gave Gerry her number. We were ready to grab at any straw—to try anything. Gerry immediately called her. Her calm and positive tone was of great help and comfort. She told us to read the story of Abraham and Isaac. She said, "Our faith is often tested by worldly circumstances, but God's love is always there behind the circumstances. Know that your son is fine. That he is already healed. Hold no other thought." We prayed intensely that night and followed her directions as best we could.

The next morning, she called and asked Gerry, "Are you going to bring your son home now that his temperature has broken?" Gerry and I stared at each other, stunned—could this be true? Within the hour, Dr. Lindley called and elatedly confirmed her words, "Robby's temperature is down and I feel we have passed a very critical point." Gerry mentioned the practitioner's help and he said he was not at all surprised, that he'd seen the power of prayer and positive thinking act as a beneficial force too often.

Robby remained in the hospital for two more weeks for what Dr. Lindley called "mopping up time," and he warned us that the meningitis would probably leave Robby with a serious aftereffect . . . a physical or mental disability. Thank God he had neither. And forty-seven years later, he's happily married to Lynne (who is very committed to our cause of Ecolonomics, along with her many other good causes) and they have given us Jennifer, our beautiful sixteen-year-old granddaughter, an athlete and equestrienne, of whom I am very proud. They say she has some of my competitive genes.

However, the next ten months of his tiny life were not easy. Robby fell prey to every bug that came along as the result of a weakened immune system. It was then that we were told that if we wanted to save his life, we may have to move away from the city, removing him from any contact with all infectious diseases. The doctor suggested that he might even have to become a "bubble baby" and live his life totally isolated from worldly activity.

I was shocked. How could I find a place that was totally void of infectious diseases? Even if I was willing to give up my career, how could I afford the move or the bubble solution? It would all be very expensive and I was broke. I seriously asked God for help.

When Robby was eleven months old, we almost lost him again. He contracted typhoidic dysentery. Again, from who knows where? He was put in the isolation ward and, because the doctor feared that dehydration might affect his brain, he attached IV tubes to the sides of his little head. It was a terrifying sight—another nightmare.

Dr. Lindley was considered a diagnostic genius, and he came up with a first-time diagnosis that definitely saved Robby's life. He determined that he may have been born with agammaglobulinemia, which, in March of 1954, was extremely rare. He suggested that we give him gammaglobulin shots. So every two weeks for over six months, we took Robby to the doctor's office to get his gammaglobulin, which looked like thick corn syrup delivered with a "horse" needle. It was a painful and traumatic experience for him, but it saved his life. The good part is that his immune system became so strong afterward that for years it defeated every bug that came along. He was a perfect rough-and-tough kid!

The two years between 1953 and 1955 was a time when life's tests came fast and furious *and* our cash dropped to $1.50. It's during times such as these that you find out how important your friends are. Shelley Winters helped us with our medical expenses. Our neighbors, the Wooleys, from across the street, loaned us two hundred dollars. Our landlord let our monthly rent slide, and Lew Brown generously dumped a huge load of groceries on our kitchen counter.

My Aunt Madge and her husband, Mike Turk, owned the George Barnes Flower Shop on Ventura Boulevard, and they gave me a part-time job delivering flowers. My customers included Lucille Ball, Jack Webb, John Ford, and Herbert Yates—the president and owner of Republic Studios. I was envious of them. Why hadn't it happened for me? Had my chance slipped past me? I was angry.

Up to my eyeballs in debt, we were barely skimming by. My career seemed as though it had hit a brick wall. I was desperate and decided to have a heart-to-heart talk with my agent . . . to prod him, goose him, challenge him. He was doing nothing for me, and I wanted some answers.

7

"Look Out, Mr. Dillon, He's Gonna Shoot!"

I walked into my agent's office, trying to be calm, remembering my mother's words, *you can attract more bees with honey than with vinegar.* He sat behind his desk, fiddling with some contraption. With great pride, he explained it was a miniature "duck blind." The heat began to rise in my neck as I repeated his words, "a duck blind?" And with uncontrollable excitement he explained, "Yeah, it's something you hide behind so you can get a good shot at the unsuspecting ducks." And then he went into great detail about how he planned to go duck hunting and give his new blind a try. I stood there looking at him, thinking to myself, "I'm here with no work, trying to feed my family, and this guy is telling me about his duck blind! Something is very wrong!" I didn't even sit down. I just said, "You're no longer my agent, forget it. I fire you!" And walked out. I went home and immediately called Milt Grossman, who a couple of months earlier had seen me play the lead in *The Big Knife* at the Las Palmas theatre in Hollywood and had suggested if I needed an agent to look him up. But Milt was in Mexico with Anthony Quinn—a client of his—and was not available.

So there I was, without an agent or an acting job—I did have the job my Aunt Madge gave me delivering flowers, paying sixty dollars a week.

Then I ran into a friend of mine on the street, who said, "You know, they're doing a series over at CBS called *Gunsmoke*. You ought to go over and see if there is anything in it for you. Charles Marcus (Bill) Warren is directing it." I was pretty excited about the possibility, because I had worked with Bill four or five months earlier in *Seven Angry Men*. So I called his office at CBS that very afternoon, and he took my call right away. He said, "Where have you been? I haven't been able to find you." (Because I had no agent.) "There's a part here that I'd like you to read for."

I went up for an initial interview and they—Bill and the other producer, Norman McDonald, told me the part paid three hundred dollars an episode, one a week. It's industry policy to settle on price before the actor reads, just in case the reading is sensational. They don't want the actor to be in a strong negotiating position.

Well, as I said, I was delivering flowers at sixty dollars a week, so three hundred dollars sounded outa-sight! Nevertheless, I was a little hesitant, thinking what I could get if I had an agent.

I knew that a friend of mine, Guy Williams (who later played "Zorro" in the television series) had read for the same part. So, I called him up and asked him what he was offered.

He answered, "Four hundred dollars an episode."

I said, "Thank you very much."

Then I called Bill back—I was trembling at the time—and said, "No—no, hey, listen, no way I can do this for three hundred dollars an episode. I've got to have at least four hundred dollars." He said, "Oh, no problem—okay $400. We'll go for that." I breathed a huge sigh of relief.

The first time I read, I knew I had lost the part. They gave me what they call "sides," just a little scene, not the whole script, and told me to go out in the hall and look at the part of Chester.

Well, I went out and I looked at the sides. I've got to tell you, the character was so inane it was on the borderline of being really stupid. I said to myself, "With all my Actors Studio training, I'll correct this character by using my own experiences and drawing from myself. I'll read it straight."

Always, when you finish a reading, you take a quick look at the director and the producer and you know right away whether you've scored or not. Well, my quick look told me that I had definitely not scored. Disappointment was written all over their faces.

Bill said, "You know, Den, we were hoping for a little more humor from this character." And the minute he said "humor," the lightbulb went on in my head. I flashed back to the University of Oklahoma where I used to have fun imitating a guy I went to school with. We could hardly understand him, because his accent was so broad. I would get huge laughs at parties by saying things like, "Alice, git the dysh rag and wipe under that ba-aby's nose. If'n neres nothin' I cain't stand it's nastiness." Or "Git that youngin' in off 'in the streets she's out dar necked as a jaybird and dat t'ere Simpkin boy's takin' it all in, too."

I said, "Oh, humor. Listen, I think I know what you mean. Could I try it again? Just let me go back outside for five minutes." They said, "Fine."

I went outside and I put that accent to their words, and it changed my entire psyche. My whole way of thinking changed—and it began to get a little funny even for me. So, I ran back in and I read it again with that attitude and that accent, and they went right on the floor. They could not contain themselves. They were laughing all the way through it! The change was unbelievable.

They said, "Thank you very much."

I left their offices and went back to delivering flowers.

A day later, I was loading up the flower truck when Mike, the owner of the shop, said, "You're wanted on the phone—!" I went in, picked up the receiver, and heard Charles Marcus Warren's voice on the other end.

"Den—this is Bill Warren. Want you to know that you got the part of Chester."

With deep relief and gratitude, I said, "Ah-ah, thank you very much."

Since I was the first one cast, I was asked to help in the tests for other actors. I tested with maybe four or five potential Matt Dillons and a couple of Docs—I didn't test with any possible Miss Kittys, because they didn't use a scene with her and Chester.

One day after one of the tests, Bill Warren came to me and said, "Do you mind if we have a little conversation after we finish?"

I said, "No."

He invited me across the street from CBS to KELBO'S—a restaurant. We settled at the bar. "You know, Den," he said, "I've got a problem."

The thought flashed through my mind . . . was I going to be fired?

I said as calmly as I could, "What's the problem?"

He said, "You see, in the past, historically if you have a sidekick in a film, he's usually too old or too fat or too young or too something, to really get involved in the action. Usually he's considered to be rather helpless.

"My problem is that I have cast you as the sidekick, and you're a leading man, physically. Six-two, hundred-and-eighty pounds and you've competed in the Olympic trials in the decathlon. I don't want people writing in and saying why doesn't Chester get more involved in the physical stuff? In the fights and helping Matt Dillon out more? We want to make him a nonviolent character that doesn't wear a gun—which also goes against tradition.

"So, I was just thinking if we could give him some kind of a handicap so people wouldn't ask those questions, then I wouldn't have to answer them."

I didn't take that as a very good reason for creating a handicap, but I did think it was a rather interesting challenge for me as an actor.

As a matter of fact, I had done workshop stuff where we incorporated physical controls into the character we were working on until that control became such a habit that we no longer had to think about it. For instance, a control might be a dialect, like an Irish accent or a speech impediment—a stammer or stutter. Or maybe just a backache or headache or some physical thing that would make the character more interesting.

The challenge of creating a physical control for Chester stimulated my creative juices. So I said to Bill, "Let me go home and think about it, and do some experimenting, and I'll get back to you."

I knew that I had to select something that I could easily control and make consistent, something I wouldn't have to worry about. I decided a stiff leg would do it. So, for a few days, I practiced running and jumping over things in the backyard stiff-legged, and it seemed to work well. I went back and showed it to Bill, and he quickly agreed. "That's it. That's perfect."

Well, had I known that I was going to be playing Chester for nine years stiff-legged, I might have thought differently about it. Have you ever tried to build a campfire stiff-legged or put your boot on and not bend your knee? To manage that, I had to be in really good physical shape. As a matter of fact, I practiced hatha yoga in order to be able to do it.

Chester's stiff leg became an unbelievably strong identifying characteristic. I think that was part of the reason why Chester was received with such love by so many people—they sympathized with him.

One thing that I made sure of with Bill Warren was that the characters (that were in the television family: Matt Dillon, Doc, Kitty, the bartender, the townspeople) would never comment on Chester's handicap—that they would just accept it as normal. He agreed. So I walked stiff-legged for nine years.

One of the main reasons why people enjoyed and smiled at Chester was because he allowed them to feel superior. You see, he wasn't the brightest person in the world, but there was a simple goodness about him—a naïve honesty that touched people. He wasn't strong in the intellect department, but his intuition was right on. He had a sense about people and would say things like, "Mr. Dillon, I don't think you ought to mess around with that person. You better watch out for him, don't go down a dark alley, you know, Mr. Dillon?"

And Chester loved women. I think women were attracted to him because he really respected and honored them—because he trusted them a lot, and that sometimes got him into trouble. He was an easy touch.

I would go out on personal appearances, and ladies would bring me all kinds of things that they had made themselves, like homemade pies, little doilies, socks, and belt buckles—all for Chester. I had no idea that that character was going to have the kind of impact that it did. It was incredible.

The cast of *Gunsmoke* was like a close-knit family. We worked beautifully together. Our weekly shooting schedule helped make it that way.

We had a day of rehearsal, which was a luxury. I don't know of any shows today that have that luxury—sitcoms certainly, but not dramatic shows. We had an opportunity to read the script and say, "Well, this part doesn't work," or, "This scene needs an overhaul," or, "The relationship is not consistent here," and we would change it. We would use that day, not to rehearse necessarily, but to approve of the script and to alter it if we felt that it needed it. Even on the set when we were shooting, if the scene wasn't working or wasn't believable, we would improvise, ad lib, and change it.

It was all play and no work! At least, as I look back from a distance of forty years, that's what it feels like. I can remember nothing but the fun times. Of course, we had to memorize lines, work out glitches in the script, work with the directors and the other actors, but we also found time in between setups to indulge in the pastime that will be found on most movie sets—playing cards. Now, my mother always said that I learned to count by playing Pitch . . . sometimes called High, Low, Jack, Joker, and The

Game, and that became our card game of choice on the *Gunsmoke* set.

Tiny Nichols, Jim's stand-in, who was six-foot-five and weighed well over three hundred pounds, had a love for the game also, and between us, we taught it to Jim. I think we must have developed an addiction, for we played every chance we had. I'm sure some of the crew, especially the first assistant director, whose job was to control the set and bring the shows in on time, thought we came to work just to play Pitch.

Now, after the principal actors finished blocking the scene, they would normally relax while the stand-ins took over. Their job was to mimic the movement of the principals so the lighting crew could light the scene properly. But after Jim finished his blocking, the three of us would hustle over to the card table, and by the time the stand-ins were called, Tiny was in the middle of the game. Now, if Jim had a good hand and didn't want the game interrupted, he'd say, "Tiny, sit down. They can find somebody else. The second assistant can stand in for you." And the second, not wanting to disturb the "boss," would willingly comply. After a while, the company just gave up and hired a stand-in for the stand-in!

We also played during our lunch hour. Jim would send Tiny up to his room to fix the steaks a half hour before our lunch break so preparing the food wouldn't cut into our valuable Pitch time. By this time I was a vegetarian, so I brought my own lunch, which Gerry packed everyday with loving hands.

We played for quarters, and Jim always kept his in a leather marble bag which he stowed away in a cabinet. Every day, almost without exception, he'd enter the room, stride to the cabinet, reach for his stash of quarters, wave the marble bag in our faces, and challenge us, "Alright, you sons-of-bitches, get this!" And before dessert was finished, inevitably, his marble bag was flat.

Years later, I heard Jim remark to a mutual friend, "You know, I paid for Den's swimming pool."

"What happened with Milt Grossman—did he ever return from Mexico?" I asked curiously, wondering seriously if Dennis has done his own negotiating for the past thirty years.

He smiled. "Yes. Milt came back from Mexico. And, yes, he did become my agent. He even got the network to rewrite my contract for *Gunsmoke* the second year, and upped it considerably."

"I'll bet he did," I said with a sudden and new understanding of how things worked. "Do you keep in touch with the other cast members today?"

Jim (Arness) and I are the only ones left of the original cast, and we do keep in touch. When I talk to him, we remember how much fun we had during that period of television—when the actors had more control. All decisions didn't come down from the networks. The sponsors also had more to say about what shows went on the air . . . and what didn't. Looking back on it, it was a great creative time—a fun time.

Talking to Jim the other day, he reminisced, "You know, Den, we were just a couple of kids having fun growing up on television and playing the game!"

And it truly was like a game for us, and a well-paying game. How fortunate I am to have had that. And, of course, that character of Chester, because it became so incredibly successful, created all kinds of opportunities for me. Chester was my "door-opener," and I give thanks to him everyday.

Gunsmoke became the longest-running dramatic show in the history of television. It went on for twenty years. I stayed with it for nine. I felt at the time that, if I didn't break loose, I would never play anything else the rest of my acting career. If I was going to have an opportunity to do what I really got into the business to do—to play a leading man with the responsibility of the show on my own shoulders—I had to break loose.

8

. . . You're Turning Down Orson Welles? . . . Saying "Yes" to Spielberg . . . There Ya Go, Marshal Sam McCloud

Well, before I left *Gunsmoke* in 1964, I made sure I had a bird in the hand. I had a guarantee of twenty-four shows with NBC for *Kentucky Jones*.

I thought it would be a winner. Buzz Kulik, one of Hollywood's more talented producer/directors was on board. The very talented Harry Morgan played my sidekick . . . great theme—all the elements were there—but after we shot the twenty-four shows, they cancelled it. I was in shock. I just assumed that the next series I did would be as successful as *Gunsmoke*, but it wasn't.

That was an eye-opener for me—I realized that I had a large nut to crack. I had a lot of responsibilities with the family, the house, mortgages, etc., and it certainly gave me a moment to think, "What did I do? What kind of choice did I make—? Was I totally stupid to leave the security of *Gunsmoke*?" But as the jobs came and my career continued to develop, I realized there was life after *Gunsmoke*.

I free-lanced for a couple of years and did some films—one of them was *Duel at Diablo* with James Garner, Sydney Poitier, and the Swedish actress, BiBi Anderson, who played my wife. I did a movie in Spain and Italy called *A Man Called Sledge*, again with Jim Garner, a number of television appearances, and a summer stock tour.

Then came the series *Gentle Ben*—from the movie *Gentle Giant*—that I had made with Vera Miles, a story about a family with a pet bear. I have many wonderful memories of the two years I worked in Florida. Skimming over the Everglades in the airboat certainly gave me a charge. Even the four or five times I sunk it trying to make a more exciting shot was a thrill of a kind.

I was pleased that it was a family show, not only for the families viewing it, but for the Weavers and the Howards as well. Robby, who got his feet wet in *Kentucky Jones*, continued his growth as an actor in several episodes. Rusty earned his spurs and his Screen Actors Guild card playing various scenes with my television son, Clint Howard. Clint's brother Ron, who was to become one of our industry's most talented directors, guested as an actor on one episode. Their father, Rance, played my neighbor, Boomhauer, all the while coaching and keeping a close eye on Clint.

Here's an interesting side story. While I was at the University of Oklahoma directing *Derricks on the Hill*, I cast Jean Speegle in the female lead, and I also cast a young actor in the role of the young man that came to Jean's home to tell her that her brother had been killed in an oil-field accident. It turned out to be a fortuitous bit of casting. Later, Jean married that young actor, who happened to be Rance Howard. I've often said I played some part in creating my own TV son. A couple of other people made *Gentle Ben* special. Beth Brickell was one of the prettiest and most talented TV wives I've ever had. The other was my sweet Gerry, who showed off her considerable talent playing a fortune-teller/lady panther trainer under the watchful eye of our longtime friend Lou Antonio, who was directing his first show.

The first day of shooting was reserved for the title shots—shots that would appear each week at the beginning of each episode. What the director, George Sherman, wanted was the airboat traveling fast through the everglades with the family on board. The technical advisor, an expert with airboats, ran through the "dos" and "don'ts" with me for half an hour. He allowed me a short spin through the glades and then said, "Okay, Dennis—you're a seasoned airboat pilot—you're ready to solo."

It was a piece of cake, particularly in the swamps for which it is designed. An airboat has a flat bottom with no conventional rudder, but rather an airplane-type, at the rear of the boat above the water and an airplane propeller mounted in the back that pushes the boat. You turn the rudder one way and the wind from the big fan in back pushes the nose of the boat the other direction. We skimmed across the water like a flat rock skipping across a smooth pond.

So I had the whole cast on the boat, including the bear and his trainer—hidden in the bottom of the boat, so he couldn't be seen by the camera. I did the run-bys without a hitch in the morning. The afternoon, however, was a different story. They needed to get some close shots, so they set the camera up on the bank of a small, deepwater channel.

The director said, "Dennis, you can just run by and we'll pan with you and get some close-ups of the family."

Now, because it's a flat-bottom boat with no rudder, it has no stability in deep water. The cockpit sits extremely high. It's made that way so the pilot can see above, and maneuver through, the tall everglade grasses. This makes the center of gravity high, which increases the instability.

There I was, perched in the high driver's seat in the deepwater channel doing a run-by, and everything was cool. We went past the camera about fifty yards, and I heard the director say, "Okay, you can turn around now."

I had too much weight on the boat to begin with—there was the bear, the bear's trainer, Beth, Clint, and myself up in the cockpit. The boat was so deep in the water that when I turned it around the wake caught up with us, went over the side of the boat, and sunk it! It flipped upside down like a flapjack! The bear, the trainer, my "family," and I all went crashing into the water. I thought the whole cast was gone the first day of shooting!

I didn't even know if Clint could swim since I had just met him—so, as soon as I surfaced, I frantically looked for him. To make matters worse, he had an iron chain wrapped around his waist that he used to lead the bear, and it was heavy. I moved fast, concerned that he might drown. I found him and grabbed him, but I was having a little trouble myself because my boots were full of water and all my clothes were soaked. I struggled to keep hold of him and swam toward something we could grab on to. I caught a brief glimpse of the shoreline, and saw that the crew was in an absolute panic! They were running down the bank yelling and screaming! I heard one guy shout, "Get a hold of the bear! The bear's a great swimmer!"

I thought that made sense—I wondered only briefly if the bear would object—but I was desperate and I thought it was the best option I had. So, swimming with Clint in one hand, I made it to the bear. I started to reach out to grab him, but instead of letting me hold on, he started slapping at me—thinking I was playing with him. I immediately realized I needed an alternate plan—Gentle Ben was going to drown us. The headlines of the *Miami Herald* flashed before my eyes: "Gentle Ben Sinks *Gentle Ben*!"

Somehow, I found the strength to swim back to the capsized boat and hang on. When the boat flipped over, a pocket of air was trapped underneath and kept it from sinking. We all held on for dear life until they hauled us out of there. It was a miracle that we all survived.

Dennis leaned forward then with his arms opened wide and flailing. He was very animated.

"The funny thing was that Ivan Tors (the producer) thought this whole event would be bad publicity for the show and he kept saying to us, 'Don't nobody say not'ing— not'ing—not'ing! Ve don't vant this in d'papers!'—I thought it would have made great publicity! What a terrific story, as long as they spelled our names right!"

He relaxed his arms and continued. . . .

Gentle Ben was an immediate success, but at the end of the second year, CBS chose to change their programming policy. They explained that they were going to cater to a more "adult" audience. So they cancelled *Gentle Ben* after only two years—while it was still in the top ten!

I was disappointed at the time, but it was a blessing in disguise for me, because *McCloud* was just on the horizon, and I would never have had the most satisfying role of my career had *Gentle Ben* continued to run.

It was while I was filming *McCloud* in Hawaii, in 1973, that I received notice that I had been elected president of the Screen Actors Guild (the first time an independent candidate had ever won). While I was in office, the guild achieved two major breakthroughs. We attained residuals in perpetuity for actors, and we were able to open up committees to the membership at large. If a member complained about what they perceived to be a problem, I simply put them on a committee and asked them to "help fix it!" and it worked.

The presidency required much time and energy, and so did *McCloud*—I needed an assistant on the set and in my office at Universal Studios. I mentioned my problem to my stand-in, John Sistrunk, and he quickly replied, "I've got just the girl for you!" John had the answer for most anything. The girl turned out to be a former girlfriend of his named Alice Ornstein Weaver Haskell Billings . . . well, at the time it was just Alice Ornstein. But after she came to work for me, my son Rick, who was working on the lot as an editor, saw her, and it wasn't long after that wedding bells rang. So, for seven years she was my daughter-in-law. Her next trip to the alter was with Don Haskell, the project engineer of our Earthship and surrounding property. I don't think that lasted seven years. Then she met John Billings, an artist who designs and manufactures the Grammys and the John Wooden awards, among others. I don't know if it was because they were married by Dik Darnell, a Lakota Sioux medicine man, or not, but this one has lasted over ten years.

On second thought, I guess my relationship with her constitutes the longest. It's been over a quarter of a century since she became my "deputy" on *McCloud*. She's done everything from creating my schedules, answering fan mail, photographing me, listening to my problems, picking up my e-mails, designing the I.O.E. Newsletter, and teaching me to line dance, and she does the same for Gerry. She became an important part of our lives when Sistrunk introduced us.

Speaking of John, when he applied for my stand-in's job, it didn't seem as though he had much of a chance of getting it. A stand-in for camera reasons is supposed to be the same height as the actor he's standing in for—John is six inches shorter than I. But John also has a silver tongue, and he convinced me that the six-inch differential would not be a problem. The first day he came to work, he was wearing specially designed boots with six-inch heels! I thought he was walking on stilts—he wobbled around on them for two days, and then decided he'd carry a six-inch apple box to stand on.

John worked for me until I moved to Colorado. He eventually became my stunt double during my fourteen years as the spokesperson for Great Western Bank and served as our stunt coordinator on *Stone* and *Buck James*.

For seven years, *McCloud* was pure joy. It allowed me to do what I got in the business to do: to play the leading man—to put the success of the show largely on my shoulders—to assume greater responsibility. I am acutely aware, however, that the success of a show depends on the talents and skills of all of its parts.

The *McCloud* TV family was exceptionally talented, and, without the contribution of each, the show would never have worked. J. D. Cannon, who played cigar-smoking, hard-nosed, smoke-in-your-face Police Chief Clifford, was a perfect foil for McCloud, who was supposed to be learning how big-city cops fight crime, but was really teaching them—a source of frustration and embarrassment to the chief and a real thorn in his side.

Terry Carter was perfect as my partner, Broadhurst, who was always trying to keep me out of trouble and show me the correct path. It was simply an overwhelming task. He just couldn't take the "country" out of McCloud.

Then there was Diana Muldaur (Chris Coughlin). What a doll! She gave the show such class—her cosmopolitan air was the perfect balance for McCloud's country ways. The chemistry was electric. They made the show special, and I'm grateful to all of them for the three Emmy nominations I received. Again, my sons Rick and Rob guested in several episodes.

"What was it like riding a horse through the streets of New York—or was it really you on the horse?" I asked, taking advantage of his pause.

Oh, it was me, and it was great fun! No one else was dumb enough to do it. Actually, that sequence wasn't in the original screenplay. The script called for McCloud to "borrow" a policeman's horse and "exit the shot," hot on the trail of the bad guys. The next shot, according to the script, called for McCloud to "enter camera right" at a full gallop into Central Park.

While we were setting the camera to film McCloud "borrowing" the horse, the producer came over to me with a very creative suggestion.

"Dennis, it sure would be a great shot if we could get you riding your horse down Sixth Avenue on your way to Central Park. What do you think?"

"What do *I* think? I think you're absolutely right. Let's do it! Lead me to my horse!" I answered without thinking twice.

"Well," the producer mused, "there is a slight problem . . . we don't have a permit and we don't have time to get one."

"Do we really have to have one?" I suggested.

The producer didn't hesitate. "Why don't we find out?"

With that, I mounted the horse, they threw the camera in the back of the station wagon, and we took off—with no permit, no crowd control, nothing. Whatever happened, happened. If the traffic light turned red, we just stopped, waited for it to turn green, and took off again. To make matters worse, as we galloped down Sixth Avenue, a light drizzle fell on the blacktop. It wasn't the kind of rain that was picked up by the camera, but it was enough to make the pavement super slick. The horse came close to going down three or four times—fortunately, close only counts in horseshoes. We continued to chase the bad guys, urged on by the hoots and hollers of cabbies.

What's interesting, is that this gallop down 6th Avenue, which was not in the script, wasn't planned, and was strictly impromptu, became the signature shot for the entire series. Sometimes a person will come up to me and say, "You know, the show I really like was . . . I forget the name of it . . . you know, it was the one where you rode your horse down the streets of New York City." That scene they never forget . . . and it almost didn't happen.

Come to think of it, we did the same trick in Sydney, Australia (again without a permit), and I was nearly arrested riding my horse across the famous Sydney Bridge. We filmed it very early Sunday morning before too many cars and police were around. . . . It was a dynamite shot!

113

"Did you do all your own stunts?"

I've always been a frustrated stuntman, so I did most of them. But there was a shot of McCloud hanging onto the bottom of a helicopter flying over New York City that made me quickly say, "Better get Bill Catching (my regular stunt double) for this one."

Now, to make that shot effective, it was necessary to get a close shot of me that made it look as though I was actually hanging on to the helicopter while it was in flight. We made this shot on the back lot of Universal Studios. All that was necessary was for me to get a good grip on the landing gear, set the camera low, so that all that could be seen behind me would be blue sky. In other words, the helicopter would lift me so that my feet would only have to be two to three feet off the ground.

The communication between the director and the pilot of the chopper was flawed. The director yelled action, and the helicopter kept going up and up and up . . . until I was hanging 150 feet in the air—with no safety harness! I hung on for dear life! I knew if I slipped, this episode of *McCloud* would probably end my career—not to mention my life! At that moment, as my palms were beginning to sweat, a black limousine drove up, and our executive producer, Glenn Larson, leaped out and yelled, "What the hell is Dennis doing up there?" The pilot got the message and I began descending. Terra firma never felt so good. My only comment to Glenn was, "D'ya suppose there's another chopper pilot available?"

"Well, how many lives is that? Five? Five lifetimes you've used up," I said, laughing. "Whoa, you were really meant to be here!" He settled in his chair. I said, "You're on a roll, Dennis. Tell me more."

My kids were crazy about John Denver, so even though I wasn't too "hip" to him at the time, when Larson suggested we cast him as Deputy Dewey (his first acting job), I said, "Sure." One day on the set, I said, "Hey, John, I understand that you are a pretty doggone-good songwriter, and I'm making an album—and I just wondered if you had any songs in your trunk that you haven't used that might be good for me."

He was eager to help and said, "You know, I just wrote one, which I recorded last night with my guitar at home. I'll play it for you. If you like it, you can have it."

I played the tape and I thought it was a great song. I called my producer, Marty Cooper, who was a hit songwriter himself, and said, "I've got a John Denver song here I'd like you to listen to," which he did and later got back to me with this comment, "You know, Dennis, it would be great to have a John Denver song on the album, but I don't think this is the one."

So as politely as I could, I said "thanks, but no thanks" to John. He then recorded it, and it was voted the Country Song of the Year. Do you remember the song that went, "Hey, it's good to be back home again"? Yep, that was it— and I turned it down!

"You *didn't!*" I gasped.

"Yeah, I did. That was the stupidest thing I ever did— well, no maybe not . . . *maybe*, it was turning down the David Janssen role in *The Fugitive!*"

"No—no, tell me you didn't do that, *too?*"

"Yep," he said, laughing. I cracked up, too. It was funny. After we both stopped laughing, he went on.

I read the pilot script sent to me by the producer, Quinn Martin, and I thought it was "nothing but a bad soap opera." Quinn explained to me that "it has to be written this way, Dennis, to sell it. We don't intend to do this kind of script once it's sold." In my mind, I said, "Oh, yeah, sure." I figured he was giving me a snow job, so again, I politely said "no thanks" to what turned out to be one of TV's classic series.

Getting back to Denver. John and I became close friends. He was one of the first to make me take a serious look at what we were doing to our Mother Earth. His music became a powerful influence in my life. He walked his talk! In the late '80s, he formed the Windstar Foundation—its purpose was to promote peace around the world and to inspire us to honor the planet that gives us life. I had the privilege of speaking on numerous occasions at his annual Windstar Conference. They were always imbued with his buoyant and irrepressible spirit. Gerry and I looked forward to the conferences with great anticipation, knowing that would get our spiritual batteries charged.

His sudden death in October of 1997 left us devastated. His leaving the Earth so soon was an immeasurable loss to all those who are trying to build a more humane, global society . . . one that is safer, kinder, and more just for all.

He was excited about the philosophy of Ecolonomics (which I will go into presently) and was one of the first contributors to our Institute as well as serving on our original advisory board.

"Wow, it seems odd that John would leave Earth at a time when he was doing so much good."

Dennis as Sam McCloud, in the
television series, which ran from 1971 to 1977.
(Photo courtesy of NBC-TV)

Walter and Lenna Weaver,
taken on May 15, 1917,
in Neosho, Missouri,
on the day after
their wedding.
(Photo courtesy
of the Weaver family)

In front of a 1928 DeSoto at brother-in-law Denzil Bell's house
in 1936. Left to right: Denzil Bell, Dennis (12), brother
Howard (15), and sister Mary Ann (4) in the background.
(Photo courtesy of the Weaver family)

Dennis and Gerry singing
together on the rock wall at
Joplin Junior College in 1942.
(Photo courtesy of the Weaver family)

With his Naval squadron flight
buddies in 1945. Back Row, left
to right: Lamont Davis (Monty),
Dennis (Buck), and Ed Ryan.
Front Row, left to right:
Sam Craddock (Tubby),
Andy Latteier, and
Don Rickard (Rick).
(U.S. Navy Squadron photo)

Clearing the high-jump
bar using the
Western Roll before
the advent of the Fosbury
Flop, at a track meet at
the University of
Oklahoma, 1948.
(Photo courtesy
of the Weaver family)

Dennis as Chester Goode ,
with his 23-year-old horse,
Nugget, in a publicity photo
for *Gunsmoke*, taken on the set
at Gene Autry's Melody Ranch.
(Photo courtesy of CBS-TV)

Teaching the kids to long jump in the backyard of the house on Royal Oak Road, Encino, California, circa 1968. Left to right: Rob, Dennis, and Rusty.
(Photo courtesy of the Weaver family)

Publicity photo for *Gunsmoke*, taken on the set at CBS studios. Left to right: Amanda Blake (Miss Kitty), James Arness (Matt Dillon), Dennis (Chester Goode), and Milburn Stone (Doc).
(Photo courtesy of CBS-TV)

A 1972 publicity photo
for the television movie,
Female Artillery,
co-starring Linda Evans.
(Photo courtesy of Universal Studios)

Gerry and Dennis in their garden
in Calabasas, California, circa 1975,
part of a photo shoot
for *Ladies Home Journal*.
(Photo by Alice Billings)

Singing "Hollywood
Freeway" (written
by Dennis) with
John Denver on the
set of a music
special, in 1975
(Dennis was
shooting *McCloud*
at the time).
(Photo by Alice Billings)

Dennis and Gerry at their
40th wedding anniversary
at SRF Lake Shrine Temple
in Pacific Palisades,
October 20, 1985.
(Photo courtesy
of the Weaver family)

Publicity photo
for the TV series
entitled *Buck James*.
Dennis played the lead
character, Buck James.
(Photo courtesy of ABC-TV)

At home in Malibu,
January, 2000, for an article
in *TV Guide*
on the remake of
The Virginian.
(Photo by Darryl Tooley)

Skiing in Telluride, Colorado, with his three sons.
From left to right: Rick, Dennis, Rob, and Rusty.
(Photo courtesy of the Weaver family)

At Paramount Studios in Hollywood, Dennis stands in front of a hydro-
gen-powered BMW prototype. BMW is committed to working toward a
commercially competitive hydrogen car, perhaps in this decade. Dennis
supports the concept of using hydrogen instead of fossil fuels.
(Photo by Julian Myers)

North view of Earthship,
home of Gerry and Dennis Weaver
(Photo by Alice Billings)

South view of Earthship
(Photo by Alice Billings)

You know, Dee, there are so many things we just don't understand, that seem to make no sense at the time, but looked at from a greater perspective is more understandable. For instance, at the time I was bummed a bit that I had chosen not to accept *The Fugitive*. But if I had, I probably would not have done *McCloud* and subsequently would not have been offered one of the choice roles of my career, in the movie *Duel*.

The opportunity to do *Duel* presented itself while I was on hiatus from shooting *McCloud*.

Milt called me up and said, "Den, the studio is going to send you a script and I want you to say yes to it now before you even read it! This is a special script! Just say yes to it. Okay?"

Now that was a very surprising request, because Milt had never asked me to do that before, but when I read the script, I knew what he was talking about, and I jumped at the opportunity.

About two weeks later, the studio called me back and said, "Would you mind working with a young director we have under contract here who we feel is a real comer? He has a lot of enthusiasm, intense energy, he's willing to take risks, and has a very vivid, if not wild, imagination."

I said, "I'm not used to working with that kind of director—sure, let's go for it."

And, of course, that young director was Steven Spielberg.

Duel was his first major film. He had done some segment television—a couple of shows—one *Outer Limits* episode, a *Night Gallery*, and a *Columbo*. This was his first movie-of-the-week, and it was a great experience for him—and for me!

"What was it like to work with Steven?" I asked, hopefully not too excitedly.

"Good question—people often ask me what it was like to work with a twenty-three-year-old Steven Spielberg. . . ."

Well, I must say, he turned out to be every bit of what the studio executives said he was—energetic, imaginative, creative, all of that, but the quality that really impressed me was his fearlessness. Steven was willing to break the mold, to make new tracks. He wasn't intimidated by the large project he was given. He never felt pressured by the schedule. For him, it was a delicious game and he had these wonderful toys with which to play it.

For me, it was just great fun. When I'd finish a day's shoot, I'd say to Gerry, "I can't wait to get up and do it again."

I developed a strong trust in Steve's suggestions, and I felt he also appreciated my creative input. Making movies is a communal art. It takes all the pieces working together and giving their best to make a final product that all can be proud of. *Duel* was an example of that understanding in action.

What I've come to realize is that life itself is like that. It is a communal game. We all need to work together; each of us needs to play his or her part with the understanding that we are an important piece of something bigger than our individual selves—and, as we improve our own role, we automatically improve the larger self. When we bring benefit to the whole, we automatically share in that benefit, as individuals. This to me is the Holy upward spiral of humanity . . . ever evolving to a more advanced society where love, cooperation, peace, and justice have supplanted hate, greed, and fear.

"Hey—we were talking about S-p-i-e-l-berg?"

"Yeah."

You know, many people have asked me if I knew that he was going to take his place among the great directors our industry has produced. My answer . . . of course not! He was only twenty-three years old! I knew he would have a long career, that he was going to work and probably make some noteworthy films. But did I know he was going to have the impact on the film industry that he has . . . ? Of course not . . . if I had known . . . I would have adopted him!

Duel turned out so good, and the reaction to it was so strong, that the studio decided to release it worldwide as a feature film. Since it was originally shot for a ninety-minute movie-of-the-week (they only shoot two-hour shows now) it was not long enough for a feature film. So, we went back and shot fifteen more minutes so they could release it worldwide.

It was a huge, huge success—a great moneymaker. And it has become a classic. It played in a Paris Art House for over eight years! As an actor, if you can get one or two real classics under your belt during your career, you are pretty fortunate.

For me, *Duel* was one, and the other was the 1958 film titled *Touch of Evil* with Orson Welles, which was re-released in 1998. It is a re-edited version following Orson's personal editing notes.

The black-and-white film was premiered in the summer of '98, at the Telluride Film Festival. The original cast included Orson Welles, Charlton Heston, Janet Leigh, myself, Joseph Callia, Akim Tamiroff, Marlene Dietrich,

Joseph Cotton, Mercedes McCambridge, Zsa Zsa Gabor, and Joanna Moore—people accepted little cameos to be in the movie because Orson Welles was directing it. Mercedes McCambridge, who was an Oscar winner, had only one line! And Zsa Zsa Gabor just showed up! She was there for a moment and then she was gone. You can hardly find Joseph Cotton, a star in his own right.

It is funny, because when the studio sent me the script—Orson wanted me to play this particular part—I turned it down! All the script said was that the character was a night watchman at an off-season motel on the border of Mexico. It just didn't seem like there was anything there, so I opted to pass on it.

Afterwards, Charlton Heston visited me on the *Gunsmoke* set and said, "Dennis, you are crazy! Everybody in Hollywood wants to be in this movie, and you're turning down Orson Welles? Believe me, this will be the experience of your life, working with this man. Please reconsider this— people are not called by Orson Welles and then turn him down!"

Chuck was very convincing, as well he can be, so I re-thought it and decided to accept.

The first day of shooting, I had a ten o'clock call. Now, traditionally in the movie business when you have a late call—on set and ready to shoot is normally eight o'clock— you don't work until maybe late in the afternoon, and that was the case this particular day. After wardrobe and makeup, I had time on my hands and began to imagine what elements I might incorporate into the character. As an idea came to me, I would take it to Orson and ask him, "What do you think?" He would respond, "Yeah, that could work, and how about adding this . . . ?" This process continued all day long. I would give him suggestions and he would add to them.

He asked me what was one of the main characteristics of my character "Chester" on *Gunsmoke*. I told him that he was basically a follower.

He quickly said, "Okay, this guy never follows. He is always ahead."

And we just kept suggesting and molding the character, so by five o'clock when they called me to the set to shoot, I had this zany character all done. I remember at one point I had suggested to Orson that he was "sexually attracted to women."

He thought about it for a split second, and added, " . . . yeah, but he is scared to death of them at the same time!" So the character was at once attracted to, and frightened by, women, which gave the night watchman a rather odd behavior. Orson later described the character as a "Shakespearean loony."

Anyway, I had a ball doing it. I had a scene with Janet Leigh, which was really fun, because she was so gorgeous I had no trouble being attracted to her—however, it was difficult to be scared of her! For that, I had to use my imagination.

The film was one of the most fulfilling experiences, one of the greatest relationships I've ever had with a director. Orson was terrific—one of the most creative persons I have ever been around. He not only starred in and directed the film—for which he should have been nominated for an Academy Award—but he also wrote the screenplay and did his own makeup. It was a creative "orgy" for him.

After he finished the picture, the head of the studio thought it was trash, and they released it as the bottom half of a double bill—a "B" movie. However, the cream always rises to the top, and over the years it has become an Orson Welles classic, with a very loyal following. A lot of colleges have used it in their film departments as an example of great filmmaking. Orson was so far ahead of his time. You look at this film—and it's hard to believe it was shot in the late fifties. He broke the formula for filmmaking. And the studio head didn't know what he had—he couldn't recognize genius. His comment was, "Orson was just showing off." And he was right. He was showing off, like nobody else could!

His master shots exposed his genius. They were designed in such a way that very little film wound up on the cutting-room floor. He got his close-ups, over-the-shoulders, and points-of-views, all in his incredibly fluid masters. He moved his camera and actors in such a way that his editor had a very easy time of it. Cuts were often unnecessary; in some cases, not even an option.

A lot of moviemakers today have tried to emulate his style, but you look at this film and you still shake your head and say, "They're just now catching up to him."

Before they released the picture, they took it away from him and wouldn't allow his input in the editing of it. He was so disappointed that he wrote fifty-eight pages of notes to the head of the studio, saying, "This is what should be," . . . begging them, almost, to do some things that would even save their version of the film.

So, forty-one years later, after the film had languished in art houses and film schools, Rick Schmidlin (an editing producer) got hold of those original notes and convinced the new powers at Universal to re-edit and re-issue the picture based on Orson's suggestions. And that is what they did—and it was released worldwide to rave reviews.

The theater in Telluride (at its premiere) was absolutely jam-packed. Director Peter Bogdonavich was the master of ceremonies, and after the film Janet Leigh and I answered questions. Some people were shocked that I was there, because the character was so zany, they didn't recognize me in the film. One guy came up to me at the Film Festival party and said, "You know, I noticed the night watchman in *Touch of Evil* and said to myself, that is some kind of an actor. I wondered if anything ever happened to his career— and then I saw the credits and realized it was you!"

During that time in Hollywood, I was, as they say, "hot"—I was doing a lot of fun things, like *The Sonny and Cher Show*—I did five or six of those. Every year, I would do a *Dean Martin*, a *Flip Wilson*, a *Perry Como Show* (we sang "Up the Lazy River" rowing in a bathtub). Also, *Ed Sullivan* and *Johnny Carson* shows.

I went right from *McCloud* to a series that didn't make it, called *Stone*, even though Stephen Cannell, one of Hollywood's hottest writers at the time, produced it. It was based on a real person—the successful author, Joseph Wambaugh—whose "day job" was a detective.

The premise intrigued me, because here was a guy whose job as an undercover cop required that he be an "unknown." But as a successful writer he was required to be on talk shows like *Johnny Carson*, which made him quite visible to the public. And because of his celebrity, there was resentment toward him in the "house"—the police department. The conflicts in his own lifestyle made interesting drama.

My son Rob costarred with me, which made the daily shoots really fun. It was a good show, but for whatever reason it didn't get the ratings and was cancelled after thirteen shows. It was very disappointing. It not only had great potential for me, but I had had the opportunity to work with my son—which was very special for me. It took a little work time to get over the frustration.

Rob later costarred with Bill Katt in *Top of the Hill* and then went into directing.

I did a lot of movies of the week and two mini-series of which I was very proud. *Centennial* afforded me the opportunity to play one of my favorite characters of all time: R. J. Poteet, the man responsible for moving the Longhorns from Texas to Colorado. For that role, I received the Best Actor Award from the National Cowboy Hall of Fame, during my induction ceremony in 1980.

Pearl gave me the chance to play against type. The role was the commanding officer at Pearl Harbor when the Japanese attacked. He was a true-blue bigot, a real meathead, but the role was written in such a way that interesting layers of his character were eventually revealed. Angie Dickenson was my stunning wife and Robert Wagner my executive officer.

During the '70s and '80s, I was fortunate to be offered scripts that dealt with serious social problems that reflected my own concerns. *Cocaine: One Man's Seduction* addressed the pervasive problem of cocaine in our society and one man's willingness to try anything to hold onto his youth. *Bluffing It* dealt with the real problem of illiteracy in America and how a man's pride can drive him to the brink of self-destruction and nearly destroy his family in the process. *When the Loving Stops,* with Valerie Harper, dramatically showed the impact and devastation divorce can have on the young members of the family.

Ishi, The Last of His Tribe focused our attention on the contemptuous and callous ways we treated the first

Americans. I was the first actor to address the problem of wife abuse on screen in the powerful *Intimate Strangers* with Sally Struthers and Larry Hagman.

At this point in my career, my screen image was anything but a wife-beater. I think one of the reasons the producers, Richard and Esther Shapiro, wanted me for the part was to make the point that abusive behavior can be present in the most innocent-looking households.

But my favorite movie-of-the-week in which I starred was *Amber Waves*, which got six Emmy nominations. I was very involved with the creative team during the filming. I had a meeting with my longtime friend, and one of Hollywood's best directors, Joseph Sargent, and persuaded him to read the script, after which, he agreed to direct. Although the basic idea of the script was sound, it really needed some fine-tuning, most of which was done by Joe and me during the shooting. I rewrote two problem scenes and another that wasn't even in the original script. I even wrote a song, which Mare Winningham sang in the film, and I later recorded on an album.

I had nothing to do with the casting, but received the benefit of some very talented costars. A young Kurt Russell played the juvenile lead. Many remember him as a child actor, and I believe his role in *Amber Waves* helped him create the bridge that jump-started one of Hollywood's most successful careers as a leading man.

Mare Winningham, who played my daughter, was only eighteen years old at the time, and won the Emmy for best-supporting actress. She was one of the most natural and truthful actors I had ever worked with—and, because she was so young, I felt that it was mostly intuitive. Her ability to give so much made working with her a delight.

I like to think of a scene with another actor as a Ping-Pong game—you bat the lines back and forth, playing off of each other, and you take from and give to—and she was one of the best at doing that. She was a great "Ping-Pong" player. When an actor does that, it just builds and builds the scene, allowing it to increase in believability and in realness. Mare continues to bring that wonderful sense of truth to her work to this day, and it's beautiful to watch.

The Shapiros were a very successful writing and producing team. They offered me the lead in their new series, *Emerald Point N.A.S.* I played an admiral who had problems with his family. It was really a nighttime soap opera. It should have been more successful than it was, for the concept was quite good. The network thought so much of it that they wanted it on the air as quickly as possible. All they gave us time to do was a "presentation" instead of a full-blown pilot.

It was May and the network insisted that the show make the fall schedule, rather than putting it on in midseason. Everything was rush, rush, rush—we were always trying to catch up, and by midseason it showed. During the time when we were going into production, the pool of writers available was not very large, and many that we would have liked to have been part of our team were already locked into other shows. We simply had a large Achilles' heel that we weren't able to overcome. You have to start with good writing. That is the foundation of any project, whether it's a movie, television series, book, play, or Broadway musical—it's the writing. The demands on our small group of writers were simply too much, and the show was cancelled after one season.

Not long after that, I played a wonderful character in a series called *Buck James*. Buck was based on a real-life person named Dr. Red Duke—a maverick medical doctor from Houston, who operated with his cowboy boots on . . . a fun character to play . . . and it was fun working with Shannon Wilcox, who played my former wife, and a great cast.

We hired Mimi Leder, a very talented young director, who was just getting started in the business. I quickly recognized her talent and wanted her to direct as many episodes of *Buck James* as her availability allowed. But producers, such as Steven Spielberg, also recognized her talent, and soon, she was directing major movies for the big screen.

Mimi and I worked together again just recently on *The Beast* (2001), a new series for ABC, which she served on as both director and executive producer. I played a "Mike Wallace" type character—another terrific role.

Buck James was a well-written show, and by all standards it should have been on the air for at least three or four years. But, after one season, it was cancelled. You have to have a strong lead-in for a show to be successful, and we followed the *Dolly Parton Variety Show*. ABC, thinking her show was going to be a big hit, dumped millions into its publicity and promotion. We were on the hour after Dolly, and both shows competed with a movie-of-the-week on other networks. Anybody who didn't watch Dolly Parton did not watch us—they were into the movie-of-the-week. For some reason, Dolly didn't get the ratings necessary to be picked up for a second year, and *Buck James* didn't either.

"Do you think you will ever retire?"

I get that question a lot, and it always stops me for a minute. The thought pops in my head, why would I retire?

I'm having as much fun as I've ever had, and I'm doing what I consider some of my most creative work.

In our present culture, retiring seems to be the goal in life for so many, and the earlier one can retire the more successful he or she is considered to be in the eyes of society. It's really a shame, for with retirement so many people lose incentive—they no longer have the "fire in the belly" for life. When we no longer have challenging goals to reach for, life becomes dull, and that condition is so often a precursor to the deterioration of the physical part of us.

No, I will never retire, and the blessing that comes with acting is that an actor never has to. We are never a victim of forced retirement. As a matter of fact, in many cases, we get more valuable with time. That's why since 1997 I've been the host of Starz/Encore's *Westerns* channel, introducing all the old, classic western movies.

Good heavens, if I had retired, I would never have been asked by Starz/Encore to host *Hopalong Cassidy, Public Hero #1,* or played Buffalo Bill in the *Lonesome Dove* series . . . or the grandfather trying to survive in the wilderness with my grandson after a plane crash in *Escape from Wildcat Canyon.* I would not have had the opportunity to counsel Tom Skerritt to get out of town while he was still alive in the remake of the classic *High Noon* for TBS . . . or I would not have had the chance to work with Bill Pullman, both as director and actor, in the first western of the new millennium, *The Virginian*, for TNT.

In *The Virginian*, I was cast against type by producer Dan Blatt. I played the land baron, Sam Balaam, who caused all the trouble by cowardly sending his hired hands to do his dirty work. I'll never forget the scene where Sam was trying to beat some sense into his horse because he wouldn't behave—and of course the horse acted in kind by trying to bite and throw me. The more he thrashed, the more Sam beat him, and the struggle to determine who was boss kept escalating.

I spun and kicked him down a steep hillside and right into a close camera shot, at which point I jerked hard back on the reins, and the horse went straight up on his hind legs, perpendicular to the ground. What a surprise to me! I came darn close to flying off and kissing Mother Earth— maybe good-bye! But I stayed with him, barely. Nobody told me that the horse was trained to rear when the reins were pulled back hard! I think it took a few years off Gerry and the crew watching behind the camera, but my stunt double just smiled and drawled, "Nice work, Dennis. Nice stunt." When my agent, David Shapira, saw the film, he thought I was crazy for not using the stunt double.

"So, let me get this straight—all that kicking the horse down that steep hill that *Sam* did was in the script, but the rearing up part wasn't?" I asked.

Exactly.

I feel so blessed to have had such a rewarding career . . . for the opportunities I have had in movies and television . . . for the talented and creative people who have shared the "stage" with me. And to realize that my earliest childhood dreams have come true. It's been an exciting life . . . a terrific run, and I'm most grateful.

Even though my "outward" life was great fun, and prosperous, and my lifelong material goals were being satisfied, I began to turn inward more and more. I was grateful for my success and, like so many others that "make it," I had the urge to give back. It was as though certain circumstances or events were gently prodding me in that direction.

The year 1983 was a time of a growing number of what the media called "new homeless." People, who never thought they would ever be such a statistic, found themselves out of work and without a place to live. Whole families were sleeping in their cars.

It was a series of news stories on television about these new homeless that caught Gerry's and my attention. I turned to her and said, "Honey, surely there is something we can do to help these people." I don't know anyone who is more touched, more concerned about the plight of others, than Gerry. One of the things I dearly love about her is her heart . . . it's as big as a watermelon.

She quickly replied, "Of course, there is!"

Coincidentally, at the time, I was costarring in a movie-of-the-week with Valerie Harper—*Don't Look under the Bed*, produced by Aaron Spelling. It so happened that Valerie was involved in a hunger program. I remember thinking, "How fortuitous." I asked her if I could attend the next meeting to see what she was doing, and she was delighted. I had no idea how much that simple request would impact my life.

For the next ten years, we drew closer to each other, bonded by a common goal—to alleviate hunger in Los Angeles. In many ways, she became an inspiration and teacher for me, and I perhaps served her the same way.

I know now that there can be no lasting peace, no security, nor can we as human beings begin to touch our full potential, so long as hunger overwhelms the human spirit around this planet.

The Presidential commission on world hunger stated, "Whether one speaks of basic human rights or basic human needs, the right to food is the most basic of all. Unless that right is first fulfilled, the protection of other human rights becomes a mockery."

Second to love, self-preservation is the strongest human motivation, and if hunger pains are strong enough, all man-made laws are ignored, our moral values are discarded, caution is thrown to the wind, and we do whatever is necessary to survive. Therefore, a community, a country, a world permeated with hunger, can find no peace, no stability, and no security. It is a world at risk, for hunger is a disease of this Earth that threatens us all.

Human beings are capable of creating an incredible world of peace, productivity, and justice—but let us realize that the major building block to that kind of world is food. Without it, we build a world of disease, bitterness, despair, and crime; everyone suffers. Hunger will directly damage some more than others, but make no mistake about it, it will eventually affect us all! For our own well-being, we must end it.

As we look around the world today, the problem seems overwhelming. I like the sign hanging in the fix-it shop that says, "The difficult we do immediately, the impossible takes a little longer."

We have never created a problem to which divine intelligence hasn't also given us the solution—we simply have to dig for it. Perseverance is essential.

So in 1983 Gerry and I, Valerie Harper and her husband, Tony, business people, lawyers, accountants, and other concerned citizens created a nonprofit group in Los Angeles called LIFE (Love Is Feeding Everyone). The purpose was to help those who didn't have the resources to buy sufficient food to prevent hunger and malnutrition. Originally, we picked up food from supermarkets such as Vons, Ralphs, and Hughes, that would have otherwise thrown it away because it was perishable—such as dairy products, baked goods, and produce. Eventually, we received dented or mislabeled cans from manufacturers, and growers often shipped directly to us.

Christopher Hills, who developed a company called "Light Force," gave LIFE over a million dollars' worth of nutritious Spirulina. Mobil Oil had fund-raisers, whereby they gave LIFE a percentage of their gas sales for a period of time. As I mentioned before, for fourteen years I was spokesman for Great Western Bank, and my good friend and chairman of the board, Jim Montgomery, donated office space to LIFE as well as a yearly financial contribution.

May Company had annual food drives, as did many of the area schools, churches, and temples. The Milken Family Foundation kept us afloat with generous financial donations at several critical times. Without its help, LIFE would have more than likely sunk. We had the help of hundreds of volunteers doing food drives all over the city. Gerry organized a group of ladies I called my "Life-Savers," who raised money with dinners and fashion shows. We only had to pick up the phone, and we got help from celebrities such as John Voight, John Forsythe, Harvey Korman, Dick Van Dyke, Susan Sullivan (who was a super wife to me in *The Ordeal of Dr. Mudd*), Maud Adams (my girlfriend in *Emerald Point N.A.S.*), and Susan Dey (who played my daughter in the same series). They all showed up on the big fund-raising day and modeled for our big fashion shows. I love them all, and if there are any I've left out, please forgive me.

LIFE is a living example of the power of cooperation and the strength of numbers, for when people come together to support a worthy cause, the impossible becomes possible.

It has certainly strengthened my faith in human beings. People do care, and when they know they can make a difference, know that they can lift the burden from someone else's back, and are shown a sensible way to do it, they are eager to pitch in and help. It is that quality that has made it possible for LIFE to survive. In 1983, we started out feeding less than four hundred people a week; fifteen years later, LIFE was helping to feed over 180,000 a week.

It is a bittersweet feeling for me, for while I am pleased that LIFE has been able to help so many, I am distressed that the need for such an organization still exists.

At the World Peace Conference in Rome in 1973, Dr. Henry Kissinger was moved to say, "The profound comment of our era is that for the first time we have the technical capacity to free man from the scourge of hunger. Therefore, today, we must claim a bold objective: that within a decade no child will go to bed hungry, that no family will fear for its next day's bread, and that no human being's future and capacity will be stunted by malnutrition."

It's been over a quarter of a century since Dr. Kissinger issued that bold objective, and yet there is more hunger now, even in our own country, than there was in 1973. There are more homeless, more soup kitchens, more people holding up "Will work for food" signs. Why? It certainly isn't because our technology hasn't surpassed that which we had in 1973. Then why haven't we eliminated the blight of hunger in the strongest, most economically advantaged country in the world?

George Bernard Shaw said, "The worst sin to our fellow creatures is not to hate them but to be indifferent to them. That's the height of inhumanity."

The simple truth is that we haven't eliminated hunger in this country because we haven't wanted to badly enough. We haven't had the *national will* to do it.

> If there is any central theme of the great religions of the world, it is for each of us to reach out, feed the hungry, uphold the poor and to love one another.
>
> —Anonymous

Of course, to give love to one another is the most important. If we could realize the great truth that we are all threads in the one fabric of life, that we are indeed one, all connected, and that we share each other's pain and joy, all our problems would soon disappear, including hunger.

Giving love only lip service is worthless. Love must be expressed. It must be coupled with action, for love without action is dead.

Albert Einstein said, "Not until the creation and maintenance of decent conditions of life for all men are recognized and accepted as a common obligation for all men, shall we be able to speak of mankind as civilized." The answer lies in each one of us making the personal commitment to become civilized.

For too many, it's a world of never-ending fear, pain, and despair. We have the power to change that. For when we take up a righteous cause, one that serves not only ourselves, but others as well, Providence supports us, and all the forces of nature come to our assistance, and the obstacles in our path melt into opportunities.

Goethe said, "Whatever you can do or dream you can, begin it. Boldness has genius, power, and magic in it."

Let us begin. Let us end this horror of hunger . . . let us have the will.

The LIFE program showed me the power of "togetherness," of people joining hands to achieve a single purpose, a specific goal.

John Denver received the Presidential End Hunger Award by President Reagan in 1985. On behalf of all those dedicated volunteers who made the LIFE program successful, I gratefully accepted the same award in 1986, and Valerie was honored the following year.

All of this stimulated me, and my interests and passion were beginning to expand—to include things philosophical, spiritual, and environmental.

9

"Never Mind the Earth, Let's Save Our Own Ass"

—Ed Begley, Jr.

Passion is a grand word. Everyone should be passionate about something—a new business, correcting a social wrong, learning to paint, surfing the Internet, or cultivating a garden patch. If we do not have passion about something, a commendable goal, a worthwhile cause, life becomes dull and boring, and nothing significant is accomplished.

Passion is the energy that fires the engine of our creativity, and without it that engine sputters and dies.

A passion that began fifteen to twenty years ago still burns strong within me—to be part of the great wave of people that have become aware of the way we have trampled and abused this beautiful Earth and are determined to correct it. I have joined those who wish to create a sustainable future so that generations to come can enjoy the sweet, pure air, sparkling clear water, and the great diversity of life our Creator has lovingly placed in our care.

Now, I am not an expert on the environment—and I don't pretend to be. I don't have a long line of letters after my name, but I did graduate from the College of Common Sense and I have learned one thing . . . every living thing needs a proper environment in which to live. If it doesn't have it, it dies—and we human beings are not immune to this law. Right now, out of ignorance and greed, thinking no farther than next Tuesday, we are doing the unthinkable . . . we are destroying that which allows us to live. How stupid can we get?

A very sobering warning was issued by the Union of Concerned Scientists, first in 1992, then re-released in 1997 at the Kyoto Conference in Japan, a warning that was mostly ignored by the media and one that is more pertinent today than when it was first issued. They said:

> Human beings and the natural world are on a collision course. Human activities inflict harsh and often irreversible damage on the environment and on critical resources. If not checked, many of our current practices put at serious risk the future that we wish for human society and the animal kingdoms, and may so alter the living world that it will be unable to sustain life in the manner that we know. Fundamental changes are urgent if we are to avoid the collision our present course will bring about. We the undersigned senior members of the world's scientific community, hereby warn all humanity of what lies ahead. A great change in the stewardship of the Earth and life on it is required if vast human suffering is to be avoided and our global home on this Planet is not to be irretrievably mutilated.

This statement was signed by more than 1600 of the world's most renowned scientists from seventy different countries, with 101 of them Nobel Prize laureates. This was not a group on the fringe—these were not radical extremists. They were respected scientists who had done their research, gathered their data, and felt in their conscience that they had to let us know the danger we are in, and what the result will be if we don't act quickly.

What they're telling us is that we must change the way we relate to this Earth. The problems we have created can only be corrected by us—the monkeys can't do it. An old Chinese proverb says, "If we don't alter our course, we're going to wind up where we're headed."

The good news is, we *can* alter our course, for we have the ability to think, to reason; and every moment of our lives is a moment of choice. The bad news is, we don't have much time, and we don't seem to understand the severity of the crisis at hand. To too many, environmental problems seem remote; and, as Einstein said, " . . . thus we drift towards an unparalleled catastrophe."

Not too long ago, a lady, with a rather concerned and disapproving tone in her voice, asked me, "Are you an environmentalist?" I knew I was going to have some explaining to do if I answered truthfully. But, throwing caution to the wind, I said, "Yes."

The look on her face was somewhere between pity and rebuke as she replied, "Oh, really?"

"Oh, yes, I am one of those, I am an environmentalist, but so are you."

"What do you mean by that?" she asked, suddenly looking a bit confused.

"Well, what I mean is that so is the taxi driver, the farmer in the field, the CEO of a large corporation, the school teacher, homemaker, the shop owner, and so on.

Everyone that walks on the planet is an environmentalist, in that every choice we make, every action that we take, has an impact on the place we live. We make the environment what it is; we're responsible for it.

"So it's not a question of whether we're an environmentalist or not—that's a given. The only question is . . . are we a good one or are we a bad one? Are we doing those things that contribute to the health of the planet so that it can sustain life for generations to come, or are we doing those things that continue to abuse it, so that future life is in great jeopardy?"

The lady responded, "Well, you may be right, but I've got other things to worry about. Besides, by the time it gets really bad, I'll be gone. I'll let the next generation worry about it. It's their problem."

What the lady didn't understand is, we *are* the next generation. And if we continue our callous attitude towards the Earth that sustains us, destroying our own life supports, it won't be long until there won't be a "next generation."

Another reason why we don't respond to the warnings from scientists is because the environmental problems have come on slowly and we've gotten used to them. We accept smog as normal, acid rain as something we can deal with—thinking someone else will handle it. And global warming? We don't really believe what the scientists are telling us, and so we drift closer and closer to the edge of the precipice.

I'm reminded of the experiment the scientists did with a frog. They put the poor fellow in a container of water and arranged it in such a way that the frog could get out if it cared to; but it liked the water and was content to swim around and enjoy itself. The scientists then began to heat the water, very slowly—so slowly that it was hardly noticeable. The frog adjusted to the rising temperature, thinking it was normal. It kept adjusting, adjusting, and adjusting, until finally the frog could adjust no more and cried out, "My God, I'm in really hot water!" And indeed he was, but by that time he was so enervated that he didn't have the wherewithal to save himself. He adjusted one time too many.

We, the people of the world—particularly in the United States, for we are by far the greatest per capita users of the Earth's natural resources, the largest consumers, and the most prolific polluters in the world—are in a dilemma not unlike that of the frog. Are we going to keep adjusting and adjusting until we adjust one time too many? Are we going to step so close to the precipice that we inadvertently slip and fall?

We are very good at dealing with crises when they are obvious. Let us be faced with a hurricane, flood, fire, or earthquake, and we come together as a group, roll up our sleeves, and handle it. One of the redeeming aspects of tragedy is that it brings people together, and the concern and love for each other shines through the façade of indifference. Our true nature as human beings is then revealed. But somehow the environmental crisis is viewed as distant, not an immediate threat, so we keep ignoring it. We "sweep it under the rug," as my mother would say.

I read Daniel D. Chiras's wonderful book, *Lessons from Nature*, and his opening paragraph left no doubt in my mind of the seriousness of the problem we face. I quote him here:

> If this is a typical day on the planet earth, 116 square miles of forest will be destroyed. In the third world, where much of the cutting occurs, only one tree is planted for every ten cut down; in the tropics of Africa, the ratio is one to 29. If

this is a typical day, seventy square miles of desert will form in semi-arid regions subject to intense population pressure, overgrazing, and poor land management. Already one-third of the world's cropland is threatened by desertification. As if that is not bad enough, today 250,000 newborns will join the world population. Each new resident requires food, water, shelter, and a host of other resources to survive. On this day, at least 1.5 million tons of hazardous waste will be "disposed" of—released into our air, water, and land—and Americans will throw away enough garbage to fill the Superdome in New Orleans two times. By various estimates, ten to forty species will become extinct today, mostly as a result of tropical deforestation. At the day's end, the Earth will be a little hotter, the rain a little more acidic, the water a little more polluted. The world's already crowded cities will be more crowded, and the air in and around them, now choked with pollution, will be a bit dirtier. And at the day's end, the web of life will be a bit more threadbare. Tomorrow, it starts all over.

We do indeed have a problem—a problem that we are continuing to aggravate. The irony is, it doesn't have to be this way. We have the knowledge, the technology, and the resources to truly make this Earth a "Garden of Eden" for all its inhabitants; what's missing is the vision, the wisdom, and the will.

Earth is four to five billion years old, and the human species has only walked on the planet for 150,000 to 200,000 years. We're the new kids on the block. During that time, we have lived, for the most part, in harmony with all other life forms until the advent of the Age of Scientific Materialism, which produced the Industrial Revolution. With its birth, life on the planet changed as it had never changed before. And it will never be the same.

We humans were given a unique role to play in this earthly drama. We are the "creative species." We are made in the image of the Master Creator; we have been given the ability to think, to hold an idea. We are the "master of our fate, and the captain of our soul." We are the caretakers of the planet. Its future is in our hands because we have free will—the power to choose. We are stuck with it. Even a decision to do nothing is a choice.

We are the only species that can significantly alter its environment, and actually destroy it. It can truly be said that we have been given "dominion over all things"; everything on Earth, in a sense, is held hostage by us. We decide what lives or dies, by the choices we make. We have great power, but with great power comes great responsibility. To be given dominion over all things does not mean we have the right to destroy the very things over which we have been given dominion. Surely it means we have the responsibility to preserve them, to nurture them, to honor them, and to glorify them.

I saw a commercial once that applauded my generation for its achievements. It said that when faced with the Great Depression, we came together, exercised great national will, pulled ourselves up by our bootstraps, and came through victoriously. It proclaimed that we did the same when we were confronted with World War II. Then came the ultimate accolade: that we have built more in the past hundred years than was built in the previous two thousand years combined.

Well, I suppose that's something to brag about. We have certainly developed unbelievable technologies. We did what some, just a few decades ago, were saying was impossible . . . we put a man on the moon. We've built airplanes, skyscrapers, computers, automobiles, hydroelectric plants, the Internet, and on and on. But, on the other hand, we've created some things for which we shouldn't be applauded—atomic bombs, land mines, poisonous gas, acid rain, global warming . . . air, water, and soil pollution . . . the list goes on. It's not *how much* we've built that's important. It's *what* we've built, and how it's used, that defines us, that reflects the level of our collective consciousness.

Our transportation systems, along with our communication technologies, have truly made the world smaller. With the shrinking of the planet, our interdependency with all things has become more obvious. Two examples of the oneness or the connectedness of all life on the planet are our environment and our economy.

What people are doing to their environment on the other side of the globe either directly or indirectly affects us on this side, and vice versa. No matter how many times we arbitrarily divide the planet with manmade boundaries, nature ignores them.

The deadly fallout from the Chernobyl meltdown didn't stop at the Polish or Finnish borders. Acid rain from U.S. manufacturing plants doesn't need a passport to enter Canada. The environment is a world problem, which this entire world of six billion people must address.

The same is true of our economy, for it, too, is global in its scope, and recognizes no people-made boundaries. The prolonged recession in Japan had a devastating effect in the Far East, infecting all the surrounding economies and even threatening the stability of our own. When people in recession-stricken countries have less purchasing power, the customer pool for our manufactured products shrinks, and our economy suffers.

Remember the acronym NIMBY—Not In My Back Yard? It came into common use because people were intent on getting anything that was detrimental to their health or pocketbook into somebody else's backyard. Let somebody else suffer the downside of slaughterhouses, landfills, prisons, nuclear plants, and manufacturing operations that pollute our air and water. Let someone else suffer the depreciation of property and the threat to human health.

What the world must realize is that NIMBY no longer makes any sense, for there is only one backyard. We all share it, and it is up to all of us to keep it clean.

How we do that is one of the great challenges we face today. There are those who say, "It's too late . . . we've done too much damage . . . the destruction is irreversible." I cannot accept that. I think we have the technological tools to reverse the tide. I believe we can be optimistic—not to the degree of the fellow who jumped from the Empire State Building and, on his way down, as he observed the people looking at him in horror from their windows, said, "Don't worry; everything's okay so far." Be optimistic, but, for goodness sake, let us not ignore the evidence that is so obvious, stick your head in the sand, and pretend nothing is wrong.

Science is very clear. We can't continue to behave as we are and survive indefinitely. The sand in the hourglass is quickly slipping away, and we must not waste a minute.

I believe this incredibly beautiful Earth, with its amazing interrelationships and its life-sustaining resources, was designed to support all living things that dwell on it. It is one grand tapestry, and we humans are just one strand and need all the others to complete the picture. Out of ignorance, we act as though we are somehow not a part of the tapestry, that we can damage it without damaging ourselves. We have developed the attitude that nature is "over there" and we are "over here," and "never the twain shall meet." The truth is, we are an integral part of nature, and our own health is dependent on the health of the Earth.

Do you remember Pogo—my favorite philosopher? The endearing cartoon character created by Walt Kelly said, "We have met the enemy, and they is us!" Nobody is responsible for our situation except us. By our thoughts and actions in the past, we have created our present circumstances, and by our thoughts and actions now, we will create our future. Pogo also said, "We are surrounded by insurmountable opportunities," and indeed we are. Our opportunity is now . . . not next year, not next week, not tomorrow . . . but now.

This is the most exciting time in the history of the human species. The potential for human growth, for true happiness, and sustained fulfillment has never been greater. However, it is also the most dangerous time, for we humans are in charge; we are at the helm of the ship. Whether we get safely through the rough waters that lie ahead depends on the choices we make now.

10

Lights, Revolutions, Action

If a man does not keep pace with his companions, perhaps it is because he hears a different drummer: Let him step to the music which he hears, however measured or far away.

—Henry David Thoreau

Dennis shifted in his chair, positioning himself for the next question.

"When exactly did you take action? Did you just wake up one morning and say 'today is the day'?"

Have you ever had the experience of a lightbulb in your head flashing on, and you say, "Oh, my God, why didn't I think of that?"

Do you know what that is? That is the intellect, the mind, recognizing and accepting what the soul has always known. We knew it all the time—and certain circumstances allow us to remember it.

Life is an evolving process—an unfolding. Every thought, every action proceeds out of, and is affected by, previous thoughts, actions, and circumstances. So, no, I didn't wake up one morning and decide to do something about the environment. My whole life, the sum total of my experiences—the people I've met, the discussions, the debates, the books I've read, the movies I've seen, my own observations, and my conscience (which I believe to be the voice of God within)—made me at some point say, "I can no longer stand on the sidelines and watch the parade. I have to do what I can to lead it, to correct that which seems to be terribly wasteful and destructive."

For many years, I had practiced meditation—and I emphasize *practiced*, for it takes a lot of it to reap benefits!

One evening, while I was practicing the stillness, the Divine Presence of God came in a very sweet and loving way, and I was moved to mentally speak to that Holy Consciousness, which I often referred to as "Divine Mother."

I simply said, "Mother, you have given us this incredibly beautiful playground in which we can experience and enjoy life, reach our highest good, and grow closer to you. And now, like unruly and ungrateful children, we are in the process of destroying it. Beloved One, I choose another direction—I choose to correct the pain we have inflicted on this Earth, and put healing and harmony in its place. But I cannot do it alone. I recognize that all that I have, the life force that flows through me, my energy, intelligence, and even my consciousness, are all gifts from you. And I could not *be* without your grace. Therefore, in the largest sense, you are the Doer. However, you have given your children the same power that you have, the power to hold an idea, to create, and you have given this planet to us to manage. Yet we are in the process of mutilating it. I choose to manage it in a more protective and nurturing way, but I need your help. I need you to supply me with the right ideas, thoughts, and like-minded people. If it be Your will, I stand ready to receive your guidance."

That was a defining moment in my life, for, within two weeks, confirmation came from different directions and in different forms—people, books, news releases, conferences, and common-sense ideas that appeared to come to me out of the blue. I hesitate to say that God was speaking to me through these channels, but there seemed to be a very strong "yes" to my call for help.

After NASA completed space flights, astronauts were reporting holes in the ozone layer, that ultrathin protective shield that screens the Earth from the deadly ultraviolet rays of the sun. With each succeeding examination, NASA reported a widening of the holes and the increased thinning of the ozone layer. This really got my attention, for scientists explained that, without the ozone layer, life as we know it would cease to exist here on Earth.

"Then you took action because of scientific information you were receiving?"

Yes, but beyond that, I've been hanging around the planet for a good number of years and have seen some disturbing changes. When I was a kid, I never heard of acid rain, smog, deforestation, or species extinction. Very few people understood the ozone layer, and "global warming" would become part of our vocabulary in the distant future.

In the 1930s, I could go hiking in the mountains and drink the pure, crystal, clean water from nature's fountains with no fear of getting sick from pollutants. I can't do it these days.

In those days, the thought of paying good, hard-earned money for drinking water was unheard of. If someone had said, "I'm going to start a multibillion-dollar industry selling drinking water," people would have thought his brain was a little fuzzy. Today, it's a fact of life. In order to ensure our own health, we carry our favorite brand of bottled water. Either that, or we buy a water filter (which has also become a huge business) and purify our own.

And so, we do indeed have a multibillion-dollar drinking-water industry. It wasn't the man who suggested it whose brain was fuzzy, it was *ours*, for *creating the conditions that made it possible.*

The air was much purer back then, but with the ever-expanding Industrial Revolution, and particularly the proliferation of the automobile, along with an unprecedented population explosion, we soon took care of that.

There's no question that we developed a social structure that needed a transportation system. People needed to be moved. The question was—what was our most sensible means of doing that?

Rather than focusing on mass transportation, which is vastly more energy efficient and therefore more environmentally and economically attractive, we opted for the automobile as our transportation of choice. The fact that automobiles were more profitable, I would suggest, weighed heavily in favor of that decision.

Then we added insult to injury. We foolishly made sure that that choice would become indelibly ingrained in our culture by making the motorcar more and more seductive to the consumer. For instance, we spent huge amounts of taxpayers' dollars lacing the countryside with superhighways and chewing up great hunks of precious nature in the process.

It is evident that this choice has proven to be highly damaging, not only to our environment but to our pocketbooks and health as well; particularly in large, population-dense metropolitan centers where, during rush-hour traffic, on six-lane expressways, a sea of automobiles, one passenger in each, "creeps in this petty pace from day to day to the last syllable of recorded time" (*Macbeth* by William Shakespeare), spewing endless pollutants into the air.

Shortly after I asked for Divine Mother's guidance for answers and direction, I began to get many requests to speak at conferences, colleges, and seminars. Early on, I mostly talked about the damage we were doing to our Earth and about how a change in our relationship to her is absolutely critical. Something has to change. We need a new direction and fresh solutions.

Yet, to correct the environmental and economic problems that confront us, we must know what caused them. They can be traced to two earthly conditions, and we human beings are responsible for both of them—the population explosion and the industrial revolution.

The ever-expanding world population aggravates every problem we have, whether it is political, social, economic, or environmental. And according to newscaster and journalist David Brinkley, we are adding 85 million new residents to our Earth each year. For each new inhabitant, the Earth must furnish food, clothing, and shelter. This constant human growth is putting a strain on the planet's ability to satisfy those needs. The question is, how many people can the Earth support? Scientists have tried to answer that question with a guesstimate, but the truth is, no one really knows for sure. What we do know is that if the population keeps expanding exponentially, as it now is, that limit will be reached shortly.

According to most scientists, humans have been living on the planet for 150,000 to 200,000 years. If it were the latter, it took us 199,810 years to reach one billion people, which happened around 1810. In just the last 190 years, we've added five billion more, and there seems to be no end in sight. At the present rate, by 2020, we will reach ten billion. If you were born before 1950, you have witnessed more births in your lifetime than all the births in the previous 199,810 years! Unless we stop proliferating, we are headed for an unimaginable disaster.

It doesn't take someone with a crystal ball to foresee a bleak future, with famines, plagues, increased poverty, civil unrest, wars over diminishing supplies, and the wanton destruction of our natural resources in the human quest for survival—if we don't stop our mushrooming population growth. We can try to ease the pressure on the Earth by using our resources more efficiently, but it doesn't do us much good to become more efficient if the number of people needing those resources continues to grow. For instance, it doesn't help to double the miles-per-gallon that we can get out of our vehicles if at the same time we double the number of cars on our highways.

Eco-efficiency is a popular buzzword for those in the environmental community who are concerned about what we're going to leave our kids. A ripple of excitement runs through us when we hear of an invention that potentially could up our gas mileage to 80 mpg. However, the reality is, more efficient solutions simply put Band-Aids on the problem, rather than correcting it. We need a cure instead of a treatment.

Eco-efficiency really only gives us more time between now and the disaster towards which we're headed. It's like my friend David Crockett says, "If we're going 100 mph towards Las Vegas, and our destination is San Diego, it doesn't help a lot to slow down to 50 mph. It simply means it's going to take us twice as long to get where we don't want to go."

As a matter of fact, efficiency is not always desirable. Look how efficiently we have raped and pillaged the Earth. Our capability in that regard is second to none. No other culture has achieved such destructive efficiency. Is that really the legacy we wish for ourselves?

When we talk about the population problem, most people will point the finger at the developing nations, the poor countries, and place the blame there, because those countries, statistically, have larger families. Although the growing population in those areas needs to be checked, as it does everywhere, those countries don't represent the greatest environmental threat. That "honor" goes to the highly developed societies, the rich countries.

It is the energy we use or misuse that creates the danger to our environment. Practically every environmental problem we have can be traced to energy use—smog, acid rain, ozone depletion, global warming, and nuclear waste.

The United States represents approximately 4.5 percent of the Earth's population but uses nearly 30 percent of its energy. We are the biggest energy hog on the planet. A baby born in America, potentially, will become twice the environmental problem as one born in Sweden, thirteen times the problem of a child born in Brazil, 140 times the one born in Bangladesh, and 280 times the problem of one born in Chad. So, each person is not born with equal ability to destroy the environment. Poor people in underdeveloped countries don't drive gas-guzzling automobiles, farm with tractors, mow their lawns with two-cycle engines, use air-conditioning or central heating, and have no nuclear plants. But as they "develop," they will want the luxuries and conveniences that we have.

India and China are countries with huge populations that are moving rapidly towards earning the label "developed." It is imperative that the United States becomes a better model. We must show them there is better energy to fuel our economy . . . to heat our homes . . . to drive our cars . . . than fossil fuel. We can't expect them to do as we say and ignore what we do. We've got to walk our talk. We have a huge responsibility to turn the corner and move towards sustainability. We not only have a huge responsibility, but we have an equally large opportunity. We must use the same American know-how, the same national will, that made us victorious in our race to the moon. We must use that same determination to move away from our Earth-destroying behavior and towards a culture that saves and protects it.

"How do we do that?" I asked, intrigued.

The specifics of how to do that, and what is needed, we'll put on hold for the moment. First, let's examine the Industrial Revolution, which many thought would usher in the Golden Age. With the development of time-saving devices and technologies, the Industrial Revolution promised more conveniences, luxuries, leisure time, freedom, and opportunity for personal growth—physically, mentally, and spiritually—a higher standard of living for all of God's children.

If we use material wealth as our measuring stick, the Industrial Revolution has certainly fulfilled its promise for some (5 percent of the people control 90 percent of the world's wealth), but, for the great bulk of humanity living on the Earth, it's been anything but the Golden Age. Poverty has snowballed—800 million suffer from hunger annually, and forty thousand die of starvation every day, mostly children. Disease has increased. The gap between the "haves" and the "have-nots" has widened. We've developed such awesome weapons of destruction that we have the ability to blow ourselves into oblivion and destroy all life on Earth, as we know it. We have disgraced ourselves by resorting to force to resolve our differences. Genocide around the globe has become commonplace, exposing the inhumanity of humans, showing us the distance we have yet to travel in our evolution towards a just, workable, and loving society. It is obvious that it will take more than advanced technology to reach the Golden Age, for technology has no allegiance to good or bad; it depends on whose hands it's in and what it is used for.

As we honestly observe the world today, it becomes glaringly clear that we have developed more intellectually than we have emotionally and spiritually. Proof of our intellectual development is in the technology that we have created. Proof that we have not developed spiritually is in the way we have used that technology. We've used it to trash the Earth that gives us life and to maim and slaughter each other in unconscionable and deadly wars. Over two thousand years ago, as recorded in Chapter 31 of the *Tao Te Ching*, Lao-tzu gave us a sensible bit of wisdom that we continue to ignore: "The more weapons of violence, the more misery to mankind. The triumph of violence ends in a festival of mourning." In the end, even the victor pays a heavy price.

After World War II, the Eastern Saint Paramahansa Yogananda wrote, "War and crime never pay. The billions of dollars that went up in the smoke of explosive nothingness could have financed a new world, one almost free from disease and completely free of poverty. Not an Earth of fear, chaos, famine, pestilence, the dance macabre, but one broad land of peace, prosperity, and widening knowledge."

We are a dysfunctional society and think we are advanced. An advanced society requires advanced thinking, and ours is still in the dark ages. We still think we're separated, that we can take from others or hurt others without hurting ourselves. We still think we are separate from nature, that we can damage the Earth without damaging ourselves.

Sir Francis Bacon, whom some call the "father of modern science," certainly advanced the hypothesis that we are not an integral part of nature when he said, "The purpose of science is to wrest nature to the ground and extort from her, her secrets for the benefit of man." That was a rather arrogant mindset, with violent implications. Wrest nature . . . ? Extort from her . . . ? It revealed a consciousness of division, and the destructive energy released with that thought permeates our society and affects our relationship with the Earth to this day.

As science developed and we became more machine-conscious, we began to think of the Earth as a large mechanical contraption that we could manipulate for our own purposes. We therefore believed that we were not a part of nature, but separate from it, and, worse still, *superior* to it. This has led to an attitude of domination, resulting in actions by us that have raped the Earth unmercifully. And, in return, the planet is reacting to the violence it has suffered, as any living organism would.

What would you do if someone tried to destroy you? You would defend yourself. You would fight back . . . unless of course you were a saint, and even then you might hiss a little.

Albert Schweitzer said, "I am life that wills to live in the midst of life that wills to live." Every living thing, from the tiniest organism to the mighty whale, has a will to live and a will to fight to survive. Self-preservation is a law common to all living things, and the Earth is no exception. Could it be that the tremendous increase in natural disasters—earthquakes, floods, droughts, tornadoes (over one hundred were reported in January of 1999, by far the most ever recorded), and extreme weather swings—are the direct result of our actions? Are "natural disasters" really natural, or do we have a large hand in creating them?

With all due respect to Sir Francis—he had it wrong. The purpose of science is *not* to wrest nature to the ground and extort her secrets, but to understand nature more thoroughly, so that we can cooperate and live in harmony with her, rather than attempting to control and dominate her. It is through cooperation and harmony that we will create a society on this Earth that is safer, healthier, and more productive for all its inhabitants.

We cannot change the laws of nature. They are forever immutable. If we try to overthrow or rearrange those laws to satisfy our human whims, we will eventually only bruise ourselves, for as Ralph Waldo Emerson pointed out, "Nature will always balance itself."

We can no longer think of ourselves as separate from nature but as a piece of the whole, and that our own well-being depends on the well-being of the whole.

Right now we are, in many ways, a primitive civilization heading toward disaster. If we are going to alter our course and create a sustainable civilization in which future generations can live peaceful, healthy, and productive lives, we must first change our thinking. Albert Einstein stated it simply, but brilliantly: "No problem can be solved from the same consciousness that created it."

The price for the good life, for a relative few, could be an environment that can no longer support human life. Unless, of course, we come to our senses before it's too late, and make some major changes.

If we keep abusing the Earth, polluting and poisoning our life supports, wasting our Earthly assets, with no thought of replenishing, it won't be long until we will bankrupt our natural resources. As economist Herman Daly has said, "We are treating the Earth as though it were a business in liquidation."

To understand the effect the Industrial Revolution has had on our lives, all we have to do is look back 150 years—no automobiles, airplanes, radar, telephones, televisions, copiers, computers, E-mail, or the Internet—and, that's a fax.

But we also didn't have some other things, like acid rain, ozone depletion, global warming, deforestation, desertification, and the poisoning of our air, water, and food source. The "good life," that the Industrial Revolution has bestowed upon us, as stated before, has not come cheap.

When the Industrial Revolution began in England about 1760, it brought with it the need for a high-quality oil to run its engines and grease its machinery. The newborn industries found it in the Earth's largest mammals—the whales.

Because it burned cleaner than other energy sources, whale oil had been a valued commodity for commercial purposes for many centuries, and whaling was considered a natural calling for robust and adventurous young men. But when the Industrial Revolution surfaced, demanding more and more quality oil, the whaling industry exploded, and whaling ships criss-crossed the oceans in greater numbers searching for their lucrative prey. The extraordinary profits to be made in whale oil created intense rivalries for the biggest catches between ships and countries.

As the Industrial Revolution grew, so did the demand for more oil. It became obvious that the natural breeding cycle of the whales could not keep up with the demand, and, as killing techniques improved, it also became obvious, to those who had a clear vision of the future, that the whales would eventually be hunted into extinction.

What saved the whales, and gave our economy and the Industrial Revolution a shot in the arm, was the birth of a new industry—oil was discovered in Pennsylvania. When scientists were able to refine the crude oil so that it equaled the quality of whale oil, the whaling industry began to decline rapidly. The last American whaling ship left port in 1925.

The oil and whaling industries in many ways are comparable. They both have supported the Industrial Revolution and our economy. And as the whaling industry found that it was unable to continue to give that support, so will the oil industry—for oil is not renewable. We can't grow it! As whaling had to be replaced, so will oil, if we are to develop a sustainable economy, for it is impossible to sustain an economy that is fueled by an energy that is not sustainable—like oil.

The major difference in the two, except for the possible extinction of the whale, is that the whaling industry created no severe damage to the environment, whereas there is a tremendously destructive domino effect from the burning of oil. It jeopardizes life on Earth. It contributes greatly to acid rain, ozone depletion, and global warming, not to mention the threat to the health of our children and the needless waste of the taxpayer's money to clean up our environmental disasters.

In the not-too-distant future, we've got to find a replacement for oil. We really have no choice. Most scientists say that, at the rate we're using it, oil will be gone in forty to fifty years. Even if it lasts sixty years, I can personally testify that that time goes by in the wink of an eye. Whatever we will be forced to do then, shouldn't we be seriously doing that now? Or do we wait until oil becomes so scarce that only the wealthy can afford it? I can only imagine the social disruptions that would cause.

It's not as though we don't have alternative fuel sources from which to choose. And practically all of them have their origin in the sun, which, as we all know, is the single source of energy that gives life to all things on the Earth—either directly or indirectly. Without it, we would have no secondary sources of energy, such as wind, moving water, biomass, and even our fossil fuels—for they were originally plants (biomass) that millions of years ago were transmuted into oil, coal, and natural gas.

The sun's energy, which originally grew the plants, has been stored in the fossil fuels for lo these many years. We are just now burning that energy. The problem is, there is serious toxic residue inherent in the original biomass that we are releasing into the atmosphere as we burn it. For a more thorough explanation of this process, I highly recommend Thom Hartmann's extremely important work, *The Last Hours of Ancient Sunlight.*

The problems with fossil fuels are obvious. However, there are limitations with the others as well. The sun doesn't always shine, the wind doesn't always blow, biomass can introduce undesirable gases into the air, and hydroelectricity requires that dams create unnatural bodies of water that disrupt ecosystems, habitats, and nature's balance.

And then there is *hydrogen.* It can be created by using the power of the sun or wind and can be stored for use when neither of those is available. It is totally clean, inexhaustible, and can be produced and used at the point of need. A hydrogen-fueled economy could easily do away with the offensive power lines that cross our country and mar our beautiful landscapes. The centrally located coal-fired power plants, one of the main sources of air pollution and global warming, would become an historical relic and join the dinosaurs, and automobiles would clean the environment as they are driven. Their exhausts would simply be water.

"Dennis, all my life I have heard people say, 'wouldn't it be nice to go back to the good old days.' I'm not so sure that's a 'good' thing—moving forward and change are all part of our evolution. Why do you think this 'good old days' desire is still here?"

Well, I've heard people say that myself, and I can understand their wanting to rid themselves of the worry, anxieties, and frustrations that are part and parcel of modern-day living; but it's senseless to fantasize that we can return to the horse-and-buggy days. In the first place, very few people would vote to leave their comforts behind. We're so attached to our luxuries and conveniences—especially the automobile. It is really ironic how we have painted ourselves into a corner. That which we won't, or, more correctly, *can't* live without, is killing us. Cars, trucks, airplanes, tractors, backhoes, etc., are all vital pieces of commerce, all made possible by fossil fuel—for right now it is the lifeblood of our economy. It is a vital part of supplying us with food, clothing, and shelter. It has infiltrated every nook and cranny of our society. Every facet of our lives is directly or indirectly dependent on the use of fossil fuel. And yet again, that which gives us our "good life" is destroying our life-sustaining environment.

Now, if we had a magic wand and with a grand wave of our hand could immediately eliminate fossil fuel from our daily lives, we would create social problems the likes of which the world has never known. Most electricity is generated by coal-fired power plants, and if coal (fossil fuel) suddenly disappeared, the result would be a dangerously low supply of electricity. Huge segments of our population would be without the power to operate their homes, hospitals, and businesses that supply us with food, clothing, building materials, health services, and other necessities of life. The world would experience mass starvation, epidemics, and a level of hysteria and fear that would lead to anarchy. Without electricity, our vast commuter systems, on which the world's economic and political structures depend, would collapse.

We are truly between a rock and a hard place, and don't have much time to make port—we've got to repair the "ship" while at sea. No question about it, eventually we've got to get rid of fossil fuel.

If we have any chance of creating a sustainable future, we must develop an energy to fuel our economy that is *sustainable*—one that is clean, inexhaustible, and economically feasible. On all three counts, hydrogen fills the bill.

"Come on, is hydrogen *really* practical? Isn't it dangerous?"

No, not at all—if used correctly. It's been thoroughly tested by the American Hydrogen Association, as well as some of the most respected companies in the world, . . . such as Mercedes Benz. Buses and automobiles are now being powered by hydrogen. As a matter of fact, hydrogen can replace petroleum in all its various applications.

Fossil fuel made the Industrial Revolution possible, and it's time for both of them to go. The Industrial Revolution has had its day, its moment in the sun. But we're hanging onto it after it's served its purpose, after it is in many ways not only not useful, but has become a real threat to life on the planet. It's like a worn-out car going downhill with no brakes that is about to crash into the ashcan of history. Now, we shouldn't throw away the worn-out car, but salvage it, take it apart, and re-use the items that are still good, and recycle the material left over, reform it into products that people need. Neither should we discard the Industrial Revolution, but save the workable parts and reform the rest into something more practical that serves us better. Mold it into the revolution that the world is in desperate need of— the *Ecolonomics Revolution*.

11

Ecolonomics . . . Think Anew, Act Anew

We were entering uncharted territory, and I was excited. "Dennis, would you please explain Ecolonomics now?"

His face brightened and then relaxed into a certain serenity, the kind that comes when the answer to an old problem is discovered, uncovered.

"Ecolonomics" is a combination of the words "ecology" and "economics." It's a word I coined to express the truth that our ecology and economics are interdependent—they are two sides of the same coin. Proponents of both our environment and industry can come together to form partnerships that bring benefits to both our environment and our economy.

The "Ecolonomic Revolution" is a movement away from societal and industrial activity that destroys our environment and threatens our economy towards behavior that nurtures, saves, and honors our environment, while strengthening our economy. It is bloodless. It is a revolution of the mind and heart. Its goal is prosperity without pollution.

The old Industrial Revolution will naturally phase out as we evolve toward a culture that is based on Ecolonomics. That evolution will stimulate the economy and create a tremendous amount of meaningful jobs—jobs which will make us feel good, because they will protect, rather than destroy, the place we live. We will honor those jobs, for they will be part of an exciting, historical movement—a movement that will create a place in which our children and their children can live healthy and productive lives.

Since World War II, we've experienced a "cold war" between not only the U.S. and the Soviet Union, but also between businesspeople and environmentalists. Each has pointed its finger at the other and declared, "you're the problem." Business has blamed environmentalists for business woes, while environmentalists have warned us that business is destroying our environment. They've been like two horses in the same harness, pulling in different directions and getting nowhere. Now, the Ecolonomic Revolution will allow them to pull together in the same direction towards a sustainable, safe, and just future for all of us.

What environmentalists and businesspeople must understand is that they need each other. In the complex world of today, one cannot thrive, or even survive, without the other. Every economic system that has ever existed in the history of human civilization has depended, directly or indirectly, on the environment. If we take away the environment, there can be no economy. Think about it . . . there is no such thing as a post-environment economy.

As we look around the world today, we will see that wherever the environment is destroyed, jobs are also destroyed, and the economy suffers. As the economy weakens, we see that the environment is in great jeopardy, for people will do whatever is necessary to survive, even if it means destroying their environment, the very foundation of their economy. People don't look very far down the road when they are hungry.

And so, we see in many places around the world this ugly cycle of environmental and economic degradation—one feeding off the other. To break this cycle, Gerry and I, along with Bob and Katherine Saltzman, formed the Institute of Ecolonomics in 1993.

Since then, we've had our victories and our defeats, but in the overall picture we've steadily moved forward, lifting—through our educational programs and networking ability—the collective consciousness, and helping to create, support, and identify new Ecolonomic business activities. But, as with the LIFE feeding program in Los Angeles, nothing is accomplished without the help of others, and I must recognize my buddies Linda Gray and Ed Begley, Jr., who have been there every time I've called on them to do something for the Ecolonomics Institute. They traveled to Missouri Southern State College in my hometown, Joplin, for the Institute's first major fund-raiser—and Joplin hasn't been the same since. Other friends, Ann and Harry Cornell, made sure the fund-raiser was successful by guaranteeing that the college had the funds to make our Ecolonomics program a winner. It takes a team to get things done and the Ecolonomic team is growing stronger every day.

The Institute of Ecolonomics mission is to create a sustainable future. To accomplish this, we know at least two things are necessary—a sustainable environment, which supports human life, and a sustainable economy, which also supports human life. Both are essential for human welfare, and if we fail in achieving either, we will suffer, and suffer greatly.

Ecolonomics is our future; it is the future of civilization, the future of business, the future of our environment . . . for they are all hooked together.

I think of Ecolonomics as a "stool." Now, a stool won't stand unless it has three legs, and the three legs of the Ecolonomic stool are business, government, and education. All three must work together to build a world where each global citizen is assured a clean, productive, just, and sustainable future.

Earlier, we noted the warning of the Union of Concerned Scientists. What were they trying to impress upon us? Simply that we must change the way we relate to the Earth.

"Dennis, give us some examples of this—how do we relate to the Earth?"

Through business, basically. But remember, neither business, government, nor education—which includes scientists and inventors—stands alone. Everything we do as a society filters down through business. We grow things, manufacture, transport, build, and develop things, all through business. Business is the strongest, most influential institution on the planet, and as such, it is incumbent upon it to take a leadership role in shaping a sustainable future. It is in the best position to "midwife" us through this incredibly fast-moving transformational period the world society is now experiencing.

Business has always been the manager of our earthly resources, and if business doesn't accept its responsibility and change the way *it* relates to the Earth, there will be no significant changes made. And we know it won't change unless there's a profit to be made. That's the way it should be, at least under our present economic design, for business may be the strongest institution on Earth, but if it makes no profit *it's out of business*, and of course would then *have no power at all.*

"So, the question is, from a business standpoint, how do we change the way we relate to the Earth and still make a reasonable profit?"

"You got it right! That's the million-dollar question."

There are numerous opportunities to do that, but it will require a major shift in our thinking, for everything proceeds from thought. We've got to examine the world around us and clearly assess it and ask ourselves, is it really working? If we are absolutely honest, we must conclude that it's not. We can do better.

We don't have to accept the hunger and starvation running rampant in many areas of the globe, nor the poverty, nor the endless cycle of wars, and the trashing of our planet. We can make better choices. However, nothing will change unless we see the perilous direction we're headed and have the burning desire, coupled with will and action, to change it.

We've got to be open to new ideas—new concepts. Remember, the bumper sticker that said, "The mind is like a parachute, it's no good unless it's open"?

The Ecolonomic Revolution represents a new model for living. It's a bloodless revolution in which everyone and everything wins. The environment wins, the economy wins, and the Earth and all its inhabitants win. It's a revolution of consciousness.

Design is the key to constructive change. The greatest percentage of the environmental problems we face today results from faulty design. If we are concerned about the wanton waste of our resources, we must examine the design—of our making—which allows such a result.

Right now we design things so that *waste is inevitable.* We're a throwaway society. We make disposable items, such as pens, diapers, paper napkins, paper towels, cameras, etc., for the purpose of throwing them away. This is called "planned obsolescence," and the reason it has been so eagerly adopted by the bottom-line watchers is, of course, that it forces consumers to buy more.

Built-in obsolescence is as American as apple pie and Mom. Just when we get the refrigerator paid for, it's worn out. It's all in the design—a design that disregards the limited resources we have on the planet, or what price we will have to pay for the damage to our environment later on.

It costs money to clean up our pollution and our waste, and it always falls on the shoulders of the taxpayer. Even if the government fines business for violating regulations, the business can and often will simply pass that cost on to the consumer in the form of higher prices.

Our challenge is to design an Ecolonomic Industrial Ecosystem where government regulations to control waste and pollution would be *unnecessary* because *the design of the system itself would produce none.*

The model for the Ecolonomic Industrial Ecosystem must be nature itself. We might ask, "Why has nature's ecosystem sustained itself for millions of years with no end in sight?"

First of all, it's cyclical in its character. What goes around comes around. It produces no waste. What might appear to be waste simply reforms itself and serves another purpose in the never-ending cycle of life.

Take the tree as an example—to the casual observer the falling fruit and leaves might seem like waste, but to the roots of the tree they are anything but waste. They become nutrients on which the roots and trunk and even the fruit it will bear in the next season feed, and the cycle is complete.

William McDonough, one of the truly brilliant minds of today, says, "If people are to prosper within the natural world, all the products and materials manufactured by industry must, after each useful life, provide nourishment for something new." Of course, that's exactly what happens in nature. What we take from the Earth must return to the Earth to once again be part of nature's magnificent ongoing cycle of give-and-take. We're talking about what McDonough calls "biological nutrients."

If all we used in our society were natural products that biodegrade easily, as the Native American and other indigenous civilizations around the world used (and in more remote areas are still using, although they are fast disappearing), we would have no problem. However, we not only manufacture products that are not biodegradable, such as tires, cans, plastics, metal tools, etc., which McDonough calls "technical nutrients," we also make many that are highly toxic, dangerous to our health, and that disrupt and destroy the Earth's fragile ecosystems.

In nature, everything is connected, everything supports something else and at the same time is supported by something else—nothing lives in isolation. It is this interdependent quality that has allowed nature to survive indefinitely.

Also, nature's ecosystem is energized by a fuel that is clean, inexhaustible, and free—the sun.

We must copy nature's ecosystem and create an Ecolonomic Industrial Ecosystem. The first step is to develop Ecolonomic technologies, products, and processes, which then can be used to establish Ecolonomic businesses and industries. Again, ones that give us good jobs and a healthy economy while nurturing, protecting, and honoring the environment, rather than destroying it.

We then need to bring Ecolonomic industries together to form Ecolonomic parks where the chosen industries support each other. Where one industry's waste becomes a resource for another. Where the entire Ecolonomic park is designed as a closed-loop industrial cycle that generates and emits no pollutants. Where the power that operates the park is clean, limitless, and economically attractive (solar-hydrogen). Where the manufacturer is responsible for the goods it manufactures. Where the products made in the park either return to the Earth as biological nutrients after their useful life, or, if they are technical nutrients, return to the Ecolonomic park to be truly recycled.

In other words, as McDonough again explains, "Technical nutrients will be designed to go back into the technical cycle. Right now, anyone can dump an old television into a trash can. But the average television is made up of hundreds of chemicals, some very toxic. Others are valuable nutrients for industry, which are wasted when the television ends up in a landfill. The reuse of technical nutrients in closed-loop industrial cycles is distinct from traditional recycling, because it allows materials to retain their quality. High-quality plastic computer cases would continuously circulate as high-quality computer cases, instead of being down-cycled to make soundproof barriers or flowerpots."

Ray Anderson, CEO of Interface, the largest commercial floor covering company in the world, is responsible for the product he manufactures. He no longer sells his floor covering—the customer buys the service that his product provides, and when the customer is finished with it, Interface *takes back* the old product and *recycles* it into new floor covering. *None of its manufactured goods reach a landfill.* This is sound business, for in the first four years of eliminating the waste in its operation, Interface increased its profit by over sixty million dollars.

"So, Dennis, the answer to our dilemma is—?"

Correct the design—mimic nature.

Before we leave the subject of business and move on to the second leg of the Ecolonomic stool, it is very helpful, even exciting, to realize that business itself is beginning to become conscious of the important role it must assume if we are to safely negotiate the challenging waters that lie ahead. This understanding has manifested in the formation of business organizations such as Business For Social Responsibility, investment funding groups like The Calvert Fund, and The World Business Academy (WBA).

The new role for business is clearly defined by the late Willis Harman, WBA cofounder. He stated:

> Business has become in the last half century the most powerful institution on the planet. The dominant institution in any society needs to take responsibility for the whole . . . as the church did in the days of the Holy Roman Empire. But business has not had such a tradition. This is a new role, not yet well understood or accepted.

171

Built into the concept of capitalism and free enterprise from the beginning was the assumption that the actions of many units of individual enterprise, responding to market forces and guided by the "invisible hand" of Adam Smith, would somehow add up to desirable outcomes. But in the last decade of the twentieth century, it has become clear that the "invisible hand" is faltering. It depended upon a consensus of overarching meanings and values that is no longer present. So business has to adopt a tradition it has never had throughout the entire history of capitalism: to share responsibility for the whole. Every decision that is made, every action that is taken, must be viewed in light of that responsibility.

And that, to me, is what the World Business Academy is really about. It is not just another association of business people to exchange information and foster collegiality. It is about investing ourselves in a task of historic proportions. Some will be called to this task and many will not. Those who are will find it extremely gratifying and fulfilling.

Willis Harman, Emeritus Professor and President Emeritus of the Institute of Noetic Sciences, passed away peacefully January 30, 1997. His contribution to many fields and many people is beyond measure. He had a robust zest for life and a deep concern for the planet and all life on it. To know him was not only to admire him, but to love him.

"As long as we are still on business, is there another ingredient we might have overlooked for sustainability?"

Yes—equity. The need for a sustainable environment and economy is more obvious to us, but the component necessary for sustainability that we are not taking seriously enough is just plain fairness. People must feel that they are getting a fair shake. We must develop fairness in our relationships with each other. If that quality doesn't permeate the fabric of our society, the chances of that society enduring are very slim.

I'm not talking about absolute equality, where people become automatons and the goods of the Earth are divided up equally. That's nonsense, for the nature of creation is individuality. Sameness can never be attained, nor is it desirable, for it ignores the immutable Law of Diversity and our basic nature as creative human beings.

However, people must feel that they have an equal *opportunity* to use their God-given talents and achieve, through the exercise of their will and the sweat of their brow, their honest share of the Earth's abundance. This is an essential building block of any social structure that is lasting.

Fairness is not easily legislated. Certainly women, minorities, and the handicapped have benefited by certain laws, but government is limited and can only do so much to promote fairness. It can't change the hearts of people, and that is where the real change needs to take place, where the real work needs to be done, for the most well-intended laws will be circumvented if the heart is not right. We will come back to this later, but it is important to remember that the bottom line problem in the world today is one of consciousness.

Since business is the most influential and strongest institution on the planet today, it is in the best position to serve as the catalyst to establish equity between management and labor, where so much conflict has historically been felt.

Capitalism as it has developed today has a serious flaw in it. It is basically unfair. If it continues down its present path, it will eventually self-destruct. It's digging its own grave.

Both capital and labor are necessary parts of our economy. Both contribute to the development of a company and both should be rewarded as the company succeeds. In other words, for the good of the whole, we need to broaden the base of capital owners. The way capitalism is structured now, that base consists of capital owners or investors who receive the newly generated money. With this scenario, wealth will always flow from those that labor to the rich. Money will continue to go to money.

Access to new capital by a broader base of people, who have historically been denied that access, energizes and strengthens our economy, and everybody gains. This is so because everyone in the company is interdependent and connected. Directly or indirectly, we share our good fortune as well as our bad.

What is needed is a mechanism that fairly and equitably allows salaried employees to acquire their share of the new wealth that is generated by a successful company. One such mechanism is with us today. It's been tested and it works. It's called an "Employee Stock Ownership Plan" (ESOP), which I'll get to in a moment, but first let me point out that this nation has already experienced the benefits of an expanded capital base.

In 1863, we had millions of acres of what we perceived was virgin, fertile, and unused land west of the Mississippi. Our perception was absolutely wrong. It was used very intelligently and lovingly cared for by Native Americans. The abuse they then endured, while most assuredly a horrible stain on our history, should not blind us to the economic lesson to be learned.

In 1863, President Lincoln signed what is perhaps the most important piece of economic legislation in our nation's history—The Homestead Act, which encouraged young men to take Horace Greeley's advice and "go west." Anybody who was willing to work 160 acres for five years could claim it as his own. Millions seized the opportunity, and the rush to settle the West was on. Some expanded their land holdings. Some sold their land and became merchants and shop owners. Some became producers of products and services.

In the thirty years following 1863, the U.S. enjoyed great prosperity. It was the result of more money in more hands.

After World War II, again we saw a great surge in our economy, when again capital was distributed to the "have-nots." This time, the returning GIs were the recipients of the windfall in the form of the GI Bill that provided the opportunity for young men and women to receive the education that moved them up the economic ladder. Through the FHA and the VA, they also were able to own their own home, which became collateral they could use to satisfy their material needs.

During these periods of great prosperity, capital was more equitably distributed, and we witnessed the growth of a very strong middle class, and the gap between the haves and have-nots was not so extreme. In most cases, a family could be supported by one breadwinner, which is a rarity today. And children benefited by having more time with their parents.

The underlying principle that created the "good times" was the same: a more equitable distribution of capital . . . more money in more hands.

Today we see that more and more of the Earth's wealth is finding its way into fewer and fewer hands. The gap is getting greater. The rubber band can only stretch so far before it snaps.

Until management and labor understand that they are essential to each other, that they share a common goal, and divide the fruits of their efforts in an equitable manner, there will always be problems.

Some very far-thinking businesspeople have understood the need for a new economic model, a change in the relationship between capital and labor, and have accepted their responsibility and have taken advantage of the opportunity to establish equity in their businesses while creating a more stable and profitable company.

One example is my friend E. Don Rott, who operated Computer Circuitry, a company based in Dallas, Texas. At one time, Don owned 100 percent of his company. However, he had met in 1971 and was greatly influenced by Louis Kelso, who some call the Father of the Employee Stock Ownership Plan (ESOP), where everyone involved in the company has a piece of the action. It brings the power of incentive to the company's players. It is fair.

The ESOP

Don Rott, after a two-year association with Louis Kelso, realized that what Kelso was saying made good sense. He was convinced that if ESOPs were "broadly applied in the United States, the capital base of our country could be expanded and extended to people who had not previously experienced any significant ownership of capital. This would address and solve many, if not almost all, of our economic and social problems."

So, in 1981, Don changed his company to an ESOP. "No longer was it *my* company, it was *our* company." The result was very gratifying, the "we" company in its most profitable year earned 500 percent more than in its most profitable year as an "I" company. This was due in a large part to the workers' understanding—that the more profitable the company became, the more money went into their own pockets. Efficiency increased, absenteeism decreased, the work environment was more harmonious, and labor-management disputes faded to practically zero.

This amicable relationship between labor and management is due to the fact that the workers have an elected representative sitting on the Board of Directors of the company. The workers now have an understanding that they are an important part of the success of "their" company. Many, for the first time, realize what stock ownership means—the value of profit sharing, and the responsibility that comes with ownership.

In 1971, there were, according to Kelso, between thirty and forty ESOPs in the United States. Today, there are over 11,000, benefiting not only eleven million employees, but current stockholders, the corporation, and other interested parties. The significant rise in numbers is due to the fact that it works. Everybody profits.

Louis Kelso once said, "The right to acquire property (capital) must be a realistic prospect for all citizens in a free and democratic economic system. If not, power concentrates, and freedom is taken away." He also said, "The only time a man feels comfortable about being replaced by a machine is when he owns it."

With the creation of more ESOPs, corporate America and employees will realize their oneness—that they are two halves of the same whole. This evolutionary change in the relationship of management and employees will be an important step towards a sustainable future, and, as my friend Don Rott has said, "It will focus the consciousness of our citizens on an exciting vision of the future, which they can passionately believe in. They will actively participate in rebuilding the American dream."

Mondragon Cooperatives

Another model for the corporate world to take a close look at is tucked away in the remote regions of northern Spain. I'm referring to the Association of Mondragon Cooperatives, which is made up of 160 cooperative enterprises. The jobs of more than 23,000 members are virtually guaranteed for life because they are the owners. The modern factories they operate produce everything from robots and plastic rulers to computer chips. They are the biggest manufacturers of home appliances, and the profit enjoyed by the cooperatives is twice that of the average corporation in Spain.

In many ways, the Mondragon Cooperatives are similar to an ESOP. The basic energy that propels them both is cooperation rather than competition. In both cases, the employees share in the success of the company. However, in Basque (Spain) each employee/owner makes a financial investment in the cooperative, which gives the worker a greater incentive to make sure the company succeeds.

When a new business is formed, each employee/owner invests approximately $10,000. If that person does not have the cash to ante up, they are not denied membership. An agreed-upon amount is deducted from their payroll, interest-free, until their investment is paid.

One major difference between the Mondragon Cooperative and an ESOP is that a Mondragon is a new venture started by a group of friends that have established a close bond. They then take their business idea to the entrepreneurial division of the cooperative, which will then supply the venture capital for the new cooperative. If the business idea is accepted, the entrepreneurial division doesn't abandon the cooperative if it falters. If necessary, they nurse it back to life with business training and advice. And the cooperative will make arrangements with the bank for the new cooperative to have more money at lower rates when it is needed. The bank only benefits when the new business is successful.

The Association of Mondragon Cooperatives is cyclical in nature. All the different parts are very closely connected. They are interdependent, "all for one and one for all." You might say they have observed what works in nature and have decided to mimic it in their economic model.

It must be working, because, as I said before, the Mondragon Cooperatives generate twice the profit of the average corporation in Spain, *and* employee productivity in the cooperatives is higher than any other business in Spain, *and* the success rate for new cooperatives in the Association is nearly 100 percent. On the other hand, venture capitalists in the United States feel a 20 percent success rate is acceptable. They figure the 20 percent of venture capital they invest successfully will compensate for the 80 percent that fails.

Author Terry Mollner, who has studied the Mondragon Cooperative extensively, has pointed out that the two elements in the Association of Mondragon Cooperatives that make them successful are cooperation and incentive. It is truly the relationships that make it work, and the understanding of their oneness. Mr. Mollner contends it is essential that we move out of the Material Age and even the

Information Age into the "Relationship Age," if our civilization is to reach its full potential as a peaceful, productive, and just society.

In an article written for the World Business Academy Perspectives, of which he is a fellow, Mr. Mollner states:

> If we are moving out of the *Material Age* and into the *Relationship Age* in our thinking, is Mondragon revealing the future that we will all someday share? And if we are skeptical about this happening soon in our country or business, would it not be wise to ensure that the changes we do implement are at least heading down this path rather than another? After all, it is not necessary for business to become a cooperative, or even substantially employee-owned, to begin operating from the relationship world view and to incorporate many of Mondragon's structures and procedures in the management of conventional corporations.

12

The Ecolonomic Stool

"Dennis, what is the second leg of the Ecolonomic stool?" I asked.

It's education.

No matter what problem we are facing, whether it's economic, environmental, political, or social, our worst enemy is ignorance. And to rid ourselves of it, we must first identify the problem. If we stick our heads in the sand to ignore it, and live in denial, it will only fester and grow. For too many of us, this is what we're doing with our environmental disaster. We're denying it. We're not heeding the warnings of our most renowned scientists. We're not listening to Mother Nature herself.

Ecolonomics is a holistic approach to solving our complex dilemmas. It recognizes that there is no such thing as an isolated, independent problem. Nothing stands alone. In other words, if a specific part within the whole is malfunctioning, the root of the problem is systemic and must be examined in that light if a lasting cure is to be gained.

This is easily recognized in ourselves. If one part of our body is diseased, it affects our entire being. It is the same with our global society. If the disease of poverty, hunger, or war exists, we can't solve any of those problems unless we address our political, religious, economic, and environmental problems as well.

Unquestionably, one of the major threats to sustaining the quality of life on the planet is overpopulation. The proven antidote for it is education. Wherever education has become a strong component of a woman's upbringing, the birthrate has fallen. There are other reasons for this besides the woman's being made aware of different methods of contraception.

With education, a woman will, in all probability, enter the mainstream of society—politics, religion, business, and/or academia. These pursuits take time, energy, and commitment—and raising a large family while maintaining these time-consuming activities is discouraged.

Statistics show that in areas of poverty around the world, more children per family is the result. It is also known that with greater education, poverty is reduced. It is also a fact that where poverty is pronounced, the environment is threatened. The importance of education is significant if we are to reach sustainability.

It is essential that businesspeople and politicians also be educated—this isn't to say that they are not. There's a plethora of degrees floating around in both institutions, but Ecolonomics is a new discipline in which most have not been schooled. Since the primary focus of business at the moment is increasing quarterly earnings, businesspeople must be taught how to make more money by preserving the environment, rather than destroying it. That is exactly what is accomplished by the programs that the Institute of Ecolonomics is helping to establish in colleges around the nation.

Businesspeople also have consciences. They care about their families, their children's future, the Earth, and what legacy they might be leaving. It is important that they understand the damage business has been, and in many cases still is, inflicting on the Earth, plus the strong position they are in to reverse that damage. It is then that business may be moved to take positive measures to help repair it.

Let me identify two colleges that have understood the important role of education in establishing a sustainable future, and have therefore created Ecolonomic courses.

The first to offer such a program was Chattanooga State Technical Community College in Chattanooga, Tennessee. The other is Missouri Southern State College in Joplin, Missouri, which was the first four-year college to create an Ecolonomic course.

In the fall of 1997, Chattanooga State offered a Certificate of Ecolonomics in partnership with the Institute of Ecolonomics. The target audience for the certificate is managers, community leaders, and city planners, and those who aspire to these positions, who seek a comprehensive introduction to sustainable development, and those who aspire to these positions.

All courses are team-taught and supported by the liberal arts, mathematics and sciences, and engineering technology divisions. The certificate is available through classes on campus and via distance learning using video and Internet options.

It was under the sound visionary leadership of President Dr. James Catanzaro that Ecolonomics became part of the curriculum at Chattanooga State. He clearly expressed the importance of Ecolonomics in an article in volume 2, issue 3, of the Institute of Ecolonomics newsletter:

> A Great Divide has developed in American society. For some, it has been raised to the level of a struggle between cultures: the culture of business and industry—bottom-line, return-on-investment-driven—versus the culture of environmentalists—Earth care, protection-of-the-planet-energized. Ecolonomics will end the struggle! It will provide the means of embracing principles of sustainability while strengthening business. That is why we at Chattanooga State in Tennessee have stepped forward to adopt this program and develop it as a national model and offer it worldwide via the Internet. Finding common values and beliefs is a new and challenging venture. It is critical to Americans at the dawn of a new century.
>
> We at Chattanooga State believe this is an urgent cause! The consequences of furthering the Divide for nature, our communities, and our nation are grave; the rewards of coordinated efforts will be extraordinary.
>
> What principles will enhance corporate profitability and simultaneously guide nature-sustaining activity? The dogmatism of the priests of both cultures has made the quest for these principles and for concerted action difficult. For this reason, we need a new starting place. Perhaps the best point of departure, though difficult, is a step back from our preconceived notions, from our strongly held biases. We must first view both conflicting worldviews with cold eyes, the eyes of detachment and perspective, and then warm eyes, the eyes of understanding and empathy.
>
> How do we know the mutually beneficial course? We must begin each decision-making process not by identifying the problem and solution options, as management gurus advise, but with a review of what we *value* most and what we would wish *every* decision-maker would do facing similar challenges. This approach will provide a context for

making specific business, personal purchase, even Sunday afternoon decisions that will lead to both efficiency and care for our world. *Then* we will respect our environment as we seek to optimize our position in it. This is the Ecolonomics Revolution!

As Abraham Lincoln (through composer Aaron Copeland) said so eloquently, "The dogmas of the quiet past are inadequate to the stormy present. . . . As our case is new, so we must think anew and act anew."

Ecolonomics is a new and powerful idea. We can do justice to our planet and we can enhance corporate profitability if our decisions are based squarely on enlightened values, most notably, values which ensure a full range of options for my grandchildren, Sarah and Trey, and their contemporaries.

Now is the time to come together as business leaders and advocates for sustaining the planet, to forge a resourceful future for many generations to come.

Missouri Southern, under the watchful eye of its forward-thinking President, Dr. Julio Leon, has also developed a certificate program in Ecolonomics to help businesses develop ways to provide goods and services in an environmentally friendly way.

It is the feeling of Missouri Southern that by understanding these concepts, government officials, industry personnel, and others can develop better policies and procedures that make sense for business and the environment.

It is the college's thought that the certificate adds a distinctive credential to degrees in business, political science, biology, environmental health, and any of the several other areas. So, new graduates should have a "leg up" in the marketplace when competing with applicants with other similar skills.

Government (the third leg of the stool) can also play a pivotal role in moving us towards an Ecolonomic society—by working in concert with business, education, and consumers. By doing this, it can be a powerful and constructive force. By establishing tax breaks and subsidies, it can encourage businesses to develop Ecolonomic Industries. Right now, the government has its priorities slanted toward environmental disaster. The lion's share of our tax dollars support those industries that are destroying our environment, damaging our health, and threatening our children's future . . . tobacco, nuclear power, and fossil fuel.

If an equal amount of money was earmarked to fund development of clean renewable energies, Ecolonomic Industries, products, and technologies, we would unquestionably alter our course and begin to seriously reduce the depletion of the ozone layer, acid rain, global warming, and the pollution of our sinking water tables along with the air we breathe and the soil that grows our food. The proponents of clean, renewable energy are simply saying, "Just give us a level playing field, an equal opportunity, and we'll win. We will reverse the destruction of our environment, strengthen our economy, and show all humanity that we can live in harmony with nature."

As I speak these words, the 2000 Presidential Election Campaign is in full swing, and of course the most predictable issues the candidates are embracing are the economy, health care, social security, a strong defense, and balancing the budget. Don't they understand that none of those things will matter if we destroy our environment? The most important job we have in the twenty-first century is to rescue our planet. We need elected representatives who truly understand the magnitude of the problem and are willing to roll up their sleeves, make the hard political choices, and do the job that must be done.

To do this, we also need an informed and eager citizenry. One of the worst problems we face is civil apathy. Gandhi said, "When the people lead, the leaders will follow."

If our elected representatives don't have a clear vision and the will to chart a sustainable course, we can't place all the blame at their feet. We aren't leading them!

"Education is so important! How ignorant are we?!" I blurted out in a fit of angry passion.

"Well, I hate to admit it, but we're either very ignorant or we simply don't care."

Ignorance is the worst. None of our problems can be solved without knowledge. Knowledge is power. But only if it is coupled with action guided by wisdom. We can have all the information in the world, but if we are not willing to do something with it, to use it in a constructive way, it's worthless.

Quality education is directly related to freedom. The great gift the framers of the Constitution gave us is the freedom to speak our minds, to express in words our honest reaction to the free flow of ideas we encounter.

Education should teach us *how* to think rather than *what* to think, particularly the young whose fertile minds have not yet become bogged down in the mire of dogma. Today, more and more, we are being taught *what* to think instead of how. The diversity of thought, so precious to our growth and freedom, is on the wane. We seem content to let someone else do our thinking and choosing for us as long as the paycheck keeps coming, the beer is cold, and we don't have to shoulder any responsibility.

Education should encourage the young to always be curious, to question the status quo—to always probe for a better way. We should teach them how nature works and the significance of all its interdependent parts of which we are only one of its billions of pieces.

We should teach them that we are the only species with the power to think and therefore the only one with the power to destroy our environment or preserve it. We should teach them how our thinking and subsequent actions affect the Earth and how we are then affected by it in return; that we can't consume more resources than the natural world can produce. If we continue to attempt to do this, which is our present policy, we will not only exhaust nature's supply, but in the process destroy our economy.

Let us teach our youth to honor themselves, and to continually remind them of who they truly are, made in the likeness of the master Creator and capable of being what they choose with the capacity to create the world of their grandest vision. Most of all, let us teach them to love themselves, for unless they do, they don't own that love. It is not theirs. And they cannot give to others that which they themselves do not possess. Let us teach them it is the giving and receiving of love that is the answer to all our worldly problems.

13
The Earthship

"You took action in an Ecolonomics way in your more immediate personal life," I said, "by making an environmental stand on how you live. Could you please tell us about that—about the Earthship?"

Our Earthship home in Colorado has become a celebrity in its own right, having been the focal point of many newspaper and magazine articles around the country. It has also attracted many film crews from a variety of TV shows and networks, such as The Discovery Channel, *The Today Show*, Home and Garden TV, and *Lifestyles of the "Poor" and Famous*.

When you build a house out of cans and used automobile tires, it gets a lot of attention. Our son Rob produced a film starring me, Rusty, and the inventive "out-of-the-box" architect Michael Reynolds of Taos, New Mexico, along with Contractor Bob Allison of Ridgway, Colorado, and a wonderful crew. It documents the building of the Earthship, from the laying of the first tire to the finished and decorated home. It has been used by service clubs, schools, churches, environmental organizations, and was played on PBS for over three years. We have transferred the film to videocassettes which are available to the general public. All the proceeds from the sales go to support the Institute of Ecolonomics.

The video can be ordered from our websites, www.dennisweaver.com, or www.ecolonomics.org.

"Dennis, what exactly is an Earthship?" I asked.

Primarily, it's a solar/mass house. Most people understand the solar concept and the need to use it as an energy source—it's clean, inexhaustible, and, amortized over time, is very cost-effective. The sun's energy is captured through photo-voltaic cells which transform it into electricity, which is then stored in batteries and used to operate the appliances in the house. But the mass aspect of the house is really more interesting, and mass is desirable because it tends to stabilize temperature—it holds energy. If you've ever been in a cave, you know the air is cooler in the summertime and warmer in the wintertime relative to the outside air. That's because of the huge amount of mass around the cave. The Earthship operates on the same principle.

We created the mass in the Earthship in a very interesting way. We took an environmental problem—used automobile tires (we throw away 250,000 a year in the U.S. alone)—and made a resource out of them. We rammed dirt into the tires with a sledgehammer to produce density, and the greater the density, the greater the mass. Each was pounded until the tire actually swelled. When we finished with a tire, it weighed close to 400 pounds. We called them "tire bricks," and each one easily held over three wheelbarrows full of dirt. The tire bricks would then be laid in courses just like regular bricks, overlapping each other for strength to form the walls of the house, both inside and outside. So every living space in the house is surrounded by a huge amount of mass. Therefore, we have no air-conditioning or heating ducts, which would produce undesirable positive ions. Entering the house, it feels like walking into nature, and plants love it. Our ferns are huge. In our planters—which run along the south side of the house in year-round sun—we grow organic tomatoes, peppers, lettuce, chard, cucumbers, and spinach, *and* tons of geraniums.

The temperature in the house ranges from 58 degrees during the coldest night to 78 degrees on the hottest day. I know 58 degrees is not the most desirable temperature for human comfort, but a person would never freeze to death at that temperature, and 58 degrees is attained without using any backup heat. A sweatshirt in the early winter mornings feels good, but fifteen minutes after the sun hits the glass, it's toasty warm.

We spent a good chunk of money building a 10,000-square-foot house, which the county building officials classified as "experimental," so we wanted to make sure the experiment worked. We put water pipes beneath the floors in certain areas of the house, through which we could run water preheated by the sun and then boosted by propane, to create a very gentle nonobtrusive heat source, but we rarely need to use it.

Gerry always asks me to be sure and tell people that we don't advertise Goodyear or Firestone . . . that we have no exposed tires. However, I should mention that Armstrong-Pirelli sent us an eighteen-wheeler full of "blem" (blemished) tires. There are 3,000 tires used in the house, and the walls are finished with several coats of adobe to give the house that beautiful Santa Fe look. Michael Reynolds built us another smaller one in Taos, but we got so busy with Ecolonomics that we never had time to go there, so we sold it to another pair of "pioneers."

Our Earthship is the best house we've ever lived in, and we've never tired of it. I don't know that I could confidently make that statement if it weren't for our "project engineer," Don Haskell, who helped with every aspect of the Earthship and has seen to it that every detail worked like a well-oiled machine from the day we moved in.

People often ask me if there are any problems with it. Now if we're honest, we will admit that there is nothing mankind has ever made that doesn't have some flaw in it, and the Earthship is no exception. When you make a house of tires, there is a small problem . . . every six months, we have to rotate the rooms!

14

One Person Can Make a Difference

Be the change you want to see in the world.
—Gandhi, 1869–1948

"Dennis, what was it about Kindness Week that inspired you to come to Dallas two years in a row and talk about it?"

He held the words just on the edge of his lips, as if waiting for the right beat to let them fly. "Kindness is very powerful," he said. "It is a tool with which we can change the world. . . ."

Gandhi showed us all that one human being can change this world. For as we change ourselves, we change others, and that will eventually lead to a change in collective consciousness. People should understand the power that they have as individuals—in the thoughts that they think, the emotions they hold, and the hopes and dreams that they are carrying within them. Those things shape their consciousness, and as their consciousness grows and moves more into alignment with what I call "spirit," mass consciousness will shift.

It's important to understand that a shift in consciousness can be productive or destructive. It depends on what is in the hearts and minds of those initiating the shift.

What happened in Dallas, Texas, is a perfect example of a constructive shift. The idea of Kindness Week was born in the mind of one person, who shared the idea with two friends, and the three took action.

"Dennis, why did you get involved?"

Well, I could say I joined the Dallas Kindness Movement as an honorary cochair because I thought I could help bring kindness to Dallas, that I could touch many lives, and those lives would be changed for the better, and the people would be happier, and Dallas would be a nicer place. That may be the surface reason—but if I'm truly honest with myself, I would have to confess that down in the deepest part of my being, I did it because I felt it would be fulfilling for *me*.

You know, altruism is really a questionable concept. We do things because we think it will please us. We think it will relieve us of some pain or gratify us in some way—bring us happiness. And if we are honest, we will realize that this is why we do *everything* that we do.

But the "wise" person understands something else—that we are all connected and, therefore, his or her own happiness must include the happiness of others. When we reach the point where people in droves begin to understand that, we will create Heaven on Earth. Man, what a tremendous world this would be if that simple truth were understood and honored!

When we realize our connection with another person, we realize that the joy or the fulfillment that we give them is something in which we are going to share, and that changes everything. We no longer fear the feeling of being separated, instead we feel the joy of togetherness. The fear that we are isolated, that we are by ourselves, creates judgment, anger, jealousy, suspicion, hate—all our negative emotions.

Love is the answer to any problem we have—whether it is environmental, social, economical, or political. If we, as human beings, were motivated by love, it wouldn't matter what form of government we had. Anything would work, if people were truly acting from love. Why? Because it would actually do away with the need for *any* government. With the understanding of our connectedness, our oneness, we would naturally and automatically take care of each other, for we would realize that, in doing so, we would be taking care of an important part of ourselves. Nobody would suffer from poverty, be denied food, want for shelter or clothing or the basic necessities of a safe, creative, and productive life. And, hopefully, that is where we will ultimately evolve as a society. Unless, of course, we go the other way, which is an option.

My strong conviction is that love will conquer. And I see us moving in that direction—with things like the "kindness movement," The Human Kindness Foundation, The Shoah Visual History Foundation, The M. K. Gandhi Center for Non-Violence, The ReCreation Foundation, and the rush of millions to give something back to the world—whether it is money for disease research, gathering supplies for disaster victims, the homeless, or saving trees. It is a wonderful time to be alive! Probably the most exciting time we have ever known. The potential available to us to make this world something that is absolutely magnificent is beyond anyone's dream!

It is possible, but it all depends upon our ability to establish a constructive change in our consciousness.

One great Saint said, "You change yourself, and you will change thousands."

So what happens when we do something "kind" for others? We feel tremendously fulfilled. And our fulfillment spills over to others.

During "Kindness Week," I was able to talk about kindness on different television shows, to large groups of people—young and old—and attend diverse religious services. Just my own behavior—of making personal contact with individuals and treating them kindly—certainly had an effect on them, and on me! The more I interacted with those people and saw that they, too, were acting in a kind way or giving back to me, the more fulfilled my heart became. It was a glorious time to spread the philosophy of kindness. We all benefit from that, and that feels incredible.

I hesitated, then asked, "Dennis, what do you think truth is?"

"Whoa, that question has been debated for eons. All I can do is tell you what works for me."

There are two kinds of truth: *relative* and *absolute*.

Absolute is not of this world. It is well beyond vibratory creation. Relative truth, however, mimics the physical world. Both are constantly changing.

In life, we deal with relative truth. I know that what is true for me today is different from what was true yesterday or what will be true tomorrow. When we know that we have attained the truth and nothing but the truth, that now our search for the truth is finished . . . we are indeed finished! For truth is continually evolving, always expanding, and allowing that process to flower is extremely satisfying to the soul.

If you resonate to "my" truth, if it excites and feeds your growth, bless it. If you are beyond it or find it not your truth . . . forget it, and search elsewhere. Know this, as I speak of these following "truths," they are truths for me now, based on my experience. And I know that it is somewhat danger-ous to write them down, for tomorrow they will no doubt change. If they make your light go on, then accept them as an important part of your journey, but never shut your mind and heart down so that your soul is not open to greater truths—greater expansion.

It is the journey . . . the continuous unfolding and real-ization of what we are and our ever-deepening relationship with God, and all that there is that fills us with such bliss.

15
The Tender Trap

> I swear by my life and my Love of it, that I will never live for the sake of another man, nor ask another man to live for mine.
>
> —John Galt, in *Atlas Shrugged*

"What a wonderful segue into your spiritual journey," I said, thinking to myself that now we're getting to the heart of the matter.

Dennis sat looking at me for a moment. He drew a deep, cleansing breath. "One of my first experiences—conscious experiences—with Spirit happened back while I was doing *Gunsmoke*. . . ."

I have always been fascinated with horses. The Kentucky Derby was always a special event for me when I was young. So, when *Gunsmoke* came along in 1955 and a few loose coins were burning a hole in my pocket, the attraction of Santa Anita, Hollywood Park, and Del Mar racetracks was just too much for this country boy to resist.

Then, there was Tiny Nichols (our card buddy, Jim's stand-in), who was a real racetrack fixture. During racing season, he would always come to work with a racing form under his arm. He taught me how to read it and how to select the horses by using his handicap "system." Of course, it rarely worked, but picking the winners was a challenge that titillated me, and it wasn't long before I was bugging the first assistant to shoot my scenes early so I could at least get out to the track by the fifth race.

I never became a heavy better, maybe a six-dollar combination or a win, plus a couple of place tickets—just enough to prove what horse I had picked. And, I must admit, it was a thrill when I got a winner. However, even though I had fun and the excitement was often intense, I frequently developed a headache before the day was over. It clearly wasn't over the stress of losing money—I didn't bet that much. I really believe it was the environment that produced it, an environment filled with a vibration of greed and frantic restlessness. Then one day, as I was driving away from the track with a nagging headache, I had an experience that affected me profoundly.

At that time, I'd been practicing meditation for only a short while and I was still much more interested in the outside world than what resided inside me. I was inching my way down the boulevard in the usual crush of angry cars jockeying for a position, anxious to free themselves from the gridlock, when suddenly it happened. . . .

My forehead became alive with an unexpected feeling that I can only describe as a holy vibration. It was so comforting, loving, and peaceful that I later came to refer to it as "the pull of God's sweet love." When that presence came over me, I was at once surprised and comforted. I wanted nothing to interrupt it, and I immediately exited the stream of cars and pulled over to a grassy shoulder and became deeply absorbed in that Divine Consciousness. I had never experienced anything that was so powerful. I just sat there—as all the cars rolled slowly by—floating in what seemed to me to be a sea of peace.

One thing that I knew for sure then was that that Divine Presence comes through "grace." I didn't consciously try to conjure it up through meditation or prayer. I realized that the going-home traffic from Santa Anita was not the environment that one would normally associate with such a spiritual experience. A dear friend of mine had often said, "God comes like a thief in the night." In other words, that Energy is unanticipated and cannot be confined to the rule of logic. I had just encountered an example of that truth.

Later, as I was driving down the freeway, I wondered why that experience came to me at that time and place. The thought came back to me that God truly is omnipresent and that "that" presence is not restricted by time and place. It cuts through the turmoil, restlessness, and chaos of this world.

The other thought that occurred to me was that I was dramatically being shown the difference between outward consciousness and the presence of God within. It was as if God was asking me, "Okay, you have a choice—which do you prefer?" There was no question which was preferable . . . it was definitely God. Sri Yukteswar (Paramahansa Yogananda's guru) said, "He will beguile you with an infinite ingenuity. . . . He is seductive beyond thought of competition."

Now this experience didn't immediately stop me from returning to the track. The pull of the world is not so easily quelled, but the memory of that day stayed with me and subtly changed me, until eventually the attraction of the racetrack dimmed and then disappeared.

I never felt as though I was being deprived of something. It was more like I had had the "track experience" and it was now time to move on.

The best way I can describe my dwindling desire for the racetrack is to compare it to the fun I used to have making mud pies when I was a little boy. Once I experienced the thrill of a bicycle, I naturally gave up the mud pies. It seems we always give up that which satisfies us less for that which satisfies us more.

That's what happened to me. The track began to lose its glitter. The more I felt the fulfilling power of God's presence within, the more I willingly left the mud pies of the racetrack behind.

Not long after that first experience, Lew Brown and I would make the trip to Del Mar racetrack and on the way back we would stop at Encinitas and visit the Self-Realization Fellowship (SRF) chapel—an intimate sanctuary at the edge of the highway.

We would go in, sit quietly, pull the life force up to the Third Eye, and awaken the spiritual consciousness that dwells there. We called it "cooling down." It was amazing—just totally amazing—being in that little chapel. It was like taking a spiritual bath that washes away all the worldly debris. The restlessness and anxiety-filled vibration of the track environment was gone.

I would sit there in that beautiful space, and the life force would go past the spiritual eye to the very top of my head—the crown center, which I lovingly nicknamed "Mt. Zion." It doesn't always happen, but it's a very special feeling when I can say, "Mt. Zion is alive today."

Again, this confirmed to me the difference between the temporary fulfillment we get from worldly things and the lasting fulfillment that comes to us when we make contact with our Eternal Self—that Holy part of us. And I know that if I can enjoy that consciousness through the grace of God, with all the dumb things I've done and all the so-called "rules" I've broken, then it has to be available to everyone. There is one way in which we're all alike. Each one of us is made in the image of God.

These experiences have confirmed to me, beyond any doubt, that God is unconditional love, that God is not a God to be feared, that God is not a God of vengeance and judgment, but a God of forgiveness and love.

We humans are the ones that utilize fear in our relationships with others. We are the ones that judge. God has no preference. He has given us the ability to make choices and exercise our free will. What kind of God would He be if we exercised His gift of free will and then He punished us for doing it? That wouldn't be free will at all—if such a heavy price was attached to it. Free will must be free. It cannot be given and then taken back. God doesn't change Her rules in the middle of the game. Let us understand, however, that by the choices we make we create consequences, and that sometimes those consequences are painful. (Please note that I have interchanged "He" and "She" when referring to God to emphasize that God has no gender.)

Hell and heaven are products of the way we live our lives. They are a result of our own actions. God simply observes the "movie." A loving mother, watching her children at play, doesn't really choose the games or select the teams. She might warn us that certain games could be hurtful, but the wise mother allows her children to learn by playing the game. The lessons are more deeply ingrained if experience is the teacher.

Some might argue that it isn't a very loving God that allows Her children to suffer. But God has designed this creation so that we feel both pleasure and pain. Pleasure cannot exist alone, no more than "tall" can *be* if "short" isn't present by which to measure it. Pain is that by which we measure pleasure, and one cannot exist without the other. But let us play the "what if" game. What if nothing existed but pleasure? It would become meaningless, boring, and life would become stale and dull. So, I know it's difficult when we go through the pain of this world, but the best attitude is to bless it, knowing that "this too shall pass." Bless it, for the more we condemn it, the more we rail at it, the more we make it real—the more we give it life.

It's helpful to busy ourselves with activity—both mental and physical—that lifts us to a higher and more productive state of consciousness. As Johnny Mercer used to sing:

> *You got to accentuate the positive,*
> *Eliminate the negative,*
> *Latch on to the affirmative,*
> *Don't mess with Mister-In-Between.*
>
> *You got to spread joy up to the maximum,*
> *Bring gloom down to the minimum,*
> *Have faith, or pandemonium is liable to walk*
> *upon the scene.*

The only change that is changeless is change itself!

The exciting thing for us to understand is that God, expressing nothing but love for us, has given us the power to direct the changes in our lives that are bound to come. We are in control and can make choices that improve the quality of our lives. My songwriter son, Rusty, has written: "Life is a dream within our control, not the result of dice that we roll. Choices we make riding the trail, bring lives together with a love that won't fail."

God has sent us messenger after messenger, teacher after teacher, to give us the ways and means to experience happiness, to grow and develop in body, mind, and spirit— to evolve towards our highest good. Teachers such as Jesus, Buddha, Gandhi, Confucius, Mohammed, Moses, Yogananda—and still we choose to ignore them, or distort the truth they brought us.

"Why *is* that?"

One reason is that we fear that in following their truths we will have to give up our pleasures, which we are obviously reluctant to do. The irony is that following these enlightened beings' suggestions would bring us the happiness that continually eludes us by depending on the outside world for it.

Jesus said, "Seek ye first the kingdom of God . . . and all these things will be added unto you." He even told us where to find it—that the kingdom of God is within. I think if He were here today, he would probably say the presence of God is within, or God's love, God's consciousness, is within.

But such truths seem vague to us. They are too ethereal, too remote. They're just not practical for the person facing "real" problems. More practical for us are the things we can experience through our five senses. And that, as all great Masters will tell us, is the grand delusion. Our sensory experience seems so real—we can see it, touch it, hear it, etc.—but the magic trick of the illusionist also seems real. So does our dream at night. Nobody can tell us that our dream isn't real while we're dreaming it. It is only when we awaken from the dream consciousness that we can say, "Oh, that wasn't real at all; it was only a dream."

The same is true of this waking consciousness that we are now experiencing. Only when we wake up to the consciousness of God that dwells within each one of us can we truly say this worldly experience is a delusion. It is only through meditation, putting the world aside, going within, and communing with that grander, more fulfilling presence of the Holy Vibration, or Holy Ghost, that we will begin to awaken. It is a process, a journey, which is satisfying beyond anything the world can give us.

No doubt about it, however, the delusion is extremely strong. God designed it that way intentionally. For if it were easy to awaken from God's dream, the whole cosmic movie would end, and God, being the Master Magician, says, "The show must go on." It's easy for us to wake up from *our* dream at night because that's *our* dream, but it's not easy to wake up from the cosmic dream, because that's God's dream. The only way to do it is to become one with the consciousness that is dreaming it—God.

The world with its infinite number of attractions has got a hammerlock on us. When I used to go to the Hollywood SRF (Self-Realization Fellowship) temple on Sunset Boulevard, I would drive by a little cocktail lounge called "The Tender Trap," and I would think, "Boy—do those words apply to the whole world or not?" It's not always tender, but it certainly is a trap.

Life keeps teasing us, keeping us stuck in worldly consciousness by saying, "Look what I've got for you; this is going to satisfy you," or, "Come over here; this is what you've been waiting for; this will really bring you happiness." But all those "things" are fleeting. They might satisfy us for a little while, but since all things in this world are transient—come and go—the pleasure from worldly things also is transient. The fulfillment fades and disappears, and we again search for "something else" to satisfy us.

Swami Sri Yukteswar said it so beautifully. "How quickly we weary of earthly pleasures! Desire for material things is endless; man is never satisfied completely and pursues one goal after another. The 'something else' he seeks is the Lord, who alone can grant lasting happiness.

"Outward longings drive us from the Eden within; they only offer false pleasures that impersonate soul happiness. The lost paradise is quickly regained through divine meditation" (from *Autobiography of a Yogi*; by Paramahansa Yogananda, page 172).

Often, there is great disappointment in what we think is going to fulfill us. But not with God's presence within; it always satisfies and is always there. It doesn't come and go like the things of this world. The mistake we make is in believing that the power to fulfill us is in the object of our senses. It is not.

If the things of this world contained the power to make us happy, if those things outside of us really contained the power to fulfill us, then everybody would be satisfied with the same thing, and it would satisfy us always. Think about this.

Obviously, the power is not in the *thing*, or we wouldn't have so many garage sales! *We* give things the power to satisfy us or fulfill us by our attitude towards them. We are conditioned when we are kids to say, "I like this . . . I don't like

206

that." We are taught to judge, and, out of habit, we hang on to our judgments.

Please don't misunderstand me; this isn't an argument for poverty. This doesn't mean we can't and shouldn't enjoy worldly stuff—we should perform our part in this great cosmic play of God's with great purpose and enthusiasm. But the paradox is that we can enjoy it more if we know the world for what it is, a passing show, and not the source of our greatest fulfillment—that lies in the core of each and every one of us. The trick is just don't take this old world too seriously.

It's the attachment to worldly things and the expectation of the fulfillment we think certain circumstances will bring us that set us up for the pain.

As an actor, I've always been given everything I've needed to play my parts—wardrobe and props, even a mustache and beard from time to time, but I wasn't attached to them. I knew they weren't mine, but only on loan to me. And when the curtain came down, I willingly gave them back to the prop-master and the wardrobe mistress.

We should have the same attitude about the things of this world—they're only on loan; they're only for us to use to enhance our role in life. But when the final curtain comes down on this life, all those things we have accumulated, that we have worked so hard to acquire, are taken away. They go back to the great prop-master in the sky. The great tragedy of the human species is that we spend so much of our time, money, and energy collecting all of our stuff, thinking that those things will bring us happiness. And so many discover at the end of the trail that their search for happiness has not been unlike a dog chasing its tail.

I love that great country song, "Looking for Love in All the Wrong Places." That's what we do. We continually look outside of ourselves in the things of this world for a love that keeps eluding us, when what we really crave is as close as our own consciousness—the presence of God within. It is discovering *that* which will satisfy our hearts and soothe our souls. And here's a great truth: it is when we find it *within* first that we have the best chance of finding it *without*.

I know now what the English novelist Somerset Maugham was talking about when he wrote the book *The Razor's Edge*. The path to God *is* a razor's edge—it is very narrow, very sharp, and we can fall off of it very easily. We have to constantly recharge our "spiritual battery"—by accessing that consciousness which the world does not offer, and which the senses cannot give us. That is our shield against the illusions (the pains, the tragedies) of this world—the door by which we can escape the "Tender Trap."

16
Journey into Spirit

As we let our own light shine, we unconsciously give other people permission to do the same. As we are liberated from our own fear, our presence automatically liberates others.

—Nelson Mandela, 1994 Inaugural Speech

As a young boy, others made my decisions and choices for me—mostly my mother and father. I went to a lot of different Protestant churches. Whichever one was the closest—Christian, Methodist, Baptist, or Presbyterian. We would also go see evangelists shout "hellfire and brimstone" from their makeshift pulpits. There was no television in those days, so the preachers would bring their tents to town—for a revival. My mother never missed an opportunity to attend, and I was always with her. They would stay in town for about a week or two, until they exhausted their audience, then they would pull up stakes and head for the next town.

These fellows were really theatrical. They were so emotional, so wrapped up in what they were doing, they gave themselves over totally to the moment. I didn't particularly understand what they were saying—it was their passion and the drama that held me spellbound and I thought, "Boy, that would be neat to do someday."

I have always been attracted to the "drama"—of any kind. For as long as I can remember, I wanted to pretend, to imagine myself in all kinds of emotional situations. I was only four or five years old when I was exposed to these evangelists, and the impression they created has stayed with me all my life.

William Harrison Prather was my grandfather on my mother's side. He trained for the Baptist ministry at William Jewell College in Northern Missouri. But he fell out of sorts with the Baptist philosophy because he couldn't agree with the "hellfire and brimstone" teaching. However, he never stopped preaching and studying the Bible. He would preach to anyone that would listen. Such men were called, in those days, "stump preachers." The nearest stump was his pulpit.

He also loved to debate. As a seven-year-old, I heard him take the negative side of "Do you spare the rod and spoil the child?" Of course, in those days, sparing the rod wasn't an option, so the odds were definitely against Granddad. But he loved taking the unpopular side of an issue and playing the devil's advocate, just to heat up the argument and rub people the wrong way.

In a debate, I would see him lose himself in the passion and emotion of the moment, pounding his fist and waving his arms while his voice rose firmly to match the fervor of his delivery. It excited me, and later I often tried to imitate him in the secrecy of the barn or nearby woods. So the flame of performing was fed, and it burned deep within me even when the trees and cows alone appreciated my histrionics.

As I grew up and began to formulate my own opinions about things, I came to disagree sharply with Granddad's interpretation of the Bible. He used it to support his own prejudices, especially when it came to African-Americans, Latinos, Asians, and Catholics—or anyone who didn't come from the same social roots as he did. As a matter of fact, most of the preachers in Southern Missouri, in the late '20s and early '30s, did the same thing. One of the blessings of my time in the service was the realization of how wrong, unfair, and absurd such prejudices were. I felt that if this is what the preachers were receiving from their Bible studies, then there must be something wrong with the Bible. It never occurred to me that the error might lie in the "student." In any case, I threw the baby out with the bathwater and rejected religion totally. I became an agnostic.

I was drawn back to my spiritual search in my early twenties, when I was still in New York struggling to become an actor. It was a tough time. Gerry and our firstborn son Rick, a tiny baby, were living with her parents in Miami, Oklahoma, and the only acting jobs I was getting were mostly Off-Broadway and a few small parts in live television, which was just beginning at that time in New York City.

The part-time jobs of selling hosiery and magazines door-to-door, velocipedes at Macy's, bubble rockets at Hearn's department store, and the janitorial work I did in exchange for my acting lessons, didn't give us much. They say there are no atheists in foxholes. Well, my situation wasn't that desperate, but I needed a break and the world didn't seem interested in giving it to me. It crossed my mind that God might give me a helping hand.

George Stowell, my father-in-law, who had become the second reader for the Christian Science Church in Miami, Oklahoma, talked to me while I was in Miami for Rick's birth. He told me how Christian Science had benefited many people. It kept coming up in my mind and one day, as I passed a Christian Science reading room in midtown Manhattan, I went inside and browsed through some of their literature.

Mary Baker Eddy, the founder of Christian Science, was the first to introduce me to a God that squared with my own sense of logic. She made me understand that God was not some distant entity that looked down on me and judged me, or a God that handed out merits and demerits, but a God that was a very integral part of my being and my daily activity. She made me understand God as energy, law, principle, mind, and especially Love.

I studied, for a while, the book *Science and Health with Keys to the Scriptures* until it got too deep for my intellect to hold and comprehend. But it certainly made clear to me that there was an understanding of God that was not part of my childhood experience—a religion that dealt with the positive aspects of God and the power of the mind.

When Gerry, Rick, and I moved to California, we began to attend a church called Unity. The church published a little book called *The Daily Word*, and I would read it quite often and found it very satisfying. In the Unity service I attended, they had a period of silence where one could meditate or pray, which I really enjoyed; and so Unity held my interest for several years.

There had not been any emotion in his voice when he told this story—only the evenly spaced clarity of his words.

"Then what?" I asked.

He breathed . . .

When I was about thirty-four—the year was 1958—my father-in-law came along again (the Christian Scientist). He jumped from religion to religion—always searching. He came to me one day and said, "Dennis, I just heard a guy who you might really be interested in. He is half-Yogi and half-Christian."

I said, "Really?" It was an intriguing combination. I knew nothing about Yoga.

He said, "Yeah, he's over here on Sunset Boulevard. You ought to go hear the man sometime."

I decided to do just that.

He was speaking at a little church called Self-Realization Fellowship (SRF), and his name was Dr. M. Lewis, Vice President of SRF.

Dr. Lewis, a Bostonian, happened to be the first Kriya Yoga Initiate (in the West) of the great Eastern Saint, Paramahansa Yogananda.

After Yogananda came here from India in 1920, Dr. Lewis followed his teachings conscientiously and sincerely. And, when I met him in 1958, he was advanced spiritually, highly realized, and very inspirational.

He was an ordinary-looking man. If you didn't have an in-depth relationship or experience with him, you would think he was just a dentist—which he was. But he was also a man who had an incredible unflagging desire to know God.

When I heard him talk, he made a lot of sense to me.

He said we all could feel and experience in a tangible way the Love of God and the peace that passeth all understanding. That we were all made in that image. And that there were certain techniques that we could follow that would give us that experience.

I said, "Ooh, there are certain things that I can do—I can test—that will help me either prove or disprove?" This idea intrigued me. So, I started going to the SRF church regularly and having sessions with Dr. Lewis.

The first time we met privately, he asked me, "Can you give fifteen minutes in the morning and fifteen minutes at night to know God?"

That was an offer I couldn't refuse and said, "I think I can handle that." It seemed like very little effort to actually have an experience of something called God.

He was a terrific example of a householder on the path.

"Could you please explain to us what you mean by *householder*?"

A householder is simply a person who is active in the world, has a job, a family—someone who is the head of a household. He told me that I could find God while carrying on my worldly responsibilities.

When Dr. Lewis first met Yogananda, he questioned him about a quote from the scriptures that said, "If therefore thine eye be single, thy whole body shall be full of light." (Matthew 6:22). He went on to ask Yogananda, "So many great masters talk about that light. Can you show it to me?"

Yogananda responded, "If I do, will you spend your time and energy teaching it to others?"

Dr. Lewis said, "Of course."

Yogananda did teach him how to experience the Light within, and Dr. Lewis learned it well.

After his days as a dentist were over, he devoted the rest of his life to that teaching—helping people attain their own self-realization—to experience their own light. He was a tremendous example for people with families who had daily activities and worldly problems to contend with. He was very special, and I was extremely fortunate to have known him in the last years of his life.

I remember also that, at our first meeting, he asked if I was involved in "this television thing." I hesitated. My mind raced back to when I was seven years old and I overheard a neighbor lady say to my mother "an actor will never get to heaven." For a moment, I wondered if Dr. Lewis was going to confirm her statement and tell me I should find another occupation, if I was really serious about finding God; or perhaps . . . you see, it was my fourth year on *Gunsmoke* and maybe he was going to tell me I had already blown it. But instead he looked at me with understanding eyes, and, almost throwing it away, he casually dropped a spiritual bomb in my lap—"you will always be in the public eye . . . as long as you know who the Doer is."

For a long time, I could not understand exactly what that meant. It troubled my mind—how could I, Dennis Weaver, not be the doer if I had free will—if I had the power to choose? How could that be so? It seemed to me that there was a conflict in his statement. If something outside of me, some "god," was the doer of all my actions, what happened to my free will? Where would that be? I would be nothing but an automaton. There could be no joy in using my creative power, for I would have none. Some "god" would control all the incidents in my life. In that case, observing the worldly conditions, one would have to assume that that "god" was not a god of love, but instead an unfair god who preferred some of Her children over others—a god that chose to bless some and condemn others.

It was a long time before I came to grips with that and really understood how God, as the Doer, and my free will could exist at the same time. The Divine Dichotomy, once understood, always is simple.

Yes, we have free will, we are in control of our own actions, and are the architects of our destiny, because we have the power to choose. But how did we get that power? Where did it come from? There is one Cause, one Source, one Creator, and that Creator has given us that power. He also gives us the life force that flows through us, our intelligence, and the urge within us to love and be loved—it all comes from the one Source. If She didn't give that to us, we could not *be*. We could do nothing. So, in that sense, the Creator is the one Doer . . . but the creative power filters down and percolates through us as a gift from the One. The Creator is responsible for creating us and giving us such power and abilities—how we use this gift is up to us. We are not puppets on a string. We are responsible for our own actions.

"Wait a minute," I said. "This could be a bit confusing for some of us. Have you ever heard the phrase, 'it's all filmed and finished'?"

"Yes, as a matter of fact, I've heard Dr. Lewis make that statement."

"Do you believe it?"

"Yes."

"How can that be, then? How does that square with what you just said about being the architects of our own destiny? Now, you are saying that what happens to us in the future has already been determined. What happened to free will?"

Your question is a good one and your reasoning is right on target. It's a case where the Divine Dichotomy again comes into play. The answer came to me via my sons Rick and Rob. Fortunately, they are not only excellent filmmakers but talented writers as well. Rob's main focus is on directing, while Rick's is on producing. Together they formed InterWeave Entertainment, Inc., to create interactive video games. They were the first to use live actors to tell their stories rather than animation. Rob received the Best Director award from the Academy of Interactive Arts for his work on "Voyeur" starring Robert Culp and Grace Zabriskie, and for "Thunder in Paradise" they received the Best Interactive TV award.

"Could you elaborate on what you mean by 'interactive'?"

The person playing the game has control of how the story develops and, subsequently, how it ends. In order to make the game work, Rob and Rick had to create eight different endings, plus the scenarios leading up to those endings. So the game player could actually choose or "write" the script that he or she desired.

"Sounds complicated."

It certainly is. The point is the different choices were already filmed and finished when the player began to play; which ending became "real" was the result of the player punching the desired buttons . . . of making a choice.

Life is like that video game, and we as the players are constantly making choices as to which "button to push."

217

What choice to make. Now if my sons could film eight different endings, God in His omniscience has "filmed" an infinite number. Every conceivable situation is already in the can, filmed and finished, and we exercise our free will and decide which button we're going to push. So we're in control of our lives. Every moment is a moment of choice. We can't blame our problems or those of the world on God. They are our doing. The problem is, so many times, we "push the wrong button."

"Terrific. Your talented sons gave us a great visual."

His eyes glazed over with that lost-in-memory look, and he focused them straight at me, but I knew he wasn't seeing me when he smiled. "Speaking of my talented sons . . ."

It was always my dream, and still is, to work with all three of them, and that desire was fulfilled for me when Rick was the supervising producer of *Magnum P.I.* Mostly because of Rick's influence, I was offered the part of a "usta wuz" country singer. I grabbed the opportunity when I was told Rob would be playing the part of another country singer, this one with a drinking problem. The script called for scenes when my character was in his twenties. Obviously, no amount of makeup could take thirty-five years off me, so Rusty, my youngest son—a great country songwriter with an out-of-sight country voice—played the young me. People always ask me about my sons. Rusty manages our "Big Barn dance-entertainment facility (along with his significant-other dynamo Madison Anderson) when he's not playing lead guitar and singing with the "Rockodiles" and recording in our studio. Rick is married to Judy (a very special mother) and they have given us our two super-duper athletic/intellectual grandsons, eight-year-old Travis and six-year-old Jess. If you think that sounds like a proud granddad, you are right!!

It's hard to describe the thrill that I experienced working with all three of them. Of course, that *Magnum* job turned out to be an all-expense-paid "vacation" for the entire family in Hawaii, and that didn't hurt either.

"So, back to free will—what you were saying is that because of free will we are responsible for the consequences of our actions."

Yes! Granted, there are environmental forces and the power of habit that often dictate to us choices and actions in opposition to our better judgment and greatest welfare; however, in the final analysis, the preferences are ours.

What I came to understand in my years with SRF is that God is not some superbeing sitting on a cloud in some antiseptic corner of the Universe, looking down at us, keeping score, and judging who goes to Heaven and who is shipped off to Hell.

"Then, what does God look like to you—what are Its characteristics?"

I understand God to be a consciousness in which all things are contained—that there is nothing outside of God's one consciousness. It can be likened to our dream at night. Everything in the dream is contained in the consciousness of the dreamer, the dreamer being each of us. We can say that it is the Master Dreamer, God, that is "dreaming" all that there is. It's all contained in the One consciousness of God.

In our dream at night, weird and unexpected things happen. It's out of our control. Likewise, in a sense, this dream of God's is out of God's control, for He has endowed us with free will and the power to create as we choose. And He will not rescind that Law, for to do so would defeat the purpose of the creation—which is to experience the exchange of love between each other as well as to experience the giving and receiving of love between ourselves and God. You see, God wants our love, but He can't force us to love Him, because by the nature of Love it must be freely given. If it is forcibly extracted, it is something else. It is no longer love.

I took a much-needed breath. Then I asked, "Dennis, why would God even bother to create this world of matter with all its pain if God is Love? Why couldn't God be satisfied as being Love and just let it be?"

That is an important question and such a difficult one to answer. It certainly has baffled our greatest thinkers. I'll give you the answer that makes the most sense to me, and you can take it for what it's worth. But understand that the human intellect, which has a beginning and an end, is not capable of comprehending that which is outside of the intellect's scope—that which has no beginning or end.

There are two aspects of God: one we'll call the Absolute—beyond this vibratory creation; and the other we will call the living God—that permeates everything in and through this vibratory creation. In the beginning, there was nothing but the Absolute, nothing but the One, and it knew Itself as only Love. But knowing Itself as Love was not satisfying. It desired to experience that Love, to share that

Love; but as the Absolute, the One, there was nothing with which to share that love. Nothing to give it to or receive it from.

The Absolute determined that it would divide Itself up into the many, so that the many individualized parts of Itself could exchange and experience love and those parts could give and receive love with the Creator—who would return it. And everybody would live happily ever after. This is when the Absolute became the living God.

There was one hitch. As I said before, for this to work, the Absolute had to give the individualized parts of Itself *free will.*

I sat back and asked, which at the time seemed like a logical question, "Why?"

"Because the nature of Love requires that it be given freely."

Okay, duh—he already said that. Where was I?

So the Absolute had to give us free will in order to experience, as the living God, the giving and receiving of love through us. It is the experience that is fulfilling and, as it is with each of us, so it is with the living God—for we are made in Its image. We can know something, but until we make it our own, through experience, it doesn't fully satisfy us.

For instance, we can know that an orange is juicy and sweet, but it only satisfies us when we eat it, when we experience it. It is the same with God. He can know Himself as Love, but it's only satisfying when the Love is experienced. And that is the purpose of creation—for Him to experience, through us, that which He knows Himself to be.

It is the same in our relationship with God. We can intellectually know Her as Omniscient, Omnipresent, All-Loving, The One Source, but an intellectual concept will not satisfy us. It is the experience of God that quenches our hunger.

"Okay—this brings up another point. As a little girl, I remember hearing grown-ups talk about God's plan—"

"—Particularly if there was a tragedy in the family or a disaster in the world, right?"

"Exactly."

They would always assume that it was a part of God's plan. It was always a mystery to me why a God of Love would plan such things. For many years, I wrestled with the question, "Does God really have a plan?"

It seemed sensible to me that the Creator would have some purpose in creating this Universe with all its magnificent interdependent life forms and systems, including us.

As I have said, Her purpose was to experience that which She knew Herself to be. Now God couldn't experience that which She *was* unless She experienced that which She was *not*. In other words, we can't experience tall unless we can experience short, which tall is not! The same is true of hot, up, joy, health, victory, in, heavy, etc. Therefore, in fashioning this creation, it was necessary for God to design it as a duality (everything has an opposite) in order to have the experience, through us, of that which God is; for it is only in the physical Universe or the vibratory creation that the experience is possible. That is simply God's plan, and God was willing to "suffer" the dualities, the "hills and valleys" of this delusive creation, in order to have the experience, through the extension of Itself—us—that could not be achieved through His knowingness.

In coming to this sphere of creation, we also agreed to implement that plan, because, as I said before, as expressions of God, She experiences through us. She feels every emotion, thinks every thought, feels every feeling that we do. She feels the joy and the sadness. Remember, God had to give us free will in order to experience the giving and receiving of love. We have used that free will to create situations that are very painful, but to blame those on God is to pass the buck. What we experience in life is *our* doing, not God's. However, the experience is also His and when we are kind, happy, generous, and loving, there is great joy in "Heaven." For God feels it! It's no different than when our children are happy and uplifted; we feel it—we experience that joy along with them. God is the Grand Parent of us all . . . no exceptions.

We will always experience the dualities in this world. There is no way to avoid them, for it is simply the way the world is constructed. But we can soften the effects of their negative parts.

"Isn't it important *how* we react to the negatives?"

Yes.

Do we pick the rose and feel the thorn, or do we enjoy its magnificent fragrance?

I believe it was not God's intention that we be brutalized by the dualities, but rather to see the perfection in all things. Bless the negatives, for without the defeats we could not know the victories, or joy without knowing sadness, peace without turmoil, and stillness without the restlessness.

I know it's very difficult to see the perfection when we are going through a hurtful situation. However, how many times have we experienced that pain and then some time later looked back and thought, "Thank God for that experience. I see now how it was important in order to create this moment of now."

Life is like a jigsaw puzzle. We can pick up one piece of the puzzle and it makes no sense at all. We only see how the piece fits, and its purpose and importance when the puzzle (picture) is complete. Then we can see the perfection. The point here is to see that perfection as we experience each moment in life. Those who can do this are called *Masters*.

There's another aspect of God's plan that should be noted. We are all being drawn back to the Source from which we came . . . to God. As a matter of fact, we are there now; we just don't know it. We haven't reached that state of consciousness that Jesus had when he pronounced, "I and the Father are one." Luckily for us, He also said, "These things I do, ye can also do."

We're all on the road back. Some are consciously helping the journey, and some are throwing roadblocks in the way.

"Dennis, this may be a stupid question, but why would someone willingly throw up blocks?"

First of all, there are no stupid questions. The answer is simply: ignorance and attachments. Attachments we have acquired to things of this world, and the belief that these things are the greatest source of our happiness.

When the individualized part of God known as the "soul" took up residence in the physical form (remember it now has free will), it identified with the body and became attached to it, forgot its true nature, and became the pseudo soul or the "ego." We began to think of ourselves as the body.

But we are much more than that. We are the soul that has a body. We are forever an extension of the living God. We are at One with It and with each other, but we live in ignorance of it, thinking that we are separated.

The really important work that needs to be done is *spiritual*. We need to tear away the veil of ignorance that makes us think we are separate from each other, our soul, and from God. For that is the source of all our problems.

As I said before, we make our own heaven or hell by the choices we make while living on this Earth. However, we may not be able to control everything that happens to us, because the choices and actions of others also impact our lives. The collective consciousness, which is determined by the combination of all individual consciousnesses, is a real force in our lives. However, we can control the way we react to uninvited consequences. Attitude is the key.

The "negative" things that we experience allow us the opportunity to define and announce to the world *who we are*. We would never be able to be forgiving if there was never anything to forgive.

Consider the pain we feel as loving prods that are saying, "There is something better—we can make better choices." If we don't want the consequences of our actions to be hurtful, then let us take actions that don't continually provoke the pain. The law of "cause and effect" is alive and well in our lives—"what you sow, so shall you reap."

I let his words trail off, as I sat wondering about how we go about achieving this understanding and reach a state of permanent or unwavering peace. Then I thought of something I had very much wanted to talk about, which I felt fit perfectly into this section.

"Dennis, I have heard a lot about Kriya Yoga—could you tell us what it is?"

Kriya Yoga is one of the main techniques of Yoga meditation taught at SRF. To quote Yogananda: "The Sanskrit root of *kriya* is *kri*, to do, to act and react; the same root is found in the word *karma*, the natural principle of cause and effect. *Kriya Yoga* is thus 'union *(yoga)* with the Infinite through a certain action or rite *(kriya)*.' A yogi who faithfully practices the technique is gradually freed from karma or the lawful chain of cause-effect equilibriums."

Kriya Yoga is a technique which many have used to unite their limited human consciousness with God's.

God is everywhere. There is no place God is not. God is aware of everything. There is nothing God is not conscious of. We, according to the Masters, being made in the image of God, have latent within us the power to become one with God's consciousness. In reality, our human consciousness is an individualized piece of God's consciousness. As Yogananda described it, it is "bottled up in a phial of flesh, corked with ignorance, and floating isolated in the ocean of Spirit."

What we want to do is pop the cork. Remove it so the soul can be free to consciously merge into the ocean of spirit and float in the sea of God's omnipresence. We want to have personal, tangible contact with God's all-fulfilling Love.

As I mentioned earlier, we are all being pulled back to that place. Kriya Yoga is a technique that quickens the process by using devotion, attention, and the life force that flows through us. Devotion is essential because God can't say "no" to it. Attention is important because it is the director of the life force and, wherever the attention and life force go, that's where our consciousness will be.

In waking consciousness, the life force is directed by our attention towards the outside world. We can touch things because the life force is going out through our fingers. We can see things in the world because the life force is going out through our eyes. We can then say we're in "worldly consciousness," or human consciousness.

The Kriya technique helps to reverse the flow of life force and through the power of our attention place it on that which dwells in the deepest part of our being—the soul or God's divine presence. We can then say we're in "soul consciousness."

St. Paul experienced that, for he said, "I die daily." He didn't die as we think of it. What he meant was that he consciously reversed the life force from going outward, directed it into the spiritual centers within, and died to outward consciousness. He was able, as is the case in death, to reach the breathless state, and since the breath is the cord that attaches the soul to the body, he was able to totally free the soul and experience death in a conscious way. He experienced the Kingdom (or consciousness) of God that Christ said was within Him.

For anybody who is interested, it is important to go to the proper source and get more information.

"That would be the Mother Center—Self-Realization Fellowship in Los Angeles?"

"Yes—or the Yogoda Satsanga Society of India."

I'm not a joiner by nature. I really resist joining anything. It was a big move on my part when I eventually took
the SRF lessons. I put off taking the lessons for quite a while
for this very reason.

I was fortunate to meet Dr. Lewis two years before he
passed. I immediately felt what a sensitive, kind, and
deeply spiritual human being he was. From that moment
on, as I explained earlier, he greatly influenced my life.

A few months after I had met Dr. Lewis, a friend from
SRF, John Rosser, said to me, "You ought to come down to
Encinitas where Dr. Lewis lives and have some private con-
sultations with him." He told me that Dr. Lewis held meditation sessions on a certain night of the week down there
and that we could catch a session and then talk to him after
the meditation. He was giving a series of lectures on Yoga
at the time. So we went down to Encinitas together with
another friend, Vincent Shortland.

I remember that first meditation—well, I don't think
you could call it really much of a meditation. The room was
filled with devotees and followers of SRF, and I sat between
John and Vincent, who were sitting there like stones, not
moving a muscle. I was so restless I couldn't believe it! I sat
there wondering if this thing was ever going to end. My
back was starting to ache, my neck was in a cramp, and
my mind was spinning. I kept thinking they were just going
to sit there forever! It seemed like three or four hours, but
it was probably only thirty minutes. That was my first
experience with attempting to meditate in such an environment.

"Why should we meditate?"

Every person on Earth is trying to attain happiness or avoid pain, and every action we take is either a conscious or subconscious attempt to achieve that goal. Often, we make the wrong choice, thinking it will bring happiness, and end up with a great deal of unhappiness, but it is important to understand that the intent is always the same.

Meditation is a technique or device to help us remove the restlessness from our minds and reach that state of inner peace, contentment, or unalloyed happiness.

"And removing the restlessness from our consciousness is the purpose of meditation? Does this ever become easy?"

Yes, to both questions. I have learned that, with proper and sustained practice, meditation becomes easier and more rewarding. It can be defined as concentration on the presence of God within, or an aspect of God such as light, sound, feeling—or the Holy Vibration, the essence of which is pure love.

From the day Dr. Lewis asked me if I could spend fifteen minutes morning and night to find God, I have never failed to do so. It wasn't always under ideal circumstances. It could have been on a plane, on a movie set, or in a strange hotel room in a foreign country. But the habit was important to establish—to at least say "okay, God, I'm here again."

And what I found out was that God is always there, in some degree. Of course, it took some time and perseverance to break through the restlessness and realize that.

We get so involved in our worldly activity, in this dualistic turmoil, that the mind becomes so restless that it can no longer tune God in. It's like a radio. You know when you are trying to tune in a station someplace and you twist the knob back and forth, but you only get a lot of static and you can't hear the music? That is what it is like with a restless mind— you are trying to tune in God, but all you get is static.

That "static" is our thoughts, our worries—our attachments to the things of this world. We have all heard the expression, "Let go and let God." Well, that is so helpful in meditation. Just sit there and forget everything else, be conscious of nothing but that Divine Presence, the sweet pull of God's love; become absorbed in it. We should have the attitude that this is the most important appointment of our day. This is my time with my Creator—my time with that all-knowing, all-loving, all-helpful, all-inspirational presence.

When we sit in the silence of the Holy Vibration and feel that love, then we really know that we are connected to God. The feeling of separation is what has created so many of our problems in this world. The feeling of separation, not only between God and us, but between ourselves and our family, our neighbors, the environment—the animals, even our "enemies." We feel separated, and indeed that is an illusion—because we are all connected. I keep going back to that, but it is such a vitally important thing to understand. We are all joined together.

"Dennis, I have tried to meditate, and it's hard—how do you meditate?"

First, it is very important to have a great longing, a craving for that which the world cannot give us . . . the unconditional love of God. That burning desire is so important because everything follows desire, and without it we will not make the consistent effort necessary to overcome the restless mind. Dr. Lewis used to say, "You've got to mean business with God."

The Bible tells us, "Knock, and it shall be opened unto you." Dr. Lewis would say to that, "You gotta knock hard!"

In other words, we've got to consistently make time for our most important appointment of the day—our time with God. Our problem is we make everything else in this world more important. We think, "Let me get my life straightened out, let me get this problem solved, or this situation fixed, then my mind will be free and I can spend time with God. Then, I can meditate." And, of course, that's putting the cart before the horse. We never get our problems solved, the distractions of this world never end. We get one situation cleared up, only to be confronted by another, and before we know it, even a thought of God is gone from our consciousness, and our very good intentions are just that—intentions. And we rationalize the loss of our opportunity with, "I just had too much to do today; I'll do it tomorrow."

Christ gave us the most wonderful counsel when he said, "Seek ye *first* the kingdom of God . . . and all these things shall be added unto you."

He also said, "The kingdom of God is within." (All the great Masters have said the same thing.) And in Psalms, we find the key to experiencing that kingdom or presence: "Be still and know that I am God." That means to be still in body and mind. It is extremely difficult, if not impossible, to still the thoughts while the body is engaged in physical activity. Using the five senses will keep the mind active, and stillness becomes very illusive indeed. If, however, through specific meditation techniques we can *still* our thoughts, which alone produce worry, frustration, anxiety, and fear, and still be conscious, what is there left to be conscious of? Only unconditional love and, "the peace that passeth all understanding," which is the nature of God within each of us, for everyone is modeled after the Divine without exception, and our true nature, at the core of our being, is pure love. For some, that love is well hidden in the worries, anxieties, attachments, and material desires of this world—in other words, in the restless mind.

When Dr. Lewis was asked to describe hell, he simply said, "The restless mind." For it is the wall of restless thoughts that separate us from God. God does not hide from us; we hide from God—by choosing the creation rather than the Creator.

Meditation is such an important spiritual tool because it helps to still the mind and in that state of Divine calmness to have a personal experience of God's presence within.

One great saint said, "Of God no man can think."

"Thought can't get you there. . . ."
"Exactly! I wish I had said that."
"You did—somewhere in here; I'm sure of it."
Dennis just smiled and continued.

Now, he didn't mean that we couldn't have a theory or an idea about God. For instance, we can say God is Omniscient, Omnipresent, All in All, etc. But that idea of God doesn't satisfy our soul. As a matter of fact, by theorizing about God, we push Her away. The idea we hold of God immediately separates us from the experience of God.

What the saint was trying to tell us is that the intellect is not large enough to hold God. The intellect as part of God's creation cannot contain the Creator. He was also saying that a thought of God will not satisfy us, for *that* satisfaction we must go beyond theory. For God to have real meaning in our lives and influence our daily activity, God must be *felt*. We know God indirectly through our senses, in other words, what God has created—and that can be very enjoyable at times, but sometimes it's very painful. However, to know God directly, we must go beyond the senses, beyond the consciousness of duality, and into the unity of God's presence where there is only pure bliss, which has no opposite.

This, in most cases, will be difficult, because the mind is so restless and it will require practice to receive the benefits of deep communion with Spirit. It really is no different than most everything in life—meditation takes practice. An example would be, if we decide we're going to play the guitar, we don't just pick up the guitar and start playing it. It may come easier to some than others, but if we want to reach a high degree of excellence in whatever we decide to achieve, it requires effort, attention, commitment, and practice. And the same is true of meditation.

Don't be discouraged if at first the results of your efforts are less than you had hoped for. In my case, I had ignored God for so many years that I figured now He was ignoring me . . . and I suppose that's fair. I sometimes had the feeling that God was reserving Herself, that She wanted to make sure of my love for Her. Or maybe She wanted to find out how strong my faith was.

Sometimes, we've got to be like the crying baby that wants its mother to pick it up. The mother may put all kinds of toys and pacifiers in the crib to appease the baby, but if none of them satisfies the baby and it continues crying, eventually the mother will take it in her arms and the baby becomes quiet and is content.

So it is with Divine Mother. If we are engrossed and satisfied with the toys of this world, Divine Mother will say, "I'll wait." She always honors our choices. But if we come to the point when the playthings of this world are not enough, when we "cry" for that which the world cannot give us, then Divine Mother comes, picks us up, and cradles us in her arms of Omnipresence.

"Could you define meditation, so we can determine if we are reaching our goal—achieving success?"

As I said before, it is concentrating completely on the presence of God within.

Others have called it conscious sleep. You see, God has arranged His creation in such a way that our soul, the eternal part of us, cannot go for long without contact with its source, its grander self, which is God or Spirit. To do this without disturbing the Law of Free Will, and our power to choose, God created sleep, at which time the soul returns to God to be recharged and nourished by Spirit. This happens without the knowledge of the other two parts of our three-part being . . . the soul is aware of it, but not our mind and body.

What happens in sleep is that the life force that normally goes outward in our waking conscious state—allowing us to be conscious of the world outside of us (remember attention is the director of the life force and consciousness follows it). That life force in sleep reverses its outward thrust and goes within, and we lose consciousness of things outside of us. Now the mind and body receive some benefit from the soul's connection with God, but, sadly, they are unaware of the soul's direct communion.

The ancient sages thought if they could, through the power of their attention, *consciously* reverse the flow of life force and place it on the spiritual centers within, that they could awaken the spiritual consciousness that dwells there and have a conscious experience of the indwelling God. And that is what they did, and this is meditation. Concentrating on the presence of God within as light, sound, or love.

To achieve this (in meditation), we want to still the senses, so it helps to find a quiet place away from bright lights and noises, where the hubbub of worldly activity cannot distract us from our solitude. It is nice to have a place that is reserved for meditation, your private sanctuary. If we continually go back to that special spot, the mind will soon accept it as the place where our worldly concerns are left behind, and with each visit God's presence is more easily felt. If we routinely make it our place for meditation, the power of habit and environment will be our ally in our spiritual quest.

Hunger for God is very important to the success of our meditation. To arouse that hunger, it is very helpful to read the inspirational words of a great Master or gaze at the picture of a Holy Saint. For others, singing or chanting with sincere longing will fill the heart with love and create the urge for deep communion.

And, of course, "Gratitude is the Attitude." Be grateful for all blessings, and especially for this golden moment—this opportunity to give and receive God's love. Appreciate what God has given us—our friends, the flowers, the song of the birds, our ability to love and be loved, the life force that flows through us and sustains us, our intelligence—it all comes from the One Source. This is all very good to get us in the right psychological mindset to enter meditation, which I have personally found fills me with the love that even the sweetest music or the most fragrant rose cannot match. Know that in this sacred moment, through God's grace, you will make personal contact with God's love-filled consciousness.

Talk with God in the language of your heart, as you would to your dearest friend . . . for, indeed, She is. Withhold nothing, for He knows our every thought. Realize you are a child of God and lovingly demand your birthright, which is conscious knowledge and experience of that Divine Presence.

"Dennis, it's hard to love someone—or, in this case, an entity—that we haven't met yet."

Absolutely. You're right on. If someone sends us a million dollars, it would certainly get our attention. We would be very grateful. We could love the gift, but without personal experience of the giver, our love for him would be indirect and vague. So it is with God. Without direct experience of God's presence within us, the best we can do is love God indirectly through God's gifts. The point is, we can't love something or somebody with whom we've had no contact.

So, there is a slight dilemma . . . we can't love God if we've had no experience of Her, and we can't have the experience of Her when we don't love God. It's somewhat like my early acting days. I couldn't get a job without an agent, and I couldn't get an agent without a job.

"I'm sure many people can relate to that . . . !" I said, laughing.

That's why meditation is so important. Through definite scientific techniques, we can have that personal experience of God's presence. And as we begin to taste that, our love for God grows, and as the love grows, the experience deepens; one feeds off the other.

The consistency of making daily contact with God is very important. The example of water and a rock is a fair analogy. If we took an immense amount of water and poured it on a flat rock all at once, it would do nothing but clean the rock. But if we took the same amount of water and let it steadily drip, drip, drip on the rock, eventually it would bore a hole through the rock. It's the same with meditation. If it is consistently practiced daily with sincerity and devotion, it will eventually bore a hole through the darkness behind closed eyes and we will feel the pull of God's sweet love and see the light of Spirit.

When we sit in the silence of the Holy Vibration and feel that love, then we really know that we are directly and eternally connected to God, and that there is really no separation between us, because we are only that which we experience—that which we are conscious of. *And*, if we can be conscious of nothing but God's love, then what a sweet revelation it is to realize that God's love is our love and our love is His, and we are One in Love.

"How can we use this to better our everyday life?" I asked.

It is impossible for deep communication with God not to be helpful as we go about our daily activities. When we can saturate our consciousness with the bliss of God's presence, then it naturally overflows into outward activity. It's like suddenly putting on a pair of rose-colored glasses—everything is rosier. The car runs a little better, food tastes better, friends are friendlier, etc. Now, in reality, the car, the food, and the friends haven't significantly changed. What has? . . . Our attitude towards those people and things. And, as I've said before, attitude is the key to happiness.

When I come out of meditation and get involved in my worldly activities, if I can practice the Presence of God while executing those activities—boy, how helpful that is, because, if I keep that God consciousness on the fringe of my own consciousness, if I keep it right there on the edge of my consciousness through my daily activities, then when I go back at nighttime to feel it again, it is very close and I don't have to work so hard to connect with it. It's right there just below the surface of my thoughts.

"You say 'practicing the presence of God.' I'm confused. Does that mean you are in constant meditation, or is it like melding God's essence into our everyday thoughts and actions?" He hesitated. Off his look, I added, "Did I miss the boat?"

"No—not at all. . . ."

Practicing the presence of God just simply means that we acknowledge that we are utilizing God's power, His grace—His life force in everything that we do. If we have the attitude, "God, you're my partner in this daily activity and we're in this together. It is your life force that I'm using. It is your intelligence that I borrow from. It is your thoughts and inspiration I feel," then life becomes so much easier. If we can feel that God is working through our hands, thinking through our minds, and loving through our hearts as we go about our daily activities, oh my goodness! the day goes just so much better—so much smoother! It doesn't necessarily mean that the chaos is out of our world, but it does mean that our attitude toward the chaos is totally different. And we can manage it so much better.

It is true that our happiness depends somewhat upon outward conditions—somewhat—but basically it depends upon our "attitude" toward those conditions. And our attitude changes for the better the more we can feel the Divine Presence of God's love within us.

As we experience God (Peace, Love, Holy Vibration), we will feel more and more alive, more and more a reality that we cannot experience through the five senses. This is why we say, "God is not known through the mind, senses, or the intellect."

We have to experience God, *feel* God, and then give ourselves over to that feeling. When we get to this place, when we tap this God consciousness, out of gratitude we want to give something back to the world. We cannot feel God's love without wanting to share it. That's spiritual law. If we change ourselves, we will begin to lift the collective consciousness away from greed and fear toward love, which, in the final analysis, is the solution to all our problems.

One of my favorite prayers is: "God, fill my heart with your Divine Love and help me to give it to those with whom I come in contact." It is just so simple—because the more we give love, the more we realize that we cannot give it away! I wrote a line in a song once that went: "It may sound strange, but this I must say, to keep love ourselves, we've got to give it away." The more that we try to give it, the more that we feel it! It expands within *us*. We immediately feel it in a very real way. The more we "give it," the more we have it! It is the great irony. But of course, the opposite is also true—the more we send out hate and anger, the more we have it—the more we damage our own happiness.

We are all looking for happiness—every one of us. We are all the same in that respect. The "ego" looks around and says, "that's where my happiness lies, in those outward things of the senses, in those things that I can feel, hear, touch, and smell."

That is the "veil of ignorance" that we have to remove. That is the primary problem with the world today—it is in thinking that outside of us lies our happiness, lies the source of our fulfillment. We have talked about this before: things do not have the power to fulfill us!

I looked up at him. I was returning from an altered state of consciousness. He laughed at what must have been a very lucid expression on my face.

"It really clears things up—doesn't it?" he said.

"Yes—yes, it does," I said softly, hating to break this extraordinary moment with ordinary words.

17

Soul and Consciousness

Thus revering the soul, and learning, as the ancient said,
"It's beauty is immense", man will come to see that the
world is the perennial miracle that the soul worketh . . .
—Ralph Waldo Emerson, from *The Oversoul*

"Dennis, what do you think the soul is?"

He settled into his chair and pondered my question for
a moment. Then . . .

The soul is what we truly are. It is our real Self. It is an individualized part of Spirit that has temporarily become identified
with the body. It is the image of God within us that perfectly
reflects and holds within it all of His divine qualities—such as
unconditional Love, peace, intelligence, and harmony.

The soul is that part of our being that can never be dam-
aged, drowned, killed, burned up, or destroyed in any
way—it is constant, ongoing, without beginning or end.

241

For most people, the soul is a concept that is vague and remote. Most people have no personal experience of it. The majority of individuals feel that it is something they will turn into or understand, or be introduced to and rewarded with at the time of death. Our soul is that which we never cannot be. We can only live in ignorance of it. The highest, most precious purpose we can have in this life is to tear away the veil of ignorance which makes us think that we are this body and to allow us once again to realize that we are a soul, a spark of the Creator's one consciousness. It is in that realization that we will find true happiness, which keeps evading us in this great "soap opera" of God's—where illusion is king.

That isn't to say we can't and shouldn't relish life; we should enjoy it to the hilt. The irony is we can enjoy it more fully if we know life for what it is—God's great movie in the sky, a passing parade, and, not in it, but beyond it, is our true home of happiness. As I said before, don't take life too seriously. Don't get too deeply attached. As Lahiri Mahasaya has advised, "Live in this world, but be not of it." This is much easier done when we have daily contact with our soul, when it becomes a living reality in our lives—not just a concept, but a personal, tangible experience. Then, we can truly say we're on the path towards self-realization.

"What is self-realization—?"

I can give you no better definition than that offered by Paramahansa Yogananda: "Self-realization is the knowing on all levels of our being—body, mind, and soul—that we are now in possession of divinity and therefore need not pray that it comes to us; that we are not merely near God at all times, but His Omnipresence is our Omnipresence; and that He is just as much our essential life now as He ever will be. All we have to do is improve our knowing."

One of the great blessings of this life is the opportunity we have to improve the knowing of who and what we really are.

Of course, we are all in different states of consciousness, different levels of awareness, and we experience different degrees of realization as we consciously evolve back to God. Life is about remembering *what* and *who* we are. In other words, realizing that we are extensions or reflections of God, made in His likeness.

A true measure of our spiritual progress is the depth of bliss we feel in meditation. To the degree we feel that bliss, to that degree, we will be approaching self-realization. The easier it will be to play our part in life with courage, joy, and enthusiasm, and the less trouble we will have with attachments to the stuff of this world. We will be less prone to expect too much from a fickle world that so often pulls the rug out from under us. As we grow spiritually, we will be more apt to find fulfillment in our creative effort, rather than in the results we anticipate that our efforts will produce.

With self-realization, we will be more concerned about what we are *being*, rather than what we are *doing*. Most of the time, we get up in the morning and plan what we are going to "do" on a particular day. Although we may get done some of what we scheduled, the truth is, our best-laid plans just don't work out the way we had hoped.

Rather than getting up in the morning and asking, "What am I going to *do* today?" we should ask, "What am I going to *be* today?" What we decide to *be* is the key to change—the key to spiritual growth and self-realization.

What we decide to do may change many times during the day, depending on all kinds of unforeseen circumstances. However, no matter how the circumstances change, what we choose to *be* need not change. I'm not talking about the kind of being that requires doing to achieve that which we want to be. For instance, if we all announced that we want to be President of the United States, there would be a lot of disappointed people, for there can only be one.

However, if we all chose to be *kind*, no one need be deprived of that goal. Millions can be kind at the same time . . . and wouldn't that be wonderful? The important point here is to understand that what we *do* is a result of what we decide to *be*. If we choose to be kind, it will be impossible for us to intentionally hurt someone. That would only be possible if we changed that which we decided to be, and chose to be mean. We can always tell what we are *being* because our actions give us away every time. What we *do* is always a result of what we have chosen to *be*. The question is, can we always be that which we choose to be despite the tests with which the world will continually challenge us?

As I mentioned earlier, in 1995 I was invited to be an honorary chairperson for a newly formed event in Dallas, Texas, called "Kindness Week." I shared the honor with Rosa Parks, Martin Luther King III, and Imam W. Deen Mohammed. The Dallas Kindness Week was inspired by the movie *Schindler's List* and was an experiment to see how "what" people chose to "be" affected what they did, and how they behaved, and how *that* would affect an entire city.

The exciting thing about the week was that most of Dallas got involved, including the mayor, local television and radio stations, churches, the police department, and the public school system—200,000 students.

Billboards stating "Be Kind to Each Other" went up all over the city. Road signs saying "Be Kind" marked major intersections. Police officers handed out "Kindness Citations" to drivers and pedestrians who performed an act of kindness. Ten thousand seventh and eighth graders attended a "Kindness Rally" at Reunion Arena and listened to speakers, watched youth performers, and two area police officers rap about "kindness." Local leaders of the three Monotheist religions came together at Thanks-Giving Square and wrote a "Kindness Prayer" . . . Christians, Jews, Sikhs, Catholics, Buddhists, Baha'is, et al., attended Muslim and Hindu mosques . . . Muslims and Hindus attended Jewish and Buddhist temples, Christian and Catholic churches . . . African-American Baptists sang and prayed at all-white Baptist and Protestant churches . . . it was phenomenal. It was an event that impacted the city—and has continued to do so to this day. So what we choose to *be* has great power.

Circumstances will challenge us. Environment is an important aid to help us be what we choose. We are definitely helped or hindered by the company we keep.

Environment is stronger than willpower! If we stay in a certain environment long enough, it will affect our thoughts and attitudes. It will shape and change us. It is only common sense to seek out those environments, and especially people, who will be beneficial to us.

Even in worldly affairs, the environment is an aid in helping us to achieve our desired goals. For instance, if we want to be a musician, we should hang out with the best musicians we can. If we want to be a tennis player, lawyer, banker, or candlestick maker, we should be around the best.

I have been extremely fortunate to have had highly realized friends during my spiritual journey. Someone was always there to encourage and inspire me. And, of course, the power of numbers cannot be discounted. That is why prayer and meditation groups are so valuable. When we are in the company of people who have consistently made "contact" with God and are serious in their search, they create a very helpful environment. Their energy, commitment, and example rubs off on us, and we definitely benefit from their efforts.

༄

In 1966 my friend Gene Benveau, president of the SRF lay disciples, asked if I would speak at a Sunday service about self-realization. I really didn't feel qualified. The thought of it made me uncomfortable, so I declined. However, Gene wouldn't take "no" for an answer and countered with, "Dennis, have you been helped or benefited from the teachings of SRF? Have your meditations been rewarding?"

He had me there. I had to admit, "Well, sure, Gene, I've had some benefits—there is no question about that. I've experienced something I've never felt before. God has become more real to me. Whereas before, He was just an idea, a concept—a theory."

He smiled and gently replied, "Just tell them that. You need do nothing else."

"Okay," I had no argument. "I guess I can tell them about that."

I spoke at a small SRF group in Long Beach, California, a week later. I was so nervous that I wrote my entire talk down and delivered it word for word. I figured that was that, and I had done my duty—that my speaking was now history. But to my surprise, I was then asked to speak at the

Lake Shrine Chapel in Pacific Palisades, which is a beautiful spiritual haven with a small lake in its center. It's a very peaceful environment, and when I first walked on its grounds I felt that fuzzy, warm feeling immediately. It was wonderful, not only because of the beautiful surroundings, but also because the chapel was filled with people who were there, not for political or social reasons, but because they were on a serious quest for God. When a number of people gather for one purpose, to feel that Divine peace, then it comes like a great flood, bathing our hearts and filling us with a sweet feeling of love.

When Yogananda discovered the land in the Palisades, he brought plants from all over the world to beautify the grounds. He brought some of Gandhi's ashes from India to rest there, and had a statue of Christ erected on the top of a small hill, with a waterfall tumbling down from its base into the gardens. He put swans on the lake and placed little benches all around it where visitors could sit quietly and meditate. On those benches, key truths from the Scriptures are inscribed, such as, "Be Still and Know That I Am God" and "The Kingdom of Heaven Is Within."

Speaking of truth, it becomes real and valuable to us when we realize it through our own experience. In other words, we shouldn't accept someone else's word that "The Kingdom of Heaven is within"—what good does it do us if it remains just a concept or theory? But when we go within and still the lake of our mind and personally feel that Divine Presence and experience the love that is in it, then we truly know that the kingdom of Heaven is within us. Then we can say, "Yes, this is true! Because I experienced it." At that point, it really means something.

I spoke at the Lake Shrine once a month for seventeen

years, while Gerry played the organ. We called it our "mom and pop" church and it was one of my great blessings. It was life-changing.

It is not an organization that changes us—it is the realization of the God within us, and our ability as a child of God to tap that consciousness—that's what changes us. We can do that anywhere, whether we attend a church or not.

I'm not suggesting that we shouldn't take advantage of a church environment. I am saying, however, that it is absolutely possible to have deep communion with God whether we are in the midst of an atheistic nation—such as the former Soviet Union—or within a group meditating in a Holy temple.

Brother Lawrence, the fifteenth-century monk, said in his little book *Practicing the Presence of God*, "the time of business does not with me differ from the time of prayer. And in the noise and clutter of my kitchen, . . . I possess God in as great a tranquility as if I were on my knees at the Blessed Sacrament."

In 1985, Gerry and I went to the Soviet Union with a group called "Projects for Planetary Peace," and the feeling of God's presence never lessened there, for Spirit recognizes no man-made boundaries or political constructions. The consciousness of God is everywhere, and we cannot confine it or restrict it anymore than we can control the sunlight.

In 1974, while I was president of the Screen Actors Guild, I went to East Berlin (while it was Communist-controlled) as America's representative at the Annual International Meeting of Actors.

When we crossed over from West Berlin to East Berlin, the change in consciousness was quite obvious. The talk and manner of its people was guarded, fearful. The streets at night were totally empty. It was if everybody went into their houses or apartments and hid. However, when I meditated on my iron cot in my tiny, ill-furnished hotel room, that Divine Presence was readily available. It didn't matter where I was.

And in our daily activity, we can experience that presence just as Brother Lawrence did. Give God the credit, all the while knowing that we are a channel through which His life force and love continually flows. If we establish that partnership, it is amazing how many good things happen.

"It seems to me that each of us is playing different parts, if you will, here on Earth—the part of the lover, the hater, the murderer, the saint, the teacher, the student, the follower, the leader, etc. Do you agree, and if you do, could you elaborate?"

We *are* all playing different parts in this great drama of God's, and all of them are important. None of this would work unless all of the parts were being played well. It is like a drama on stage—each part makes the play work. It is an ongoing process, this movie of God's. With many different stories going on all at the same time, each one of us is the "star" of our particular story and a supporting actor in the story where someone else is the star. It's marvelously complicated and magnificent in its design.

Like every good drama, this movie of God's is not void of problems; otherwise, there would be no conflict and the movie would be very boring. So the problems will always be with us—how we react to those problems is a measure of who we are. If we are not pleased with who we are, we have the tools . . . free will, the power to choose, reason, intelligence, imagination, and wisdom to recreate ourselves anew . . . to select a better part to play . . . to cope with what life brings us.

The purpose of this movie or play of God's is to give us a place to grow, to expand our consciousness, to attain our full potential—to remember who we truly are.

"Now there's a question." I dared to interrupt him again. "Who do you think we are?"

Christ said, "Know ye not that ye are Gods, children of the most High?" The problem is, we don't. We may be willing to accept that intellectually—vaguely—but we don't know it experientially. If we did, the world would be a quite different place.

It's difficult for us to put ourselves in the same category with Christ simply because we have not attained the same level of consciousness that he had. However, he did clearly tell us it was possible to do so. No matter how much it might appear to the contrary, underneath all the layers of ignorance, we are " . . . Gods, children of the most High," extensions of God made in the image of the one Creator.

That doesn't mean that God looks like us physically, it means that we carry within us the essence of what God is— unconditional love. And we carry within us all the qualities of God that are extensions of, or flow from, that love.

As we are a soul that has a physical body, God is Spirit that also has a physical body. It is the entire universe, all of creation. Through our minds, hearts, feelings, and senses, we experience this world through our physical body; but we are not truly our body, nor is God truly this Universe. However, He experiences through the Universe just as we experience through our bodies. Most people believe that we are the body—that that is the "be all and end all" of everything; we're much more than that, we are a soul—an eternal part of Spirit.

When we are able to remove ourselves from the chaos of our individual "dramas" by receding into the deep stillness within and merging into Her consciousness, into that haven of peace, then the world (our "dramas") begins to lose its power to crush us. The problems roll from us like water off a duck's back. In this state, we become more sensitive to others and more understanding—more able to walk in the shoes of our friends or our "enemies." It helps us to be more understanding, more compassionate. When we are able consciously to merge in that Divine Presence, what we truly are becomes more and more apparent. We are an individualized piece of Spirit.

"Dennis, some spiritual teachings contend that life as we know it is an illusion. That's hard for us to accept because everything seems so real."

Hey, it seems real to me also, but so do our dreams at night. Let's go back to our "dreams" for a moment. Nobody can tell us they're not real as long as we're dreaming. We only realize it was nothing but a "dream" when we awaken into what we'll call *waking consciousness.* Likewise, we can only say for sure that this waking consciousness is just a dream (or illusion, as you called it) when we awaken from it. Until then, we must deal with this as the reality we perceive it to be. As Yogananda has said, "If you hit your dream head against a dream wall, you will feel a dream pain."

Now our dreams at night are easy for us to awaken from because they belong to us; we are the ones doing the dreaming. They are *our* dreams. It is very difficult to awaken from the dream we call life, because that is God's dream. If it were an easy thing to do, we would *all* wake up and this whole vibratory creation would collapse—the play would be over. But as the "Master Magician" God says, "the show must go on," because it is through the material creation and sensory experience that the Creator experiences Its knowingness, as we do also. That experience is achieved by the Creator through all that's been created, but especially through us, for we are the only species that has reached Self-consciousness. And, because of our unique brain and spinal centers, we have the ability to realize the grandest aspects of Divinity.

When we awaken at night, what happens? All the things in the dream go back into the one consciousness of the dreamer—ourselves. In other words, all things go back into the dreamer, who is then fully awake and no longer in dream consciousness.

If we want to awaken from this worldly dream—God's dream—we must do it through the same process. We must become one with the dreamer, which is God. And of course, that's what we do when we grow spiritually. We get closer to awakening as the contact with God's presence—as unconditional love—deepens.

"Is there really any hope of doing that? Waking from this dream we call life?"

All the great masters tell us it is not only possible, but that it is inevitable. Ramakrishna (a great Christ-like Master from India) said, "All will be saved." Christ, who was fully awake while still in the physical body, said, "I and my Father are One." And, of course, he also said, "These things I do, ye can also do." Yogananda said Divine Mother will eventually shake each of us awake and "every man sooner or later will have that liberating experience."

"Does that mean this whole creation will just go poof? Dissolve away?"

Yes. And then the Creator will do it all over again—for everything goes in cycles. But we don't have to worry about that happening for eons of time—that is a long, long way down the road. And of course, for each of us individually, it depends on how quickly we choose to use our free will and awaken. In other words, how soon do we truly put God first and choose the Creator over that which He has created.

"What happens to us—the individual expressions of God—when and if everything dissolves away? When and if we awaken from this illusion or dream?"

We go back to God. Then, if we choose, we again forget our Oneness with God, as we now have, and once more play another part in the next creative process.

You see, we are creative beings, and to create is an unstoppable urge within us, for that is what God is. God is the Master Creator, the Creator of creators, and we are made in that likeness. It is that urge to create that will pull us back to God's vibratory creation, for that is where the creative process takes place. It is that urge, plus our unfulfilled desires and our unfinished business.

The vibratory creation cycle can be likened to our breathing. When we exhale, we are pushing the breath out, away from its Source. Then, when we inhale, we draw it back to its Source. We can say it's expanding and contracting. God has given us a titillating clue as to how the Universe works. When God "exhales," the Universe expands. It's like the big bang theory. Scientists are telling us what the great yogi masters have said for millennia—the Universe is now expanding, and at some point God will "inhale" and draw it all back to Itself. Then it starts all over again.

Wow, I was feeling pretty small right about now—shattered into a million pieces of nonrelative matter. Question upon question came floating in and out of my mind, like the breath of God, but the only one I could latch onto was, what part does religion play in all this?

"What about religion? Where does it fit in?"

Like everything else in this world, it has its benefits and its downside. No matter how I answer your question, it's going to ruffle some feathers.

There are a thousand and one religions around the Earth, and the followers of each think theirs is the best— this is the dilemma. They believe that theirs is the true path to God. Religions tend to divide us, and that's a problem. So, I don't belong to any formalized religion.

Religions historically have utilized fear to control people and maintain power over them. Religion should have one purpose . . . to take us back to God, as unconditional Love, and thereby save us from the tremendous suffering in the world, the frustration, anxiety, and fear that overwhelms so many of us.

People join a religion for all kinds of reasons that have nothing to do with establishing a personal relationship with God. They go to church thinking that they might profit politically, financially, and socially. Now, there's nothing wrong with people advancing themselves in those ways, if that's what they choose to be, but at least let's call a spade a spade.

There's no reason to purposefully avoid the environment of religious gatherings and churchgoing if it makes us feel good in our hearts and truly brings us closer to God, for many people are helped by doing so. They are sincere people on an honest spiritual quest and receive the benefits of the original teachings from which the religions have sprung—before those teachings were distorted by human egos who used religion as a tool to serve their own interests. True seekers are usually tolerant of the religious choices of others and have realized that God, in Her infinite wisdom and omniscience, has provided countless paths back to Herself/Himself.

It is in the institution of religion where the consciousness of separation is so prevalent. If indeed there is only one Source, one Cause, one Creator, and the purpose of religion is to feel, to know, and to become one with that Creator, then there, in truth, should be only one religion, for there is only one God (Creator).

As we observe life, we see that people have different immediate goals. Each person has a different intention or desire and these desires motivate us, causing us to take certain actions. However, is there one overriding goal that is common to *all,* regardless of race, color, religion, or social status? One grand desire that we all share? One to which all our lesser goals lead? If there is, it would seem that this goal of goals would be worthy of our devotion and worship.

Now, at first glance, there may appear to be no such thing. But let's take a closer look. We all want to exist. The thought of not *being* is repugnant to us. If we existed without being conscious of that existence, that certainly wouldn't satisfy us. We all want to exist and be conscious of it. If we attain conscious existence (which anyone reading these words has) and it is filled with pain and torment, that certainly wouldn't be anybody's goal. So we want that conscious existence to be happy and blissful, and we don't want it to come and go. We want it forever. Therefore, the goal, to which all other goals are subordinate, is attaining Ever-Existing Conscious Bliss. That's as close as the human mind can come to defining God, the goal of all goals.

"And this is attainable, right?"

The masters say it is. And it is what we are *all* seeking, consciously or unconsciously.

Some may protest and say, "That is not so. I don't really care about myself. I just want to make others happy. I want to serve." Or someone might say, "I just want to be a successful lawyer or doctor," or, "I want power and position," or, "I just want to make money," or, "I just want to find the person who raped my daughter and kill him!"

Now, if the persons who have stated their objectives were asked *why* they want to achieve those goals, they may have many initial reasons. But after each answer, if they are again asked why, they will eventually wind up with the same final answer . . . "because it makes me feel good; it makes me happy."

If they are then asked, "why do you want to be happy?" they're stumped. The answer is simply, "just because I want to be happy, stupid, like everybody else." There is no answer beyond, "I want to be happy." That is the end of the line, for happiness is the native condition of our soul (what we truly are), and the soul will be completely content and will rest peacefully when it experiences that sublime happiness from which it came. When our soul feels that, only one overriding desire remains, and that is . . . to please God, who has gracefully given us such fulfillment. And of course, when we speak of pleasing God, we include all the zillion extensions of God that It has created.

So we can say that we take all our actions, either consciously or unconsciously, to ultimately reach that state of supreme happiness. In that sense, we do *all* things in an effort to please *ourselves*. We are all self-motivated. The problem is we are, for the most part, looking for ways to please the little self, not realizing that we are part of the larger Self, and that our own happiness must include the happiness of others.

Therefore, in our effort to satisfy the little self, we often make grave mistakes and choose those things we feel will bring us pleasure, and in the short term they might give us quick gratification, but over the long haul, bring us great pain and regret. Whether what we choose brings to us pleasure or pain, it is important to realize that in both instances the intention was the same—to attain happiness.

"What is a guru, and is it beneficial for us to follow one?"

A guru is a very special incarnation. He or she is fully realized. They have torn away the veil of ignorance and have completely realized their oneness with God and all His

257

creation. They have chosen to reincarnate for one reason, and that is to bring those of us still identified with the body and living in delusion back to God. To help us remember once again what and who we truly are. A guru has one desire, one mission, and that is to awaken us, to liberate us, and to unite us with eternal Spirit—to bring us to that supreme state of happiness.

A guru serves as a bridge to take us from ego, or bodily consciousness, to God consciousness. They are drawn to us through the power of love, when our hearts are right, when we truly feel in the deepest part of our being a yearning for that which the world cannot give us. Sometimes we come to that point through the pain of this world. At those times, we should recognize that pain as a loving prod from God to come home—to remember. Sometimes it comes to us because we have tried everything in this world and have become saturated with its pleasures and all its toys and still feel an emptiness in our hearts. We then cry out for that which the deepest part of us inherently knows has eluded us.

The guru is a physical incarnation of God. Although God speaks to us in many ways—books, friends, songs, motion pictures, nature, etc.—in the state of consciousness we're in, we often don't listen very well. Sometimes we need to get the message the conventional way—through a physical form, vocally. So in God's great love for us, She takes on a physical form, comes down to our level in order to speak to us in a body so that Her directions cannot be misunderstood—to guide us out of the delusion and back to our home in Spirit, back to the remembrance of who we are.

"But aren't we all incarnations of God?"

We are, but the point is (and I've gone here several times), we don't know that we are. We're asleep as to our *true* self. We're ignorant of our relationship with God. We think we are separated. It is only when we're fully awakened that we will realize totally and completely that we are indeed incarnations of God. In that consciousness, we will realize our oneness, not only with God, but with all It has created, including each other.

So a true guru is very special. We can have many teachers and guides, but an authentic guru is not found so easily. It takes earnest and sincere craving, and then, when the devotee is ready, the Master appears.

I'm reminded of a story that might help illustrate the answer to your question. It's the story of the young prince who lived his entire life sheltered inside the walls of his father's magnificent palace. His every wish was satisfied by a host of servants who were at his beck and call.

One day, he said to himself, "I wonder what life is like outside the palace walls?" The thought intrigued him and his curiosity grew so strong that one night he donned his finest garments, filled his pockets with plenty of cash, and ventured forth to see for himself what lay beyond.

As he was walking down a dark alley, he was spotted by two muggers who couldn't believe their good fortune. They hadn't encountered such a choice prospect in many a moon, whereupon they knocked the prince unconscious, stripped him of his fine clothing and money, and left him in rags.

When the prince awakened, a strange thing had happened—the blow to his head had scrambled his brain. He couldn't remember who he was or any particulars of his past. He was suffering from total amnesia.

He looked at his skimpy clothes and, noticing that he was penniless, concluded that he was a beggar and spent the next few years begging for alms.

Then one day a miraculous thing happened. He tripped and fell and hit his head on a very hard rock. The blow immediately cured him of his amnesia, and to all those within earshot he joyfully proclaimed, "My God, I'm a prince and didn't know it! I've been living the erroneous thought that I'm a beggar," whereupon he returned to the palace and into the loving arms of his mother and father, and there was great joy in the kingdom.

There is great joy in the kingdom of God also when we remember who we are and return to our eternal home— realizing that we are forever one with God. Until then, we are living with spiritual amnesia.

"That really keeps an otherwise complicated point very simple," I said. Still troubled by the "guru" issue, I ventured to return to that subject. "Dennis, going back to the guru— does he or she have to be living in the physical body to help us? In other words, can we follow a Master who is residing on the other side?"

A guru never "dies." That is also true of all of us. The difference is, the guru knows it and we don't. However, I know that is not the answer you were looking for and I do understand the thrust of your question.

No. A guru does not have to occupy a physical body. St. Francis's guru, for example, was Jesus the Christ, who walked the Earth many centuries before St. Francis. However, in most cases, it helps. It's very powerful to be in the presence of a God-realized being. Most people don't possess the intense love and devotion that St. Francis had, in which case a guru in the physical body is practical.

"Do the close disciples of a guru have the ability to pass on the guru's teachings and wipe away the veil of ignorance that you spoke of, for true seekers?"

The closer the disciple is to the guru, the better the chance for that to happen. Understand, there is nothing impossible with God, but usually the problem is, truth is passed from one disciple to the next, the egos get involved, and over time the original truth becomes distorted. We can liken it to a light. The farther we go away from it, the dimmer it gets. This is true of all the great masters who have come to shed God's eternal light of truth on the world. So when the spiritual light grows dim, God, in His infinite love for us, sends another until we finally get it.

Yogananda understood this process and tried to create a buffer against it by leaving written lessons containing specific yoga techniques and daily living and meditation instructions. The lessons are available to any sincere person on a spiritual quest.

The closest living disciple of Yogananda's is Sri Daya Mata, who met him as a teenager and became a loyal disciple when she was seventeen years old. For many years, she acted as his secretary, preserving his early lectures by shorthand. With Yogananda's passing in 1952, her duties became greater, and by 1955 she became the spiritual head of the Self-Realization Fellowship. For the past forty-five years, by her example of loyalty and devotion, she has been an inspiration and living example for hundreds of thousands of devotees around the globe, keeping the flame of Yogananda's spiritual legacy burning brightly.

"It seems to me that in the West we have developed a misunderstanding of Yoga—like we get only a part of it. Can you help out here?"

The word "yoga" comes from the same root as the word "yoke" and simply means union of the soul with Spirit or God. Of course, there are different types of yoga to suit the different individuals and their personalities. One type of yoga might be suitable for one person, while another may be more attractive to someone else. But the one that is specifically designed to liberate us—freeing us from attachments to this world and identification with the body—is the ancient science of Kriya Yoga.

18

Death, Karma, and Reincarnation

I once saw a documentary based on the life of a tribe living on a remote section of an island in the South Pacific. What left an indelible impression on me was the way they treated what we call "death." They celebrated it. It was the crowning reward for a life well lived and which now had gained freedom from the "slings and arrows" of this world. What they prayed hard for was the newborn they knew would now have to face the trials and tribulations of this world while caged in the body. They had it right.

Death is a fiction, something we've made up trying to explain a phase of life we don't understand. Many of the mysteries of life can be explained if we study dream consciousness, so let's go back to it. . . .

In our dream state, we lose awareness of our body and the people and circumstances that are familiar to us in our waking conscious state. But we don't lose consciousness in the dream. We know this, because when we wake we can say we dreamed this or that and we thus determine whether the dream was positive or negative. If we lost consciousness, we would know nothing of the dream.

As we've stated before, God created sleep in order for the soul to return to its Source and get recharged. Now there comes a time in the lives of all when the small recharges of nightly sleep are not enough for God or our Soul, and so God created death . . . or the "big sleep." And, as in the small sleep, we don't lose consciousness here either.

If we as adults have a day in which we are unkind to others, hurtful, and just plain mean, or our mind is filled with worry, fear, guilt, or shame, that consciousness will sooner or later show up in our sleep as a bad dream. Our sleep will not be satisfying. If our day is filled with violence, murder, or in any way brings great pain to others, our dream could become a nightmare.

Going into the big sleep is a very similar situation. I have come to understand that if we have lived a life that is basically kind and loving, a life of service to others, then that is basically what we will experience on the other side. Especially if, through a personal contact with the Divine Consciousness within us, we have lifted our consciousness above the "ego" and felt the unconditional love of God at will—our transition will be quite pleasant and awake, and filled with a sense of freedom and love.

When we "die," we take our consciousness—the one we have established on Earth—with us. It is neither elevated nor diminished with "death." In other words, we are not rewarded or penalized just because we "die." What we feel there, we will have earned here.

There are many planes of existence on the other side and God has more options than heaven or hell. God doesn't keep a scorecard, add it up at the end of each life, and say, "You just barely made it into heaven, son, and you . . . well, sorry to say it, but you scored a 64. Now, a 65 would have opened the pearly gates for you, but since you were short one point, it's to hell with you!"

"In my Father's house are many mansions," Jesus said (John 14:1–2). And we will go to one of them. Which one, depends on the consciousness we've attained while playing our part in this life. So it behooves us to make a sincere effort now, to be kind, considerate, and compassionate. To lift our consciousness above the ego and experience God as Love. It will serve us in the greatest way in the big sleep. As the Masters tell us, the law of cause and effect doesn't stop because we die.

And as we have the power to choose here, so we have it there. And if we have created a life here that isn't serving us, we have the power, by virtue of our free will, to undo it and recreate it. We have the power to choose again. The same is true on the other side—it's still our choice!

God in Her great love for us will never stop giving us another chance to come home to Her. It's up to us how long we want to feel the stings of separation by making choices that divorce us from Her love and comfort. For only in God will we find the lasting fulfillment that continually escapes us in the passing things of this world.

We are fearful of death because we are *taught* to be fearful of it. If we could experience it while still in the body, like the example I used of St. Paul (in the chapter "Journey into Spirit"), all fear would leave us. For most of us, in the state of consciousness we are in, this ability is beyond us. But remember what Jesus said, "He who believeth on me, the works that I do shall he do also; and greater works than these shall he do" (John 14:12). In other words, what Jesus is saying, is these things I do you can also do. St. Paul proved it. And we can, too. Of course, it is most easily achieved through deep meditation. The deeper we go, the quieter and slower the breath becomes, and the quieter it gets, the more we penetrate the stillness, the closer we get to "consciously dying"—and the more we feel the great joy of Christ consciousness.

Death is nothing to be feared any more than going to sleep at night is to be feared. For many, it is a joyous and uplifting experience.

Back in the late sixties, my friend Milburn Stone—who played Doc Adams on *Gunsmoke*—related to me an unusual experience he had during heart bypass surgery. He told me that while they were operating on him, he became aware of leaving his body. He actually watched the operation from above it. At one point during the procedure, he began entering a great tunnel of light, which he described as incredibly exhilarating and fulfilling.

His consciousness eventually returned to his body, and the operation was pronounced a success by his team of doctors. Milburn later went back to *Gunsmoke*, but that experience was life-changing for him. He told me that he no longer feared death, but welcomed it, for he knew through his own experience what was waiting for him.

Life should be lived, in a way, that prepares us for the time that we leave this physical form behind. If we have lived a life filled with endless worldly desires, strong attachments to material things, hate, prejudice, greed, and fear, we may spend our astral journey in one of God's "mansions" that isn't very pleasant.

"Okay, I'm going to ask the obvious question here. How do we prepare for death?"

Well, we don't expunge endless worldly desires and strong attachments by denying them. Not by resisting them either, but by replacing them with that which satisfies us in a greater way—the all-fulfilling power of God's love experienced in deep meditation. It will sever the pull of the world and free the soul for its inevitable journey back to God.

Know this above all else, that *no one*, no matter what state of consciousness they might be in when "death" comes, *no one* is eternally lost. Everything is, and always will be, contained in God's one consciousness. We can never be separated from it, any more than the character in the dream can be separated from the dreamer, or the thought can be separated from the thinker. By our strong attachment to the things of this world, we can live in the delusion that we are separated, but it is *only* a delusion. And that delusion must be destroyed, if we are to attain final liberation from the fears and uncertainties of this ego consciousness and return to God. Yogananda puts it more clearly: "To surmount *maya* (cosmic delusion), . . . to rise above the duality of creation and perceive the unity of the Creator, was conceived of as man's highest goal. Those who cling to the cosmic illusion must accept its essential law of polarity—ebb and flow, rise and fall, day and night, pleasure and pain, good and evil, birth and death. This cyclic pattern assumes a certain anguishing monotony after man has gone through a few thousand human births; he begins to cast a hopeful eye beyond the compulsions of maya."

I hesitated, my mind spinning. I gathered my thoughts and asked, "Dennis, can we discuss reincarnation?"

To discuss reincarnation, it is necessary to make three assumptions: (1) that there is an initial cause, a Creator, and that that Creator is a God of Love; (2) for every action, there is an equal and opposite reaction—the law of cause and effect (Karma) is operating in this world; and (3) we have free will.

Reincarnation, and the law of Karma, are correlative doctrines—neither is plausible without the other, and neither can stand alone.

When we observe the world around us, it appears to be filled with inequities. Without the law of reincarnation, it is impossible to accept God as loving and just. Why are some born with a silver spoon in their mouth, while others suffer abject poverty, some mentally handicapped, and others are intellectual geniuses? Why are some born with weak bodies, while some are extremely powerful—natural-born athletes? We see people that lead exemplary lives, kind and highly moral individuals that have nothing but trouble. We've all dealt with experiences we didn't think we deserved and cried out, "why me, Lord, why me?" And, of course, the opposite is true, also. There are those who lead mean and contemptible lives who draw to themselves an endless stream of material wealth, and we wonder, "why them?" Both cases are befuddling.

We see the effects, but the causes are a mystery, unless we consider they were created in a previous life.

An impartial and loving God could never give one of His children an advantage over another. We are what we are, as the result of our own choices and actions!

One lifetime is not enough to satisfy or complete the *effects* generated by the *causes* we lay up. Inexplicable circumstances become understandable when we realize the cause that produced the effect happened in a previous life.

The law of reincarnation is an inspiring concept and gives us great hope. It helps us to understand that if we will plant the seeds of good actions, they are bound to bear fruit—if not in this life, then in the next.

When the soul enters the body, it forgets its true nature of oneness with Spirit and is intuitively trying to remember, or return to, that state of perfection. It has sunk so low in ego consciousness, has become so encumbered with the barnacles of material desires and worldly attachments, that it can't achieve that goal of goals in one lifetime. It's a process—a journey. Reincarnation allows us time necessary to work out our imperfections and free ourselves from bondage to this dualistic turmoil.

"One of the big arguments against the doctrine of reincarnation is that people don't remember their past lives," I said.

That's a very weak argument. For heaven's sake, I can hardly remember what I did last Wednesday, and I certainly can't remember what I did at age nine months. Not to remember past lives is one of the greatest blessings God has bestowed upon us. We've all accepted all kinds of roles in this grand play of God's, and, as we say in the movie business, some of the parts we've played are forgettable. To remember them would fill us with such guilt and shame, and so depress us, that life would become a drudgery, continually tormented by the remembrance of wasted opportunities.

And so God, in Her wisdom, dulls our memory of past lives, wipes our slate clean, and says, "Here's another chance; see if you can get it right this time." It reminds me of the advice Swami Sri Yukteswar gave to a young student: "Forget the past; the vanished lives of all men are dark with many shames. Human conduct is ever unreliable until anchored in the Divine. Everything in the future will improve if you are making a spiritual effort now."

Over half the world's population believes in the doctrine of reincarnation. And so did the Christian church, until it was declared heresy by the Second Council of Constantinople in 553 A.D. The church reasoned that, if people felt that they had endless opportunities to be saved, they would not make sufficient effort in their present life to gain salvation. And so the priests sent out a very fearful message: "You've got one chance, and you'd better seize it now or your sins will drive you straight to the everlasting fires of Hell." But it's a dangerous thing to try to adjust truth. In many cases, people felt it was an impossible task to be washed clean of their "sins" in the forty to sixty years they had to live, so their attitude became, "since I'm going to Hell anyway, I'm going to live it up while I'm here"—and they recklessly indulged themselves in a plethora of "sins."

"Ah, yes—I remember reading about that in Edgar Cayce's book on reincarnation. Were all references to reincarnation struck from the Bible?"

We can still find indirect references to it. The next-to-the-last verse in the Old Testament promises, "Behold, I will send you Elijah the Prophet before the coming of the great and dreadful day of the Lord." In the New Testament, the spelling of Elijah was changed to Elias by the Greek translators.

In Matthew 17:5, it reads, referring to Jesus, "Behold, a voice out of the cloud, which said, 'this is my BeLoved Son (Jesus) in whom I am well pleased; hear ye him.'" But the disciples were confused, for in the Book of Malachi it was promised that Elijah (Elias) was to come first and announce the arrival of the fully realized Son of God, Jesus, where-upon, in 17:12, Jesus assured them, "But I say unto you that Elias (Elijah) is come already, and they (the scribes) knew him not." In 17:13, "Then the disciples understood that he spake unto them of John the Baptist." It's clear, there was no doubt in the mind of Jesus, that John the Baptist was an incarnation of Elijah.

Some will ask, if reincarnation was an accepted doctrine in biblical days, why isn't there a more obvious mention of it? Because it was an accepted axiom. No one questioned it. There was no debate surrounding it until much later. Of course, religions are malleable. Historically, they have molded their tenets to satisfy political, economical, and social pressures. Otherwise, it would still be a sin to eat meat on Friday.

Reincarnation is a blessed law. Because of it, we have the opportunity and the time to finally cleanse ourselves of the attachments and worldly desires that we have *willingly* acquired, which keep us imbedded in this worldly consciousness—with all its worries and fears. We can then enjoy the beauty and freedom of one of God's grander "mansions" as we climb the ladder of consciousness back to our eternal home in Spirit.

"That was beautifully said, Dennis—thank you. Could you address the subject of Karma, as you understand it?"

Karma is a much used word these days and one that is often misunderstood. It is the result of our actions. And actions are the result of the influence of environments, habits, desires, and tendencies acquired in this life, or brought over from previous lives.

Because we often utilize our free will in a way that doesn't serve us, our actions create many undesirable and sometimes painful results. However, it is important for us to understand that our free will is also a tool by which we can design or redesign our lives.

Through the use of our free will, our actions are continuously changing, and thus our karma is always changing. It is not static. It is not set in concrete. St. Paul is a perfect example of how the worst actions can be overcome by replacing them with good actions. He was a murderer, who became a Saint.

An experiment with blue paint may throw some light on the subject. Let's assume that blue paint represents our present "bad karma." The paint will stay blue until we take an action to change it. If we begin to add yellow paint (good actions) to it, it immediately begins to change. If we continue adding yellow, it will become green. And if we add enough yellow, the paint will change its character completely. It will become yellow. Practically every trace of its former blue self will be gone. We can live with our hurtful karma and suffer the consequences, or we can use our innate wisdom guided by our conscience and begin to change.

If I'm crossing a street, and all of a sudden I hear a loud, piercing horn and spin around to find a huge Mack truck barreling down on me, I have a choice. I can throw up my hands and say, "It's my karma" and immediately depart the body, or I can say, "Legs, don't fail me now!" and get out of the way.

Too many people equate karma with fate, and there is no such thing. For every effect, there is a cause; for every result, there is a reason. By the exercise of our free will and the actions we take, we create our karma. By the exercise of our free will and the actions we take, we can change it.

It's hard to understand the anguish we sometimes have to endure. And to be told that there are no accidents, and that whatever we are suffering is the result of our own actions, seems absolutely preposterous. We say, "Why in the world would I bring this pain on myself? And where, or what, is the cause of it?"

We have to look to karma's corollary, reincarnation, for an acceptable answer. The cause is often hidden from us in the desires and actions taken in previous lives. We can understand that the law "as ye sow, so shall ye reap" exists and seems fair. But until we are fully realized, and at one with the Creator, that which triggers the effect we are experiencing will forever be concealed in the maze of countless previous thoughts, desires, and actions that we have long since forgotten. We can't connect the effect with the cause, and so we've created a convenient and acceptable answer. We say it was just "luck"—good or bad.

"Okay, so what happens when all the individual souls *think* and *act* like a group together—as one?"

We are not always directly responsible for everything that happens to us, for in this world—there is "collective consciousness" that creates mass karma, which is a strong force in our lives. The collective consciousness is made up of the accumulation of the individual consciousnesses in a certain group—be it a neighborhood, state, nation, or world. So, by our thoughts and actions, we contribute to the mass consciousness with which we have to contend. The collective can have a beneficial or detrimental effect on us, depending on the character, or state of consciousness, the group has attained. It is very wise to seek out the group or mass consciousness that will be of benefit to us.

One of the greatest aids in creating good karma is the company we keep. Our associates and friends are the single, strongest environmental force in our lives. How many times have we heard, "His problem was, he just started running with the wrong crowd?"

We are all subject to the power of the environment in which we live. It is stronger than will power. The environment in which we stay will eventually mold us to its likeness. Only a Master is strong enough to withstand it. Only a Master can change *it*, rather than having it change *him*.

The law of cause and effect is operating in our lives, and it can be a blessing or a curse—for we are in charge of the law and it need not be our cross to bear.

The level of the world's collective consciousness is very low. As we observe it today, it is filled with hate, greed, and fear. And as a result, injustice and horror are seen throughout our society. Because we don't understand our connectedness, we cannot accept our oneness with each other. *Competition* is the energy which drives our social affairs, rather than the more efficient energy of *cooperation*. And we are still bent on settling our differences by force and violence rather than by common sense, law, and negotiation.

"Dennis, some people feel that their mistakes or sins are too great and that they can never be forgiven—or worse, they are doomed to be forever separate from God."

We can never collect enough "sins" so that we will forever be separated from God—as a matter of fact, we are never separated; we just think we are. However, this knowledge should not encourage us to fritter away our time in frivolous pursuits that keep us from our greatest good, that keep us anchored to this sea of life that alternately tosses us about on its waves of pleasure and pain. It should inspire us to use the tools that God has given us to escape the chaos of this world. We don't have to leave the body to do that. With enough deep meditation and God communion, it can be done while playing our part on the present world stage. We can reach that state of consciousness in which we can live in this world but be not of it. We can live free from its pain-producing attachments and expectations. It's really our choice. The truth is, we are our own saviors. It is not God that punishes or rewards us—we punish or reward ourselves.

"That makes a great deal of sense. Could you define the word 'sin' as you have come to understand it?"

It is rather silly to make a laundry list of what is a sin in the eyes of humans. As the need and perception of society changes, the laundry list will change. Many of the sins of the Victorian Age would no longer qualify. And, in cultures around the Earth, the lists will vary greatly. So, what is a sin? This answer satisfies my heart: anything that isolates me from my greatest good . . . anything that destroys, interrupts, or derails my spiritual journey. In other words, anything that separates me from God. For in the Holy Consciousness of God, there is only perfection. There can be no "sin."

With this as a yardstick to measure sin, it takes deep introspection and self-analysis to be honest with ourselves and determine the sins we have established. Is there something creating great restlessness and emotional upheaval in our lives? Then perhaps we should question our choices. Is the world taking away our peace and supplanting it with a sense of emptiness? Are we quick to anger? Does forgiveness come with great difficulty? Is jealousy and possessiveness normal to us? Are we deeply attached and dependent upon material things for our happiness? Perhaps we should examine our choices and priorities, for they all can separate us from God. Through introspection and self-analysis, each of us can make our own list of "sins," and, of course, what separates all of us from God consciousness is the failure to make personal contact with His Divine Presence. Lahiri Mahasaya, a great saint, has advised us to "solve all (our) problems with meditation."

"This seems like an over simplification. . . ."

Well, I think, coming from a saint that gained cosmic consciousness, reached the breathless state, and made a conscious exit from the body, it deserves a closer look.

"Okay—fair enough," I said, feeling suddenly very humble. "Please, go on."

Lahiri Mahasaya was not referring to sporadic meditation, where restlessness still fills our consciousness and the contact with God is minimal. He was talking about meditation in which we can direct our full concentration on the Divine and totally merge in Its all-fulfilling love—becoming one with it. In that state, all worldly desires recede from our consciousness and dissolve into the great sea of bliss—fading into the nothingness from which they came. And in that state, there are no worries, frustrations, anxieties, or fears. Those emotions cannot remain in God's presence any more than oil can stay in the same space with water.

"How does that kind of meditation solve our problems?"

Well, obviously they are solved while we are in that state, for they are no longer in our consciousness, and we are only what we are conscious of.

"I don't mean to be dense, but how does that experience solve our problems when we return to the world? When we again have to play our parts in this drama?"

First of all, having that experience allows us to take this world with a grain of salt. We now know that there is a haven of peace right within us that is always accessible to us . . . that there is a reality and fulfillment greater than that which the world has to offer, and we naturally don't take this world so seriously. That alone is a great aid in solving our daily problems, for the calmness it generates allows us to think better and make more sensible choices. With that experience, we are not so concerned about the little self, but are more willing to serve the bigger Self—for we cannot feel God's love without wanting to give it to others. That is spiritual law. And the more we give, the more we receive. It is like a yo-yo—throw it out, and it comes back to us.

I'm not trying to say that, with that experience, the problems of this world will completely disappear. They won't. As long as we breathe the air of this Earth, we will experience the duality of its nature. However, with deep God communion, we will react to those dualities—the pleasure and pain, the victories and defeats—in a more serene and less disturbed way, all the while knowing that they are only a part of a passing show and, not in them, but beyond them, is our true home of happiness.

To go into that sweet stillness and feel the peace that passeth all understanding—the Comforter of which Jesus spoke—filling us with great faith. And it is that faith that will give us the strength to pass the tests of this life and solve the worldly problems that will always find their way into our daily activities.

"Tell me how friendship plays into all of this. Can we talk about this relationship?"

True friendship is the sweetest of all relationships. It is the most constructive and happiness-producing. In real friendship, there is no possessiveness, nor sense of ownership. In true friendship, there is a mutual desire between two friends to help each other attain freedom and reach true happiness.

Friendship is a special energy or consciousness that God has placed in this world to draw us back to Him, and to once again realize, in a concrete and personal way, our connectedness with others. Friendship begins to tear down the walls that divide and separate us. It makes us realize our closeness with each other and God.

Friendship is based on mutual usefulness. Now, there's a vast difference between usefulness and being used. If either person, in the relationship, feels they are being used, it will bring doubt, suspicion, and resentment between them—poisoning any friendship. We are always attracted to those who help us and are useful to us. We feel safe with them and want to hang out with them. So it follows, if we want friends that are useful, our friends will want the same from us. It's a matter of give-and-take.

If we have a strong attachment to a single friend, excluding all others, the law or purpose of friendship is not working as the Creator intended, and it will curb the development of Divine Friendship. We should look upon everyone as a potential friend and offer our friendship to all those who cross our path. If that offer is rejected—and since we are still struggling with ego-consciousness, it may be hurtful—the best thing we can do is, do as Divine Mother does when we reject Her offer; say as She does, "I give you my love and wait for you to change." This can be very difficult, of course, because our love is not yet purified, not yet unconditional. However, it certainly presents us with a grand opportunity.

Giving our love doesn't mean that we become a doormat for someone to walk on. But sometimes it serves us and the other person to hiss a little, like a snake that never bites, always with calmness and love supporting the hiss. For a while, at least, it's probably sensible to direct our friendship to someone else.

Prejudice and bigotry stunts the development of friendship. These ideas curtail its natural urge to grow—to make the circle of friendship larger—and therefore, they violate God's law of friendship. We should realize that the same life force that flows through us, flows through everything and everybody in this creation, and that everything has a purpose in the cosmic design. How ignorant it is, of any of us, to hate another person, or hold a judgment against another person, just because they are outwardly different by race, color, religion, age, sex, character, etc. We are in no position to judge the journey or purpose of another soul. We don't know what has brought that soul to this particular moment in time, or the particular part it is playing right now, which is necessary to complete its pilgrimage back to the Creator. With our limited intelligence, the deep mysteries of the universe will forever remain unfathomable. Of course, that is why Christ said, "As ye judge, so shall ye be likewise judged."

We've all heard the expression, "flattery will get you no place." It certainly won't create a lasting friendship, for a relationship that is built on hypocrisy is likely to crumble. We shouldn't support a friend who is indulging in an activity that is destructive. If we do, we are not being useful, and therefore, are not a true friend, but a pseudo friend. We shouldn't agree—when we feel in our heart that our friend is wrong—just to gain favor. This is so tempting to do, for we are all looking for acceptance. However, in the long run, it will weaken the bond of friendship, whereas honesty, openness, service, and sincerity are the ties that bind us together in lasting friendship.

Spirit is continually drawing us back to Itself, and that effort is most strongly supported through the energy that manifests as friendship.

Remember friendliness attracts friendliness. What we give we receive. Yogananda says:

The sun shines equally on diamond and charcoal, but the former has developed qualities that enable it to reflect the sunlight brilliantly, while the latter is unable to reflect the sunlight. Emulate the diamond in your dealings with people. Brightly reflect the light of God's Love.

If we can do that, we will never be without true friends. The greatest, most dependable and loving friend we can possibly have is God, who dwells in the stillness within our own consciousness. If we can develop that friendship now, when this grand mortal movie is over, and earthly friends have left us, that Eternal Friend will be there to help us merge into His eternal joy of light and love.

"A lot of spiritual books I've read talk about our habits being greatly responsible for keeping us in ignorance. Could you explain this idea?"

He chuckled softly. "I'll give it my best shot."

At least 90 percent of what we do, we do because we've done it before. We've often been accused of following in the ruts that other people have made, but what is closer to the truth is that we follow in the ruts that we ourselves have made. And the more we go down those ruts, the more we repeat the specific actions; the deeper the ruts get, the more difficult it is to get out of them.

Have you ever noticed how many people are in a rut? I've been in a few of them myself. We are creatures of *habit*. But, like most everything else in this world, habit has two sides—good and bad. Hopefully, we will, through wisdom and our God-given common sense, throw out the bad ones and keep the good ones. As a matter of fact, if the law of habit wasn't available to us, life would be a drudgery—it would simply be nonworkable. Imagine getting up each morning and having to learn how to walk or tie our shoes again, or learn to read, or drive a car. We'd never make it to the office—as a matter of fact, there would be no office! So, the law of habit allows us to function in this world. It is a real blessing. However, the law can be abused, and then it becomes a curse. The law simply works. We are the ones who trigger it and set it into motion.

What is a habit? According to Webster, the definition is: "A thing done often and hence done easily." To me, it's a mechanism, inherent within each of us, that allows us to function in this world more efficiently, saving both time and energy.

The important thing for us to understand is that, by the actions we take, we establish habits. It therefore behooves us to monitor our actions closely, realizing that any initial action is a candidate to become a habit. For some people, it only takes a few repetitions of an action to lock in a habit, and then our free will—our power to choose—is gone. Of course, how quickly an action becomes habitual depends on the tendencies we bring over from our last incarnation. There are those who have become alcoholics with just two or three drinks.

Once the habit is ingrained within us, it is very hard to shake. The best way to get rid of a bad habit is to replace it with a good one.

I started smoking when I was nineteen years old, for two reasons. Number one, I knew I wanted to be an actor and every actor on the screen at that time—from Humphrey Bogart to Gary Cooper, even Bette Davis— smoked. I just figured, if I was going to be an actor, I had to learn. I know, I know, it was a rationalization. The other reason was the Naval Air Corps. Talk about the power of environment! It was about as powerful as it could get. If you didn't smoke, booze, and party, you got thrown out. It wasn't long until the habit was in full bloom.

After the war, when I enrolled in college and became a track athlete, I realized, if I was going to do my best, I had to give up cigarettes. So I made a conscious effort to stop. And you might say I was fairly successful. I cut down—way down—to one cigarette a day. But I never "cut the cord" completely. I always had that one cigarette just before going to bed. My thinking process went like this: "I've been very good. I haven't had a single cigarette all day. I should now be rewarded with one for my good effort. After all, I'm going to bed, and it won't be possible to have another before I go to sleep, and one is certainly not going to hurt me."

What I failed to realize was that I was keeping the smoking habit alive by that one cigarette. The habit was still lurking in my subconsciousness, ready to show its ugly face at the earliest opportunity. After track season was over, I went from one a day, to two, to three, to four, and by the time track season came around again, I was up to almost a full pack.

The desire to quit was really not strong enough. In the back of my mind, I knew I was not ready to stop. The commitment was just not there.

When I got to New York City, right after the final tryouts for the Olympics in 1948, smoking was ubiquitous. The environment was too strong to withstand, and I willingly succumbed to it, in an effort to belong.

Now, let's fast-forward to 1956. It was my second year on *Gunsmoke,* and we were filming out at Gene Autry's

Melody Ranch in Newhall, California. I was in between shots, and passing the time playing a friendly game of Pitch with a few of the stuntmen, when I began to cough. I was smoking at the time, and I hacked up phlegm that was mostly black cigarette tar. I thought to myself, am I stupid? Here I have a potentially long-running career as an actor ahead of me, and I'm in the process of jeopardizing it by ruining my throat and voice. It was the first time I really was disgusted enough with myself to commit to quitting. I immediately stood up, flipped the cigarette I was smoking as far as I could fling it, and announced to all those within earshot that that was my last cigarette. It gives strength to our convictions if we let others know what they are, if we publicly announce them.

Sometimes Providence steps in and gives us a helping hand, also. That is, if we really mean business. Be that as it may, in this case, I got some help. An old cowboy doing extra work happened to be on the set that day. He was standing nearby, idly playing with a short piece of rope with a monkey's paw knot tied on the end of it. He would flip the rope and make a knot in it, using just one hand. I walked over to him and said, "Whoa, how did you do that?" Without any words, he just did it again. I was totally intrigued, and asked, "Can you teach me to do that?" He said, "Maybe."

I was an attentive student until they called me for my next shot. Normally, after the completion of a scene, I would reach for my reward—for a job well done—a cigarette. This time, however, I hurried over to the old cowboy for another lesson with the rope trick. My mind was so focused on it that when the first assistant called me in for my next scene, I suddenly realized I hadn't had a smoke in between shots. For the rest of the day, I followed the same routine, and when the assistant director said, "It's a wrap" at the end of the day, I still hadn't had a cigarette. I quickly realized the importance of creating another habit to replace the one that I wanted to get rid of. I also understood how important it was to not have idle hands, and to keep the mind focused on something constructive.

As I was walking to my car, I asked the cowboy if he could make me one of those ropes with a knot on the end. With no hesitation, he responded, "Why, heck, you can have this one," and he tossed it to me.

That small act of kindness had a significant impact on my life, for I kept that little rope constantly with me for over a year. Every time I had an urge for a cigarette, I reached into my hip pocket, drew out the rope, and got my hands busy practicing my rope trick. As a matter of fact, I incorporated it into Chester's character. If you happen to catch an old rerun, one of the early half-hour episodes of *Gunsmoke*, you might see Chester doing his rope trick on the boardwalk outside of Mr. Dillon's office. It also helped me entertain kids when I would make a personal appearance at a hospital. They loved the rope trick.

It was 1956 when I learned the trick—over forty years since I flipped that cigarette and yelled, "I quit." And, much to the credit of that little rope, I haven't had a cigarette since.

19

Changing Consciousness

The disastrous feature of our civilization is that we have developed more materially than we have spiritually. Any civilization that develops only materially, and not in the sphere of spirit, heads for disaster.

—Albert Schweitzer

"So, Dennis—it's quite obvious that you agree with Albert Schweitzer in his assessment of our civilization's run toward disaster if we don't quickly develop spiritually. Can we discuss this?"

Yes. Albert Schweitzer was absolutely correct.

Now, we have to ask, "What did he mean by developing spiritually?"

To me, he certainly didn't mean that all we are required to do is to put our name on the membership list and join some church, synagogue, or temple.

Many people have done just that, and have grown very little spiritually. What I think Schweitzer meant by "developing spiritually" is that we must come to the higher understanding that we are all one, that we are all connected, and that our own happiness depends upon, and must include, the happiness of others. That not only are we human beings connected, but everything on the planet is connected—we therefore not only need each other, but we need all that the Creator has created. It is an interdependent world. If we do not think we need each other, all we have to do is look at the clothes we are wearing, and the food we are eating, or the transportation that we are using. When we do this, we realize that we cannot do, or have, anything in this society without the help of others. It is just impossible.

It is clear that the Earth, and all her inhabitants, are joined together to make a workable "one." Therefore, we should develop a "reverence for all life"—which was Albert Schweitzer's theme of his own life.

"How does one develop a reverence for all life?"

By examining life itself and realizing what a tremendous gift we have been given . . . by *changing our consciousness* . . . by changing our hearts.

Many visionaries and futurists have agreed that the underlying problem facing the Earth, and its inhabitants, is a problem of consciousness. They have concurred that our efforts to correct the dilemmas we face will be ineffective until we get at the root cause of our predicament. In other words, until there is a shift in the "collective consciousness" away from hate, greed, separation, and fear, towards love, peace, cooperation, oneness and justice, all our efforts to fix the problems confronting us, whether they be social, political, economic, environmental, will ultimately fail. Until we root out the cause, the symptom will continue to recur.

Can you imagine a world in which we as human beings realize our oneness with each other and all that there is? Can you imagine a world in which we realize that we share each other's pain and joy?

Of course, the truth is, we do already. We just don't believe that we do, and therein lies our trouble. For it is that false thought that leads to all the mayhem. And so the world is filled with cheaters, murderers, thieves, criminals of various sorts, and war—the result of fear, and the feeling of separation.

We will either come to the higher understanding that we are individualized parts of the One Whole, and that our own well-being depends on the well-being of the whole, or we will, out of ignorance, continue to believe that we are separate, that we can bring benefit to ourselves while we damage others, and, in holding onto that belief, we will eventually destroy ourselves.

"Excuse me, but this sounds a bit naïve—don't you think it's unrealistic to think *everyone's* actions could be motivated by love?"

"Let's dream for a minute. Let's play the game of 'what if.'"

"Okay," I said, happily knowing that I could do that.

What if we all truly cared for each other? What would be the practical result, if everyone came from love?

I can think of a few pluses, and I'm sure you'll add to my list. First of all, no one would want for the basic necessities of life. Hunger would be no more, poverty would be impossible, pestilence would disappear, and disease—if not totally eradicated—would be reduced to a bare minimum. And war would be no more!

There's a lot of talk these days about cutting taxes. But then the question always comes up, "What expenses do we eliminate in order to make those cuts?" Think of the billions of dollars we could save on our defense budget alone. We wouldn't need one. Who would we need to defend ourselves from? Ourselves? Remember, we are all *one*. I know that's a tough one to swallow, because we've been taught for so long that we're separate from each other, and we thoroughly believe it. We've been taught, "for me to win, somebody else must lose." The lie is so solidly ingrained in our consciousness that we simply believe anything else is impossible.

Think of the billions we spend to fight crime, which would no longer be necessary. Or the billions to clean up our environmental messes, that would no longer be required—for we would not make them. We simply would never consider destroying the natural things of Earth that give us life, for our consciousness of "oneness" would not be limited to just human beings but would embrace all things, including plants, animals, and our life-sustaining environment.

We would save billions of dollars in health care, because, as we stopped damaging and polluting the Earth, our own personal health would improve significantly.

By simply coming from love, we could cut taxes to practically nothing. Think of the time, energy, and money we could save that could be used to improve the living conditions of all Earth's occupants. Our standard of living would skyrocket.

"I'm going to play the devil's advocate here and say that's impossible—it could never work."

Well, do we really think what we are doing now is working? Maybe we need to improve our observation skills. Take another look at the world today, and we see poverty, unchecked disease, a polluted and poisoned earth, wars, and a real threat to our freedom of choice—in other words, a real mess. I'm inclined to believe the fellow was right when he said, "Love is not an option; it's an absolute necessity." Paramahansa Yogananda put it more bluntly, "We will either learn to love one another or perish." We've got to make some serious changes; if not, we're headed for environmental suicide. The answer is magnificent in its simplicity: "What the world needs now, is love, just love."

It will be argued that what I'm proposing is a "utopia," and that it is only possible in our imagination, only in our thoughts and dreams. Well, that is for sure where a "utopia" must be born, for everything ever created proceeds from thought—from an idea. To quote Yogananda again, "Utopia must spring in the private bosom before it can flower in civic virtue, inner reforms leading naturally to outer ones. A man who has reformed himself will reform thousands" (from *Autobiography of a Yogi*; page 557). Changing the collective consciousness is the answer, but let us understand, it is a personal responsibility which requires individual reform.

"And just how do we go about reforming ourselves?" I asked, not at all sarcastically, but very seriously.

"Well, that's a big question. . . ."

First of all, the problem of the world is a problem of the *heart* rather than the *intellect*. Our intellect is strong and well developed. It doesn't listen to the pleadings of our heart. It is not guided by love. You might say the heart part of us has been pushed aside. We are driven by our belief that in material things, we will find our greatest fulfillment. We fear there is not enough to go around, and our intellect tells us, "Get yours before it's too late; never mind who might be deprived." And greed motivates our actions and permeates our society.

If we are to reach our full potential as human beings and create a peaceful, fair, and sustainable world, the hearts of people must change! Our tendency is to point the finger at someone else and say, "He's the culprit, or she's the rascal . . . and they need to change their hearts . . . and if they would just do that . . . if they would change . . . everything would come up roses."

Too often we, with good intentions, make it our mission to change the hearts of others, when in reality there's only one heart that we can directly affect, only one we definitely have the power to change, and that's our own. But if we do that, if we become kinder, more compassionate, and loving—not just in words, but in our actions—we will have positive effects on the people around us. It is important that we become the change we want to see in others. Then, we will see the innate power that is in us. We will see the "power of one" in action.

"Yes, but how do we do that? How do we change our-selves?"

To begin with, we need to believe that we will benefit from the change, that it will bring us greater fulfillment. We must have the desire, for desire is the forerunner of action. It is essential to know what part of us needs to change. We have to honestly examine our attitudes, motives, and desires—to develop what I call "Third Eye" awareness. As an actor, to help me develop different characters, it's been a useful tool. I study myself. I may be involved in a real-life situation, in which emotional energy runs high, and I will still find that I am monitoring myself. A part of me may be enmeshed in the circumstances, but another part is aware of my behavior, my reactions, emotions, etc. I'm not always able to attain clear objectivity, but to a useful degree I can be both the participant and the observer. Later, in a quiet moment, I can reflect back and ask myself, "What was I being? Was I kind, stubborn, helpful, critical, loving, judg-mental . . . ?" If I was being something that I really didn't like, that took away my peace, that I was not comfortable with, then, at least I knew what it was I needed to work on—what I needed to eliminate from my character. It's a lot easier said than done, for those character traits are psycho-logical habits that are ingrained from childhood.

"I've heard that the first few years of a child's life deter-mines his or her entire personality—could you give us your thoughts on this?"

The first seven years of a child's life, and the environ-ment it is exposed to, are *extremely* important, for the young mind is like a sponge—it absorbs both the positives and the negatives, the good and the bad. It does not discriminate, and the psychological quirks it absorbs are very hard to dislodge. As Sri Yukteswar has said, "Good and positive suggestions should instruct the sensitive ears of children. Their early ideas long remain sharply etched."

An excellent aid in helping us reform ourselves is our environment—especially the company we keep. Transplant an Oriental into a western culture and it isn't long before he will be dressing, eating, and generally adopting the lifestyle of a westerner. The same is true if a westerner is moved to the Orient.

If we want to be peaceful, we should associate with those that demonstrate peace. The same rule applies to courage, honesty, or cheerfulness.

The greatest, most effective, and dependable environment for reshaping us in a beneficial way lies right within each of us—as the presence of God. It is extremely helpful to make direct contact with that presence and spend time with it. Build that relationship, and it will affect everything in the outside world. *That* environment will change our hearts without question, for when we feel the fulfilling power of God's unconditional love, we are engulfed with a deep feeling of gratitude and readily give it to others.

God's presence can change us for the better like nothing else can. That's why it is critical that we balance our outward activity with inner communion. If we fill our consciousness with God's presence, until we cannot tell the difference between God's consciousness and our own, we will awaken to the truth that there is no difference. It is all One. There is no separation. In that instant of realization, our heart is cleansed and purified, and all meanness is washed from it, for hate and vengeance cannot stay where love and forgiveness resides.

Of course, until we are totally anchored in God (few walking the Earth are), when we take up our daily activities, we will again be affected by worldly consciousness and will be drawn into its turmoil. That's why it is important to set aside time each day to make that daily communion with the presence—to continually cleanse our hearts. The more we make the contact, the more it will stay with us during outward activity, and eventually the world will not be able to shake it from us. Then life truly becomes sweeter, and we can play our parts unattached and with great enthusiasm.

"What do you say to people who say meditation is escapism—checking out?"

He gave me a mischievous smile and said, "I would say they are right."

I would go even further and say it is the most effective tool for escaping that I have discovered in my experience. If we honestly examine the motives of ourselves and others, we will conclude that we're all trying to escape the "slings and arrows of outrageous fortune" (Shakespeare) to remove the hurt in our lives. So escaping, in itself, is not a bad thing. It only becomes a problem when the escapism we choose does not serve us, or does not help us reach true happiness, but rather traps us more firmly in our suffering. Or if the means of escape we choose deflects us from our responsibilities . . . responsibilities we need to satisfy in order to reach lasting happiness.

Lasting is a key word. We know there is nothing lasting in the world. The world is always changing. The only thing that is permanent in the world is impermanence. So it's impossible to find lasting happiness in that which is not lasting. The irony is that when we realize this obvious truth, we have a much better chance of getting closer to the happiness we seek. For our expectations from our "here today and gone tomorrow world" shrink perceptively, and it's the expectations that set us up for disappointment and pain.

"Dennis, you can't be saying that we should give up our hopes, dreams—grand desires—can you?"

Of course not. To live without them is impossible. I can't imagine doing anything that wasn't preceded by a desire—a dream. Even habit was established by the repetition of an action, which originally was born of a desire. When the action becomes automatic, we can say it's not prompted by a desire, only because the desire that formed it is lost in our consciousness—no longer are we aware of it.

Should we have desires? I say, by all means! Have the grandest desires, the loftiest visions, selecting those that, if fulfilled, will bring benefit to others as well as to ourselves. Otherwise, what we think will bring us happiness often destroys it. The trick is to enjoy the action that the desire initiates. Live in the "now"—in the creative moment—not in the anticipation of what you think that action will bring. Enjoy the action without being attached to a perceived result. This allows us to live in freedom. It removes the anxiety and fear and leaves us free to "change horses in the middle of the stream." It allows us to go in a different direction in response to a gentle urging deep in our soul.

He stopped talking and looked at me. I realized he was waiting for me to ask the next question. I pushed on. "What is the role of family in shifting mass consciousness?"

It cannot be underestimated. The family is a unit of immeasurable importance—a design that is ingenious in helping us move away from separation consciousness, towards oneness. The family provides us with the opportunity to extend our love beyond the "little self" to the "greater Self." To think not only of our own needs, but of the needs of others. The family allows us to reach the grander wisdom that our own happiness and well-being include others. When we have attained the feeling of oneness within our immediate family, then the next step is not too difficult—make the family bigger, bigger, and bigger, until it includes the entire world.

We are all familiar with the expression "the family of man." It is our responsibility to make that saying more than empty words, more than just an intellectual concept—something we feel deeply in our hearts. When we act in response to our hearts rather than our intellects, the miracle will happen.

One of the major disasters facing our society today is the disintegration of the family. When the family breaks down, where is the love to nourish the young souls that have just entered the physical form? Where is the role model to teach them, through example, kindness, compassion, forgiveness, truthfulness, honesty, humility, etc.? Before young people take on the role of parenthood, they should be keenly aware of the responsibility that goes with it.

Let us understand that a family can be a commune, a tribe, or a clan. It need not be confined to the group consisting of parents and their immediate children—although usually this is considered to be the strongest family unit. However, the extended family consisting of a group of relatives by blood, marriage, or adoption is important.

If love is not the glue that holds the family together, it is a good bet that that family is dysfunctional. A small child, growing up in an environment void of love, will be badly nourished psychologically. The sense of separation will be deeply ingrained in its consciousness, and it will develop a lack of love for itself, resulting in suspicion, anger, distrust, jealousy, violence, fear, and an absence of self-worth. Once this pattern is established, it is too often inherited by the next generation.

It is natural for a child to want the support of the family. If the traditional family collapses or evaporates, the child will search for that family support in other ways. Different ones find it in different places. The fortunate ones find it in something positive—a special friend, the love of music, books, etc. But often young people attach themselves to that which will not serve them well. They take to the streets, searching for acceptance and security they should have received from a loving family. The large cities are full of pitiful stories of young teenagers selling the only thing they possess in order to survive—their bodies.

For others, of course, it is the gang that becomes their family, and they pay a heavy price just to be accepted. Nobody can stand to be ignored and unloved for very long.

I cannot help but relate the way we treat our young children to the way we treat our planet. The indifference they endure, and the lack of caring and concern we show them, are reflected in their lack of concern and caring for the place they live. The sad thing is, the children grow up to be adults and the same attitude stays with them. They grow up not caring.

There is a lot of work ahead of us if we're to be successful in changing collective consciousness away from fear to love. But I believe that we will make it—because that great shift in consciousness is already occurring. I see it in the multitude of messengers that are showing us the way and making us reach for that higher understanding of love and Oneness—messengers in the form of organizations, nonprofits, books, movies, lecturers, conferences, and even businesses.

I nodded in agreement. "So, you think 'business' is starting to think this way, too?"

Yes, I do.

There is no doubt in my mind that our only salvation is a shift in consciousness from "fear" to "love." It is definitely happening—the only question is, is it happening fast enough?

"You keep saying that we must move away from fear to love. What about hate, greed, jealousy, and intolerance?"

They are simply "children" of fear. Fear is the breeding ground for all of them—just as love spawns kindness, forgiveness, understanding, and compassion.

There are really only two basic emotions that make up the human psyche; one is *love*, and one is *fear*.

"Okay, we're learning how to step into love—. How do we step out of fear . . . ?" I asked, thinking it was a rather simple question. But there was a pregnant pause, and I could almost hear the wheels of his mind clicking as it turned the question over and over again.

Then he spread his arms wide, and, looking incredulous, he asked with a light, slightly ironic voice, "Do we really want to step out of fear? Do we want to eliminate it completely from our consciousness?"

"Well, yeah—! As you just said, fear spawns hate, anger, jealousy, and judgment. I, for one, want it gone!"

"I'm not so sure we do. Like everything else in this world, fear has a negative side and a positive side."

"I don't mean to be difficult, but what could possibly be its positive side?"

The positive side of fear keeps us out of trouble—keeps us from doing stupid things that might severely damage us.

Fear is the result of our past experiences. Why don't we go swimming in shark-infested waters? Because we all experienced the movie *Jaws*. We know the consequences. If we swam with the sharks, we would no doubt exit this physical form, and we're not ready to do that. Fear keeps us playing our part in this cosmic drama. We *fear* what may be on the other side—what might be waiting for us.

As Hamlet said, "Who would fardels (heavy loads) bear to grunt and sweat under a weary life but that the dread (fear) of something after death, the undiscovered country from whose bourn (shore) no traveler returns, puzzles (paralyzes) the will, and makes us rather bear those ills we have than fly to others that we know not of?"

God is Love. God is also all there is, so in ultimate reality Love is all there is.

"Okay—if God is everything, and God is love, where does fear come from? From us?"

Initially, it comes from the Creator. God in Her great love for us lovingly introduced us to fear—it's nearer the truth to think of fear as a cautionary device—to prevent the pain in our lives. So fear—as caution—is a product of love. To be guided by cautious fear is a wise choice. Our problem is, we have allowed cautious fear to grow into destructive or slavish fear that paralyzes our will and destroys our creative and productive impulses. For that kind of fear breeds all the bad stuff: rage, meanness, judgment, and vengefulness—the kind we were talking about earlier. And that aspect of fear we allow to manifest in us. We express it. So, in a sense, we can say that it does come from us.

It is the stifling, slavish fear that we must weed out of our lives—we must step out of.

Be cautious, but not fearful. The more we dwell on that which we fear, the more power we give it, the more real it becomes, because fear feeds on itself. It is an energy that attracts itself, so that which we fear has a tendency to show up in our lives.

Realize that fear is "False Evidence Appearing Real." We should dismiss it from our thoughts by involving our minds in positive goals. Let us put our efforts into being of service to others. Read inspiring books. Keep good company. The best company, of course, is God. We should talk to Him as our best and most helpful friend, for indeed He is. Say, "God, my beloved Friend, this fear I'm experiencing is intruding itself into my true being. It is not who I am, and I give it back to you. I am thankful in my heart that you have lovingly taken it from me." We should then go about our business knowing it has been done. Have faith that, as His divine children, He cannot say "no" to us. Remember that fear is totally washed away in deep communion with God, for it simply cannot invade that Divine Presence—that consciousness where only love resides.

The last was said with a definitive sigh, and I knew we were nearly done. Had we left anything unsaid? Was there something else? I ventured forth with what I thought was to be my last question. "Dennis, would you like to sum things up, so to speak?"

His thick eyebrows knitted together, then relaxed.

I would like to remind us that this beautiful playground—this Earth—has been put in our care. We are the ones that have scarred and defaced it. And for the sake of future generations that have to depend on it, and live with the results of our choices, we must strive diligently to leave them a productive, clean, creative, and just world.

To do that, we have to go beyond simply trying to fix our outer environment, although that effort and purpose is very admirable and essential. But what is more important is the cleansing of our inner environment—that part of us that we can't experience through our five senses. The outer environment we see, hear, touch, taste, and smell—all a function of our five senses—but our inner environment is not experienced in that manner. It is what we truly are at the very core of our being. Some might say it's our character. It's our thoughts, ideas, attitudes, emotions, our hopes, visions, and dreams. Why is that important? Because what we have created on the outside is simply a reflection of what we are on the inside. If we are carrying around within us hate, greed, prejudice, and fear, that's the kind of world we will create. But if we are carrying inside us love, peace, hope, understanding, compassion, forgiveness, and a sense of oneness, that too is the world we will create. It all starts within—in our inner environment.

"I know we've touched on this before, but it's so important—can you reiterate how we change our inner environment?"

First, we must recognize the need for change. We must understand how we, as well as everyone else, will benefit from a kinder, more loving world. This takes deep self-examination and introspection. And we must be prepared to be brutally honest with ourselves. However, we may come to the conclusion that our inner environment is badly in need of change, but that intellectual understanding rarely results in a change in our consciousness . . . simply because our psychological quirks and emotional habits may have been acquired over many lifetimes. They are solidly imbedded in our character.

The most effective tool I know for changing our inner environment is deep meditation, for it is in the immaculate stillness within, in the sphere of Spirit, that thoughts and emotions are produced. It is there that we experience in a tangible and personal way the unconditional love of God. We simply cannot experience *that* without being affected by it. It affects our thoughts, it affects our emotions, our ideas, attitudes, and dreams. In other words, it affects, and begins to change, our inner environment, which in turn has a profound effect on our outer environment. It all begins within.

It is when the hearts of people are changed that we will see the dramatic change in the "character" of the world. And the hearts will change as we grow spiritually, as we have closer communion with that eternal part of us, our soul within. It is then that we will lose the false idea that we are separate . . . separate from each other and separate from God, and all that It has created. It is the realization of our oneness that is our salvation. Remember, there is only one heart that we can change, and that is our own. But when we change our own, we begin to affect others. So, the shift in world consciousness, that is so desperately needed, is an individual responsibility. We need to light our own candle so that others can light theirs off of ours. Let us visualize candle after candle set aflame, sweeping across the world like a great prairie fire, pushed forward by the winds of love, burning away all hate, bigotry, fear, and greed— leaving in its wake a world of peace, cooperation, oneness, and justice. Change is inevitable. Do we become a product of it, or do we produce it? The choice is ours.

A Meditation

The light was shifting outside the windows, and I could tell that morning was near—a couple of hours away at the most. We had talked all night.

The house was quiet—and the phone had long since stopped ringing. Did I dare ask? Was this an appropriate time? I had no idea. All I knew was that I was being drawn toward a desire to know, beyond talking, what the experience of really meditating felt like. I also knew that I trusted Dennis to give me that experience.

"Dennis, would you be my guide—would you lead me in a meditation?"

"Now—?" He questioned me with a fleeting look of amusement on his face.

"Yes. Is that all right?"

"Well, sure. I'll have to explain a bit as we go along."

I nodded happily.

Sit in a relaxed but alert position with the spine straight. It is important to be comfortable, because we don't want the body sending messages to the brain, continually telling it of the discomfort it is in—thereby creating a host of restless thoughts. Fresh air, too, is always helpful.

Now, after a double inhalation of oxygen, gently tense the body and, as you exhale, release the tension, and watch your body relax. Repeat this several times. (We take a few moments to repeat this process.) After final repetition, check your body for hidden pockets of energy that might remain, and release them.

It's important to prepare the mind to leave worldly concerns behind. There's a song I wrote that's been a great help to me—it goes like this:

Now is the time to quiet the mind . . . leave all my worries and troubles behind. . . . Lord, I hear your Eternal Song . . . and know in the stillness I'm where I belong. . . . No place to go and nothing to do . . . but feel in the stillness my Oneness with You. . . . Lord, I shed all worldly cares . . . and know in the stillness that Your Love is there. . . . To Love you, Lord, with all my might . . . is all that will make this old world right. . . . Lord, I put you in everything first . . . and quench in the stillness my inner thirst. . . . Be still and know, be still and know . . . be still, my heart . . . be still, my soul . . . be still, my thoughts . . . be still and know that God is Love . . . be still and know.

Place your attention on your breath. Watch it as it goes in and out, in and out . . . think of yourself as the observer. Do not try to control the breath; let it flow. Watch it as though it belonged to someone else—you are simply the observer. When you catch the mind wandering, bring it back; gently but firmly bring it back to the breath. Know that God's grace and love has supplied you with the breath—that you are breathing in God's love—and allow a great consciousness of love to fill your heart. Mentally whisper, "Thank you, God. Thank you, God, for your Divine Presence." This must be done with the highest degree of sincerity. The mechanical mouthing of words will always be recognized as hollow and will not evoke the desired response from your Higher Self. God knows what is in your heart, just as you do.

Now, with every inhalation through the power of your loving attention, draw the energy (life force) in your body, up your spine, to the point between and just above your eyebrows—the "Christ Center" . . . the spiritual eye, the third eye, single eye—it's called different things, but it doesn't matter what you call it—the important thing is that it's the place in the body where the Divine Presence is most easily felt.

Remember, it is the attention that directs the energy, so pull the energy up by directing the attention upward to the Christ Center with every intake of breath. (We take several quiet moments to do this.) It is the energy that will awaken the spiritual consciousness that dwells at our Spiritual Eye. (Several beats.) Go deep into the stillness—for it is in the quietness of your soul that you will feel the great Love of the Infinite.

Don't expect—just notice what is in the darkness, deep in the stillness. Examine it with calm attention. Don't judge it. Don't think about it. Just allow yourself to be consumed by the calm stillness. Experience the experience. Feel the feeling. Focus . . . focus . . . focus. . . . Mentally whisper, "I love you . . . I love you . . . I love you . . . Let go and let God."

"Merge into the sea of peace—float in the ocean of Love. . . ." (What followed was a time of quiet, in which I completely left my body and this reality behind.)

What felt like several minutes of silence passed, then Dennis started bringing me back, by talking softly—his deep baritone voice so sweet, so gentle. After a few minutes, I was back, feeling refreshed—not at all like I had been up all night. All my fatigue had vanished into the suddenly very bright morning light that was now flooding through the windows.

"Wow, that was incredible!" I managed, while staring out the window curiously. "How long were we gone?"

He turned his gaze from the outdoors to the silver-and-turquoise watch he wore on his left wrist. "An hour and a half."

I was shocked. "Oh my! I had no idea—it felt like only a few minutes!" I exclaimed with unbelievable joy. "That was terrific. You are a great guide."

"Well, I don't know about that—."

A long silence passed between us, and then we both smiled simultaneously. We were done—finished. We had covered it all.

Epilogue

I packed up and stood for a moment before the large windows in Dennis's office, looking out. The sun illumined the sleepy valley. A gossamer layer of wood smoke hovered idly, somewhere between rooftops and mountain peaks, waiting for the morning breezes to blow it away. But I was not seeing the smoke nor the valley, nor even the snow-dusted ridge it hung below; I was seeing the world beyond the mountains—a world filled with possibilities. I was seeing people from diverse backgrounds standing together on a new city street. I was seeing the great shafts of skyscrapers looking bright and clean, sparkling against a cloudless sky like a Kodak picture, snapped by a skilled photographer on assignment for some progressive magazine, and held neatly in time. I was seeing acres of lush corn, soybeans, and alfalfa. I was seeing the eyes of young and old alike, looking toward the future with no fear on their faces.

The door opened, and Gerry entered, carrying two steaming mugs of green tea.

"Green tea—to wake you up," she announced in a much too chipper voice for this early time of day. Gerry was a morning person, up at the crack of dawn every day. She handed me a mug, and I sipped it gratefully.

Then she gave Dennis her full attention, which included a good-morning kiss and sweet hug. She handed him the other mug and stared up into his face, curiously.

"Well, did you get some good stuff for the book?" she asked him.

Dennis looked down into Gerry's smiling, childlike, green eyes and hugged her. There were no ready words on his lips this morning—they were not necessary.

I sipped my tea and watched the two of them, once more marveling at their loving relationship of fifty-four years.

Then his eyes left Gerry's and traveled to the window. They fixed themselves, trancelike, on the two tepees below the house in the damp meadow with their dewy canvases aglow in the sunlight—his eyes were smiling.

I could see that Gerry knew the exact thought he was thinking and that she would push no further. I recognized that expression on his face, too. It was the look of promise.

I quietly slipped out the door.

ॐ

We live to learn to love, and we love to learn to live. No other lesson is necessary.

—From the book of *Mirdad*

Afterword

My wonderful friends . . . thank you for once again allowing me the honor of coming into your lives, as you have done for so many years through my work on the stage, in television, and the movies. It has meant more to me than I can tell you to be able to share my story with you. Like every acting job I have ever done, this book has been for me a labor of love. Going over all the memories of my childhood, telling you the inside stories of my career, and revealing to you my very personal passions and experiences is a great privilege.

Why do I say that? Because I believe it is always a sacred thing to reveal oneself to another. It is all that any of us really want, when you think about it. We spend our entire lives seeking to know each other, and I think that is because we understand at a very deep, intuitive level that the more we know of each other the more we know of life itself, and of everything that is really important.

Sometimes we become aware that we share with each

other some of the same thoughts. We discover that we stand on some common ground, that we hold some of the same views, and that we are not so alone in our experience after all.

For example, through the years as I have talked with so many of you during my personal appearances, I have come to know that a large number of you share with me a great love of life, and for our Earth on which we live it.

Like me, you want to do all that you can to pass on to future generations the breathtaking beauty of an unspoiled natural environment, and the unlimited opportunity that is afforded us by a thriving and vibrant economy. Like me, you see these as wonderful gifts from our benevolent Creator, entrusted to our care for our children, and for our children's children, and for all those who will come beyond.

All the world *is* a stage, and the people, the players. We are now writing the script that will be acted out tomorrow on this stage of life. I hope you will join me in writing a new and exciting story—one with a happy ending. I hope you will join me *on* the stage in playing an active and vital role in the drama of our Mother Earth.

We cannot afford to stand in the wings, waiting to hear our cue. The cues are being given to us all over the place. *Now is the time to act.* Because friends, they are already taking some of the scenery away, and if we do not act now, the old Globe Theatre in which we hope to play out our human story may be no more.

But it is not too late. We can stop the curtain from falling. We can keep the "play" going for centuries to come if we are willing to change, change the *way* the human race is acting just a touch. It wouldn't take much, really. That's what's so exciting. Some of the smallest changes can produce some of the biggest results.

If you'd like to learn how you can make some of these changes—and how you can help others become aware, so that they can make them—I invite you to partner with the Institute of Ecolonomics in marrying our ecology and our economy to sustain our future.

One way to do this would be by subscribing to our newsletter, bringing you the latest news and information on practical ways to protect and preserve our environment at the same time that we enliven and enhance our economy. I hope that you will do so, allowing me to extend my visit in your home and in your life; allowing us to stay connected in a very real way. I know that there is much we can do together to keep our play going for the new, young actors who will take the stage tomorrow.

To begin receiving our newsletter just send $35 for an annual subscription to:

Newsletter
Institute for Ecolonomics
Box 500
Ridgway, CO 81432

There are other ways you can support the Institute as well. We are right now developing some extraordinary and exciting programs, such as Community Level Mediation, when business and environmental interests appear to clash at the local level in your city or town, and our Ecolonomic Incubator, in which we hope to be able to provide start-up support for imaginative and innovative technologies and businesses that provide products or services in an ecologically friendly way, expanding our educational programs in all levels, especially focusing on the young.

If you write to us or connect with us on the Internet, we will tell you all about these and other outreach endeavors— and provide you with a way to actively participate in them within your own community. You can touch the world from your home.

Our website address is: www.ecolonomics.org

My e-mail address is: weaver@dennisweaver.com

And you may reach us by telephone at 970-626-3820.

As President John Kennedy said, ". . . divided there is little we can do, together there is little we cannot do." Let's get together and save our environment. Then, all that you and I have worked for, all that we had hoped to pass on to our offspring, will be a reality, and our efforts will not have been in vain.

Tomorrow's children await our answer. Tomorrow's world awaits our creation. Join me today, for the sake of tomorrow.

Thank you for caring.

Love,
Dennis

THE INSTITUTE OF ECOLONOMICS
Touch the world from your home.

Hampton Roads Publishing Company

. . . for the evolving human spirit

Hampton Roads Publishing Company
publishes books on a variety of subjects,
including metaphysics, health, integrative medicine,
visionary fiction, and other related topics.

For a copy of our latest catalog, call toll-free
(800) 766-8009, or send your name and address to:

Hampton Roads Publishing Company, Inc.
1125 Stoney Ridge Road
Charlottesville, VA 22902

hrpc@hrpub.com
www.hrpub.com